With Luck

Douglas Hawker DFC

ISBN   190060415-9

Printed and bound in the United Kingdom

Published by Compaid Graphics.
T'otherside, Drumacre Lane East,
Longton, Preston. PR4 4SD
www.compaidgraphics.co.uk

To Margie who took a chance

**To my friends whose chances
were denied**

Contents

Foreword

Air Marshal Sir Richard Bolt KBE. CB. DFC. AFC.,
Former Chief of the New Zealand Defence Staff

Douglas Hawker and I have not known each other personally, but having survived a remarkably similar experience of war myself, I can identify with him very easily - and having been fortunate enough to build on that experience and to complete a full Service career after the Second World War, I count it a privilege to be invited to write this Foreword to the Douglas Hawker story.

The author's memories of his youth, as infant, school boy, then farm boy, are a fascinating reminder of how much change can take place in a society in one lifetime. He tells of his pre-war visit to Britain with very limited resources, an adventure not uncommon for enterprising boys in the thirties – and for him, and the host of other young New Zealanders who later served in wartime Britain, just discovering the evidence of history and heritage was quite unforgettable.

But the main focus of this story is on those war years, and since then, so many changes have taken place, in the international scene, in society and in Service life, that today there is often no more than a vague appreciation of just what Douglas Hawker and thousands of other Kiwis were doing in the RAF Bomber Command and why. Most were volunteers from all walks of life, some straight from school, and until war began few would have dreamed of the parts they were to play in battle. For those who were to be bomber pilots, the challenge of simply flying large aircraft in the black of night was itself enormous, but satisfying too. Some critics have said that it was all a case of fighting other people's wars, a hangover from colonial times. Others will still claim that because of the huge loss of life, both military and civilian, the whole bombing offensive against Nazi Germany was immoral and inappropriate. But they invariably stop short of saying what alternative there should have been, and in any case, such notions just do not reflect the realities of those times.

The Second World War was indeed a total war – not simply a conflict of military forces. It was in the final analysis, about freedoms and principles, and those like Douglas Hawker who fought alongside Allies far from home, were in fact not only representing New Zealand but fighting for New Zealand interests. As for the bombing, tragic though the consequences often were, without it there was no way in which the Allies could have successfully mounted the invasion on D-Day, or brought the war in Europe to a victorious conclusion. We can of course reflect that without that victory in Europe, and later the Pacific, life in New Zealand would certainly have been vastly different, but that is another story.

The lengthy training preparations which the author and his crew went through to qualify for operational duties were very demanding in themselves. Then came the hard realities of operating against the enemy, which he describes in graphic detail. The fears, the excitement, near disasters, and sometimes the satisfaction, were only typical of what was experienced by thousands of others. As one of the many who also flew Lancasters in battle, I can certainly share Douglas Hawker's memories of it all very clearly. They were of the kind no one ever forgets, and the casualties, so many of which he records in detail, are a reminder that those operations were far from being one-sided and that those who survived their tours were fortunate indeed.

So, while typical of many he may have been in his operational activities, I believe our author was rather uniquely different from the majority. In war, he was married, a few years older than most, probably more mature, and I suspect, possibly better behaved than some of us may have been under the pressures of war. He was certainly thoughtful about all that was going on and we can now be grateful that his memories are so clear and that he has been able to record so much in meticulous detail.

His conclusions about the whole bombing offensive, discussed towards the end of his story, are in my view, the right ones. It was something which had to be done despite the emotional costs and the tragic losses on both sides, which it involved. Since those times of course, advancing technologies have changed the whole nature of conflict and it is easy to say that many of the historical facts about the Second World War are now irrelevant. Yet some things have not changed at all. World peace is still as elusive as ever, the future just as unpredictable in security terms, and perhaps above all, the freedoms which the author's generation fought to preserve are still as vitally important to us as they ever were. Will we always be ready to play our part in defending them again should the need arise?

We are indebted to Douglas Hawker for telling his story in a most interesting and revealing way.

Richard Bolt
Wellington
New Zealand
January 2004

Preface

It has been an interesting experience in writing this book to discover just how much help needs to be elicited from many people and also the willingness they showed in responding to the requests made of them.

At the very outset of the proposal to produce this book, my wife Margie drew my attention to the volume of work that would be involved and then offered her unfailing encouragement to me to go ahead with it. I have regarded her support as indispensable.

I wish to acknowledge the unfailing courtesy afforded me by Jane Proven, the Research Curator of the National Air Force Museum's Archive and Library at Wigram, Christchurch, New Zealand, and the ongoing access to the available resources there which she arranged for me. I record my thanks to Norman Bidwell, the President of the Brevet Club, Christchurch Branch, and to Sally Randall, Administator at the National Air Force Museum, Wigram and to Laurie Turner, a fellow Voluntary Guide at the Museum for their help and advice over various matters.

I wish to thank staff at the Royal Air Force Museum at Hendon for their encouragement and interest, especially Vernon Creek, its Education Officer. I have also been grateful for the excellent services of the Christchurch Central Library, the staff without fail being always willing to help in response to my queries and search for titles.

I am indebted for the support and encouragement of my former aircrew colleagues, Alf Dawson and Jack Warwick, who, in spite of my best efforts to make them airsick, managed to offer some complimentary remarks.

With regard to the private sources used, I am grateful to Heiko Pöhland in Dresden for organising the despatch of the evidence provided by Heidrun Kramer and the supplementary text by Heidrun's daughter Inka Pöhland. I am grateful to Günter Rabe for the translations of both these texts into English, and the confirmation of German spellings and the verification of place names throughout the entire text. In Tokyo, Professor Nobuya Kinase formerly of Bunkyo University, a Zero fighter pilot during the Second World War and a kamikaze who was lucky enough to survive the war, was kind enough to arrange for the two testimonies included in Chapter 16. I wish to thank him for his interest and to thank Hisa Nomura, formerly Assistant Professor at Bunkyo University, and Keinosuke Obi, formerly Professor and Dean of Information Sciences at Bunkyo University, for being willing to relate their respective experiences. I also thank Mitsunori Sagawa, formerly Secretary to the Chair of the International Exchange Centre at Bunkyo University, for his translation of the latter's text into English.

I thank Squadron-Leader Mervyn Davies, the President, and Gordon Lodge, the Secretary, of the 57 Squadron and 630 Squadron Association for their work and Newsletters from which I have drawn. In New Zealand, May Calvert willingly sent me private papers concerning her late husband's war record. I am grateful for the trouble she took to gather them together for me.

Without the technical computer help of Sheila Smurthwaite the text would never have been drawn together in presentable form. Her skills, advice and tuition were greatly appreciated. I thank Mia Ryan the manager of Ryan Recruitment, Christchurch for the use of office facilities and Diane Alpers for the help she rendered over the preparation of the photographs for publication.

I am grateful to my wife Margie, and Wolf Rolf Just, Head of English at Villa Maria College, Christchurch for reading the text and making helpful suggestions to improve it.

Most of all, I extend to my much valued friend Dr Alan Paisey, formerly Head of Administrative Studies, Bulmershe College, University of Reading, my grateful thanks for his unending assistance and tireless research without which I doubt that this book would have been written. In also editing my text, he made the reminiscences and records of an ex bomber pilot cohere constructively with contextual events to achieve the particular historical perspective I envisaged.

Douglas Hawker
Christchurch
New Zealand
January 2004

Chapter 1

Runway Reflections

As the shadows deepened at day's end, thirteen bomb-laden Lancasters rolled slowly round the winding curves of the perimeter track, their propellers clawing at the air to maintain the momentum of their heavily-laden aircraft. On reaching the end of the runway in use the pilot of the leading aircraft stopped his engines. All the following pilots followed suit.

From the opposite direction twelve Lancasters had carried out exactly the same exercise. The station's two squadrons were now assembled, nose to tail, facing each other and almost ready to go. Take off would be alternatively from each side of the runway, designed and built to take these four-engined bombers and their heavy bomb loads. In the growing gloom the twenty five aircraft made two long black lines, each stretching over three hundred metres around the perimeter track. Altogether 175 crew members and about 150 tons of bombs were ready to go.

Petrol tankers were systematically moving slowly along the lines of aircraft, topping up their petrol tanks to their limits because the night's target was at about the maximum range of these Lancaster bombers. They would need every drop of the 2,154 gallons that each aircraft's fuel tanks could hold. Other vehicles were scurrying about the airfield engaged in the multifarious jobs with people and materials to keep the airfield operational and to get this particular night's operation successfully off on its way.

We were bound for Munich in Southern Germany. It was to be our fourth operational sortie as a crew. But for me, personally, it was to be my fifth flight over enemy territory. My initial flight had been as an observer with an experienced crew to see how things should be done.

As I sat in my pilot's seat waiting for the preparations for our departure to be completed, my thoughts returned to that first trip as a passenger, when I saw seven aircraft go down in flames. The drama and ferocity of it remained vividly fresh for me, unassuaged by the passage of the few intervening days. Especially etched in my memory was the fate of one of those aircraft in particular. It was on fire, but still flying, and it seemed that the crew must have been endeavouring to deal with the fire because I could see that it was diminishing. Eventually it seemed to be almost out, except for just a little flicker of flame, and I felt relieved that they had regained control.

Yet even as I watched, that little flicker began to grow bigger, and bigger, destroying my feelings of relief. It grew ever larger until finally the aircraft went down like a flaming torch. It would have been over the English Channel at that time. I often wondered how the crew fared. Had they plunged to their doom in the sea, or had they been incinerated along with everything else before the wreckage hit the water?

There was a chance that some may have survived as there was time to bale out. Each crew member had a small inflatable dinghy which could be clipped to his parachute harness if the need arose to bale out over the sea or if a damaged aircraft was forced to land in the sea. The dinghy offered some chance of survival, enhanced if they were fortunate enough to land in a calm sea and within reasonable distance of the alert patrolling Royal Navy or the Royal Air Force Air-Sea Rescue vessels. Their chances were slim so often, however, in the dark expanses of the North Sea, which was so seldom less than disturbed and sometimes stormy.

I reflected also on the fate of the other six aircraft I had seen destroyed that night. Each one had exploded in a spectacular ball of fire, so there could have been no survivors.

While the tankers were topping up our tanks we had time to think during that relatively quiet period. It was a time for confronting one's fears and worst thoughts, for getting on top of them in one psychological way or another.

Later on I often wondered how so many thoughts could pass through my mind in such a short time. Perhaps it was true, I mused, that a drowning man's entire past life passed through his mind in a few seconds.

I also wondered what thoughts were going through the minds of the rest of the crew just then. John Miller was the rear gunner, sitting uncomfortably in the cramped tail turret. His job was to protect the aircraft from attack from the rear by enemy fighters. I assumed that he would be uncomfortable because I couldn't imagine how he could be otherwise while sitting in such a confined space on a leather-covered piece of steel. John Miller (known as Dusty of course) was a fairly solidly built man. To keep him warm when we reached freezing temperatures at higher altitudes, he wore an electrically heated suit. Elsewhere in the fuselage the rest of us had the benefit of hot air mechanically blown in from the engines but this would not feed through far enough to the rear turret. John was thirty-one and a policeman before volunteering for aircrew. He was an easy person to get along with and got on with his job without any fuss, despite the discomfort he must have been in at all times.

Further forward, in the gun turret on top of the aircraft, sat Ron Adams, our mid-upper gunner, whose job was to protect the aircraft from fighter attacks from above. He was possibly a little less uncomfortable than Dusty because of his smaller stature. Otherwise he endured similar conditions. In peace time Ron was a market gardener in North Walsham, Norfolk. He was twenty-seven and quite understandably spoke with a broad Norfolk accent. Because of his small stature he was known as Shortie and always needed a little help in climbing up into his turret. Like Dusty, he never complained but he did get very nervous at times.

Down in the fuselage, and further forward on the port side and at right angles to me was Alf Dawson's tiny radio office. Alf was responsible for maintaining a listening watch for messages from base and watching the 'Fishpond', which was a dial to detect an enemy aircraft creeping up underneath the aircraft to attack it. In the event that we had to ditch in the sea he had the crucial job of transmitting distress messages as constant signals for rescue organisations to fix on to us. Also, he controlled the cabin heating which meant that he could set a temperature of his choice which the rest of the crew had to be content with. There were complaints of course but they were never very serious.

In civilian life, Alf had been a fireman on railway engines, which were coal-fired at that time – the probable reason why he had acquired the nickname of Digger. He had his twenty-first birthday while we were doing our tour of operations. His nice head of blond hair was always immaculately kept in place. He came from Cumbria, in North West England. He had a strong local accent and was always ready for a laugh. He was a very competent wireless operator.

Ahead of Digger on the port side, surrounded by blackout curtains, sat Jack Warwick, the navigator. We were dependent on

Jack to tell us the course to steer to arrive at every destination. His nickname was 'Earl', but invariably he got just Jack. Because Digger and Jack were mostly confined to their small offices, they saw little of what was happening outside. This applied particularly to Jack. To make it as difficult as possible for the enemy to organise his night fighters to be in the right place at the right time, we used to head in numerous different directions before finally committing ourselves to a course for the target. So Jack was always busy, calculating the next course while allowing for the effect the wind would have on the changed course. As his little office was surrounded by blackout curtains it was impossible for him to see out. Jack was twenty-two and in civilian life an auditor, so he was used to dealing with figures. He was dedicated to his job. Consequently he was an excellent navigator and always had a ready answer to any question I asked.

I was twenty-seven and in the pilot's seat. I had grown up in the countryside of Canterbury in the South Island of New Zealand but since my parents had just retired to the city of Christchurch in New Zealand, I claimed to have come from Christchurch. I sat in front of Jack but we could not see each other because of the blackout curtains. Unlike Jack, I had an excellent outlook. Being able to see all around the aircraft enabled me to keep a sharp lookout for trouble. As I flew I used to look to port as far as the port fin and rudder, then, slowly, round to the right until I was looking at the starboard fin and rudder, pausing while I was facing forward for a quick look at the instruments to check that everything was as it should be. Then I looked slowly back until I was again looking at the port fin and rudder. That was my routine for as long as the trip lasted, for up to six, eight, or ten hours.

At times I was surprised at how much I was able to see at night. In the dark we see things first with the side of our eyes rather than the middle and the natural instinct is to focus on the object with the middle of our eyes. If, in the dark, we follow our natural instinct to look directly at the object it will probably become invisible. During our training we used to practice night vision and of course on night operations we became very good at seeing with the sides of our eyes.

Beside me, on my right, sat Les Meace, the engineer. Beside him, attached to the fuselage was a large panel with an assortment of dials and switches. His duties were to keep a check on the fuel gauges and other engine instruments. He also had to change the fuel cocks from the various tanks, as required. He also fed out the strips of tinfoil, called 'Windows', to confuse the enemy radar when needed and to help the pilot when needed, as well as keeping a sharp look out for enemy fighters. As we climbed into rarer air at higher altitudes, the fuel pumps on the engines needed help to maintain the fuel supply. To effect this, the engineer needed to switch on pulsometer pumps inside the fuel tanks. Les, at nineteen, was the youngest member of the crew. He had worked in a clothing retail store before joining the Air Force. His seat was above the entrance to the bomb aimer's compartment so it had to be movable when access to that compartment was needed. Les's job was more varied and less specific than that of other crew members, so he was more of an odd job man, but he was always ready and willing to tackle whatever was asked of him.

In the early days of the war there had been two pilots in a bomber aircraft. Since the aircraft required only one pilot to fly it, the second pilot was the one who had to do the odd jobs. When a bomber was shot down, however, two trained pilots were lost. It was soon realised that as it took a long time to train a pilot but not very long to train an engineer, it would be better to replace the second pilot with an engineer to do the duties of second pilot except for any actual flying. As a consequence, sometimes the first time an engineer ever flew was when he joined an operational squadron.

Roy Griffin was our bomb aimer and like myself a New Zealander. He was thirty-two and came from Mata Mata in the North Island, and also like me, spoke with a Kiwi accent. He and I were the only two married members of the crew. He had several business interests back home in New Zealand and was keen to do his share in helping to put the world to rights. He fitted in well with the crew. His position in the aircraft was in front of the engineer but down below him, where he could lie down to look through the bomb sight at the target below.

While we waited on the tarmac our thoughts among the seven of us must have been many and varied but they were inevitably dominated by one thought I was sure we had in common: How long would we survive? As the pilot I was well aware of my special responsibilities and shared in the general feeling that as a crew we could be tested to the limit but were determined to be equal to it. Nevertheless, the statistics told us that most crews did not survive more than five operations. Three weeks before, ninety four bombers had failed to return from a night operation. In each of those bombers were seven crew members. Six hundred and fifty eight lives had been lost in one night.

For a significant perspective on that particular night's loss rate, it may be noted that during the three months of the Battle of Britain in which the fighter pilots had valiantly fought the invading bomber fleets of the German Luftwaffe, a total of five hundred and thirty seven lives had been lost.

What would our future be? The answer we gave ourselves must have been tinged with resignation. We were very anxious of course, which sounds better than saying we were very scared. Perhaps I should make it clear that I speak for myself only, but the future did not look good - and I don't have any doubts that our feelings were mutual. Anxiety was to be our constant companion for the next five months and we would have to learn to live with it.

We had survived a fighter attack during our first trip. Our second trip was uneventful. On our third trip I lost control of the aircraft while evading a fighter. Now here we were about to take off on our fourth trip. After I lost control on the third trip we were heading for the ground at nearly 400 mph. I had thought it was the end of the road coming up fast. I had extreme difficulties to deal with that emergency but the fact that I did somehow manage to regain control had helped me to feel that it might be possible to survive. I found myself asking myself: Are the rest of the crew biting their fingernails and wondering if I will lose control on this, our fourth trip, and thinking "Maybe we won't be so lucky this time"?

Why were we, along with all those other aircrew members, sitting there wondering how soon our lives were going to end? What was it that made us put our lives on the line in this way? It was certainly not for the thrill of flying because only the pilots were doing the flying. To sit for hour after hour in the darkness, staring out into the night or peering at a set of instruments, then watching anti-aircraft shells exploding round about and seeing other aircraft going down in flames, was anything but a thrilling experience. At least the pilot had a small degree of control of the situation but the rest of the crew were entirely dependent on the pilot and were exposed to all the other risks as well.

I had no doubts about why I was there and I felt sure that there would be very few who weren't there for the same reasons. My thoughts took me back to my primary school days when I heard accounts of the antics of Hitler and his 'Brownshirts'. I didn't like what I heard but it appeared to be not our problem. Opinion was that the German people would have to sort it out for themselves. I went on to high school and then back home to work on the sheep station that my father was managing. By then there was growing concern because seventeen million German people had voted for Hitler as Chancellor.

He had achieved power in Germany and was making aggressive noises but since it was only fifteen years since the carnage of the First World War, I thought that no sane person would ever want to see a repeat of those terrible times. Writings on the wall, however, became more ominous with every new infringement of the peace by Hitler in succession - the remilitarization of the Rhineland on 7 March 1936, forbidden under the Treaty of Versailles, the Anschluss, which forced the unification of Austria with Germany, the annexation of Czechoslovakia in two waves, and finally the invasion of Poland, carried out under spurious pretexts. At the same time Germany was giving substantial support to Franco in the Spanish Civil War, 1936-9.

With each step assurances were given that no further territorial demands would be made but they were calculated to deceive. In our newspapers we also began to read reports of the persecution and arrest of Jewish people and other minority groups and of the destruction of their shops and homes. There were also rumours that the people involved were being put into concentration camps.

Memories of the First World War caused most sane people to realise the futility of war, and most countries had embarked upon a policy of disarmament. Military equipment that became obsolescent was not replaced, and defence budgets were cut to a minimum.

When it was realised that Germany was secretly rearming, numerous people felt that more money should be spent on defence. Often they were branded as warmongers, Winston Churchill being frequently referred to in that way. There were many people who insisted on the virtues of disarmament and who had a naive trust that the world could be made a safer place by willing it to be so. They related to the mental state of the students of the University of Oxford Union in their annual debate of 1933 who passed the resolution "That this house will in no circumstances fight for its king and country". This resolution, which Winston Churchill subsequently labelled "ever shameful" created an impression in countries like Germany, Italy, Japan and Russia that Britain had become degenerate and decadent, which was enough, according to Churchill, "to sway many calculations" in those countries.

It was clear to me, as I am sure it was to most people, that there was no limit to Hitler's ambitions. If we valued our freedom to live the kind of life we chose to live, we would have to fight to preserve it. About 440 B.C an Athenian General said "Freedom is the sure possession of those who have the courage to defend it". Nothing has changed. I thought that the freedom we had was not a birthright but a privilege gained for us by the sacrifices of others. So it was up to us as individuals to decide whether or not we valued that privilege enough to fight to defend it.

I was in England when, on Sunday morning, 3 September 1939, Prime Minister Neville Chamberlain declared, "We are now at war with Germany". German troops had marched into Poland, and the British government had instructed its ambassador in Berlin to inform the German government that if the German troops were not withdrawn from Polish territory by 1100 hours on that Sunday morning, a state of war would exist between Britain and Germany.

It must have been a sad moment for Neville Chamberlain. From what I have read in later years I have concluded that in 1938 when he came to an agreement with Hitler to allow Germany to annex part of Czechoslovakia, he really believed that he had won "peace in our time". It seems that he was just as gullible as many peace activists.

We had a war on our hands and we were not prepared for war. I was appalled at the thought of having to be involved but I knew I had to be.

And so as I waited on the runway such thoughts used to rush through my head, trying as I might to make sense of my being in an essentially intolerable situation. I became used to the new experience of having such a review and constant internal dialogue with myself which was to last for the duration of the extensive series of combat missions I undertook in Lancasters.

Before this sortie, as it proved to be for every other sortie, the preparation and waiting time approximated for me to what I had understood of the experience of New Zealanders in the trenches in the First World War. Waiting for the whistle to blow as the order to go 'over the top' was the time of the utmost trepidation - only the whistle for us was a Very flare fired from the airfield's control tower.

Chapter 2

Lucky Starter

My arrival on this planet on the 17 November 1916 may not have been quite the joyous occasion more favourable circumstances would have engendered. Frantic battles of the First World War were being fought. Many New Zealanders were falling in battle. My mother had recently received the sad news that her brother had been killed in France. It was a merciful fact that she could never know that one day another great conflict was going to expose her newly arrived baby to the same fate.

Fig. 1. Douglas (age 2), holding mother's hand. Outside a barn at Spotswood, North Canterbury, New Zealand. Father in doorway and Jack looking at him. Circa 1918.

It was to be my father's birthday on 19 November. Since he already had a son, he was hoping for a daughter. It may be that tiny babies can react to the immediate social atmosphere. It may be that I sensed the tension that prevailed because I have been told that I would lie quietly in my cot for hours without making any noise.

The first actual memories I have, however, are of my third year by which time I was mobile and taking an interest in my surroundings. We were living on a farm in North Canterbury in the South Island of New Zealand. The fact of which I was unaware at that time was that the owner of the farm lived in Christchurch. Later on I assumed that my father was probably the farm manager.

*Fig. 2. Douglas (age 3),standing behind brother
Jack. Mother and father on right.*

Christchurch, circa. 1919.

There was a ladder leaning against a very high post. Surely
there must be something up there, I reasoned, because I had seen
my father coming down. I felt it was prudent, however, to
investigate when no one was around. As my father must have gone
inside for a cup of tea, it seemed a good opportunity to find out. I
was about two thirds of the way up the ladder when I heard a voice
say "See if you can get up to the top". It sounded like my father's
voice but it didn't have the usual growling sound. Before I got on to
the next rung of the ladder I felt my father's arm around me so I
never did find out what was up there.

Beneath me as I climbed the ladder there was a concrete area
where my brother Jack used to ride his tricycle. Jack was two years
and four months older than I, and had been given the tricycle by
the owner of the farm. It was made clear to me that it was Jack's
tricycle and that nobody else was allowed to ride it. I have no
recollection of the person who made that clear to me but it was
indelibly fixed in my mind that such was the case, though of course
I often longed to see if I could ride it. By to-day's standards,
tricycles then were primitive indeed, with all metal wheels and of
course no rubber tyres. I never did ride that tricycle.

In a shallow gully below the house ran a small stream, over
which a wide, thick, plank provided the means of crossing without
getting wet feet. We had been warned always to be very careful
when crossing it because on the lower side was a very deep pool, so

deep in fact that it was reputed to be bottomless. I remember pausing one day as I crossed the plank to peer down into the pool below. It certainly was deep and I couldn't see the bottom. But I can remember wondering why, that if it were a bottomless pool, the water didn't fall out of it.

I must have had an enquiring mind - which on a particular occasion could so easily have caused a major disaster. Jack and I had been warned that we must never touch matches. In those days all matches were wax matches, not the wooden safety matches that were produced at a later date. Wax matches were made of strands of waxed cotton twisted together to form a stem, on the end of which was a phosphorescent head. It was possible to strike them on almost anything, including such unlikely items as a pane of glass, the fabric of one's trousers or even the stubble of a well weather beaten face. Because the wax melted quickly, those matches stayed alight more easily in a wind.

One day I was able to acquire a box of matches, so I decided to find out what the mystery was all about. I crept into the sitting room (which we would now call the lounge) and hid behind the china cabinet. I carefully selected a match and struck it on the striking part of the matchbox. Of course, it burned freely. I wondered what all the fuss was about, calmly disposing of the burning match by popping it into a hole which I found in the wall. Twice more I repeated the exercise, which just about satisfied my curiosity.

That took place eighty-three years ago and the house is still standing. It needs to be explained that in those days in New Zealand, houses were constructed almost entirely of timber. A timber framing was erected on the outside onto which were nailed overlapping weather boards. On the inside were nailed rough sawn boards, over which jute scrim was stretched and tacked. On top of the scrim could be pasted wallpaper to give a final finish. It seems that one of the interior boards must have had a knot which had fallen out, leaving a hole in a most convenient place for me to post the flaming matches. There is a saying that "curiosity killed the cat". I think my cat life must have had more than the nine lives which cats get away with.

I recalled that experience when I had young children of my own, making sure that they understood matches and how they worked. The natural curiosity of most young children leads to questions to which they want some answers. Yet it was common family policy in those times to observe the dictum that "children should be seen but not heard", which discouraged children from asking questions and caused a conflict of interest, to the detriment of a child's development that normally proceeds by way of observing and experimenting.

I remember a little about my first trip away from home. My mother took us to her old home in Westland, where her parents were still living. It was on the West Coast of the South Island, where she grew up. It was a big journey to undertake at that time.

Our luggage was packed in two basket-ware containers designed for travelling. Each container had a lid, which looked the same as the one containing the clothes, except that it was slightly bigger and fitted completely over the one in which the clothes were packed. Then two straps, one at each end, which had a carrying handle between them, were fitted. We were ready for the road. There were just the three of us – mother, Jack and me. I suppose it must have been too costly for my father to come with us or it was impossible for him to leave the work of the farm. We must have travelled to Parnassus railway station by horse and gig but I remember nothing of that part of the journey.

I remember however being at Waipara railway station and needing to use the toilet. My mother took me along the platform to a separate building with two doors. On each door was a container into which she had to put a penny before the door would open. When the door was opened I was a little scared to see high up on the back wall a big metal box with a chain and handle hanging down and a strange looking seat on which to sit. It was not the sort of arrangement I was used to but it was reassuring to have my mother with me.

Again I became anxious after my mother had returned me to our seat in the carriage. She decided then to go back to get herself a cup of tea. I was very concerned that the train would start before she came back. Taking me to the lavatory had used up a considerable amount of the stop time. I had heard the guard announce that the train would stop for a few minutes for refreshments but I wasn't sure for how long. My mother duly arrived back in the carriage, carrying a cup of tea and a small cake of chocolate each for Jack and me. At that time, and for many years afterwards, one could buy a small cake of chocolate for only a penny.

Away went the train on its way to Christchurch. My mother was managing to drink her tea in spite of the lurching train but I got myself worried that she had not had time to return her cup and saucer to where she bought it and might be blamed for stealing it. She was able to put my mind to rest, however. For an unseasoned traveller there can be so many problems.

Arriving at Christchurch railway station after dark on that occasion, my mother hired a hansom cab, which was waiting on the roadside, along with several others. The driver put our luggage aboard and my mother told him where we wanted to go. This was the first time I had seen a city. Being dark made it impossible for me to see very much but everything I did see intrigued me immensely. There were so many big buildings, roads and all sorts of horse drawn vehicles with different sorts of lights and even some motorcars. I was particularly impressed by the quietness of the hansom cab in which we were travelling. I was so used to hearing the noise of the iron-tyred gig wheels on a gravel road. But to hear just the clip clop of the horse's hoofs with rubber tyred wheels on a paved road was most impressive. I was surprised and fascinated too, to see the driver sitting up so high behind us.

My grandparents on my father's side lived in Christchurch, so they were waiting for us when we arrived. Soon we were enjoying a nice meal. There were no kerosene lamps and candles in their house. All the lights were gas lights. Soon I was tucked up in bed. I was very tired. The next day we travelled back to the railway station. In daylight of course, there were lots more things for me to see, especially the huge, powerful steam engine, which I was allowed to view before we boarded the train. It scared me when it suddenly sent out a big cloud of steam.

We set off on our way to the West Coast. I was excited but still tired enough to sleep, apparently for most of the time, because I remember nothing of the trip until we arrived at Arthur's Pass after travelling for about four hours. We were then in mountainous country and as I had slept we had passed through sixteen tunnels. Our train could go no further when it reached the mountain range called the Southern Alps. We had to leave the train and board a stage coach but from that point onwards I remember almost nothing about the rest of the journey.

Of being on the West Coast and the journey back home I have only two vague memories – one, of being helped to board the stage coach with my mother and the other, of watching the wheels of the coach cutting their way through the snow. About three years later, my mother again took us to her old home and I do have some memories of that occasion.

Times were hard for most parents. Money was in short supply. Hours of work were long and arduous, especially in country areas. Children were consequently often regarded somewhat as a nuisance, so we mostly had to make our own entertainment. Our parents had to do everything the hard way. There were no washing machines, dishwashers, refrigerators, vacuum cleaners, radios, television, or any other of the labour saving devices that are taken for granted today.

This was mainly because they had not yet been invented, or if they had been invented they could not be afforded – but in any case we had no electricity to run such things. For light we depended on kerosene lamps and candles. For transport we used horseback, horse and gig, horse and buggy, or horse and dray, depending on the particular requirements. And, of course, we walked. People walked as the natural thing to do. Walking dictated so much of the pace of life.

City houses were lit by gas. Transport in the city was mainly by bicycle, horse drawn tram, or hansom cab. There were cars around but they were few and far between in the city and scarce in the country. I remember at the age of five rushing in to my mother and excitedly shouting, "Mum, I just saw a motorcar". Even in the cities there were very few telephones. Working, eating and sleeping formed the measure of life for the majority. Leisure time, entertainments, vacations and the ubiquitous sporting attractions as they now exist were virtually unknown then. Such diversions as were available were out of the reach of most people owing to their lack of leisure time or ability to pay for it.

By the time I was four we were living on a different farm on the road between Parnassus and Waiau. Apart from those who lived on the property, we saw few people. Social events were rare but I do remember one which created great excitement. Our parents organised a woolshed dance. The contribution from Jack and me must have been minimal but we found ourselves involved, much to our delight.

The area of the woolshed where the wool was classified, stored and baled had to be cleared of any paraphernalia which could be moved to provide a suitable area for dancing. Then a wool sack about one third full of wool was dragged around the area to flatten and sweep the rough floor to provide a suitable surface for dancing. This usually took a long time and looked like hard work but neighbours came in to help. The next step was to gather bush cuttings, shrubs, tree branches, flax bushes and ferns from nearby undergrowth and woodland to adorn numerous spots all round the woolshed, creating a pleasing atmosphere and helping to minimise the sheep shed odours.

The area where the actual shearing normally occurred was cleaned and decorated, making a suitable place for supper to be enjoyed. Just outside the big sliding door of the woolshed a makeshift stand was erected to hold a beer keg. Last of all, an area where sheep would often still be housed was covered with empty wool packs, making a cosy place for Jack and me and other children to be put to bed. By then nearly everything necessary had been done - but not quite. What about the orchestra? A horse was harnessed into a spring dray and my parents' old piano was loaded and transported to the Ballroom.

I guess I must have slept through all the frivolity because my next memory is of the following morning, when Jack and I saw the beer barrel sitting outside the woolshed door. Since no one seemed to be around, we sampled some of the contents.

Occasions such as this took place from time to time in the country districts in those early days. Primitive transport facilities made travel difficult, so folk had to provide most of their own entertainment and, for that very reason, probably enjoyed it all the more.

Jack and I were, to a large degree, left to our own devices to spend our time. For example, we somehow knew what a telephone was because we used to tear strips of flax and twist them together to make a 'pretend' telephone wire, which we strung up between the shrubs. We would each take hold of one end of it and talk to each other by 'phone'. Of course, we needed to talk fairly loudly because the reception left much to be desired.

Across the road from the house was a small creek. It was a natural attraction for small children where we used to spend many happy hours turning over boulders to see what creatures were hiding underneath them. I don't remember how, but one day we caught an eel. Thinking that our mother might cook it for us to eat, we proceeded to beat its head with a stick to kill it. While we were doing that one of the staff appeared and said, "If you want to kill that eel, you should hit it on the tail, because that is where its nerve centre is". We did that and immediately it became motionless. It was a surprising lesson I learned at a young age about eels. In the years since then I have realised how many people have not known that fact.

A nearby gully harboured many native trees and shrubs. One of my most treasured experiences was when my mother took the two of us up the gully in search of birds' nests. If we could get close enough to see the nest we were allowed to peer inside but we were not allowed to damage the nest or take any eggs.

We had been given a white rabbit, which was kept in a small area fenced with netting and containing a box for shelter. We called it our rabbit hutch. One morning we found that the wire netting had been cut and the white rabbit was missing. We never knew the answer to the mystery of its escape. I decided to look for it in the surrounding hills but I hoped that if I failed to find it I could replace it with an ordinary grey rabbit, so I set off to find one. I walked round the hillside putting my little arm into every burrow I could see. It wasn't easy because the grass was dry and slippery and my arm was not long enough to reach far into a burrow. I was four years old.

I met up with one of the shepherds who asked me what I was doing. I explained that I was trying to find a grey rabbit to replace a white rabbit, which we had lost. He said, "But aren't you afraid of getting bitten?" I knew that rabbits didn't bite because many times I had picked up the white rabbit and stroked it. I was surprised that a grown man could think that rabbits would bite. Surprisingly, I did find a rabbit and pulled it out of its burrow. Holding it securely in my arms, I went to stroke it but it suddenly put its two sharp front teeth right through the skin on my wrist. Later on I had an identical experience with a dear little mouse. In today's jargon I suppose I had found myself in the middle of a steep learning curve, with two bites to show for it.

On Christmas Day 1920, a man who was unknown to me came to visit the family. He was a jovial man. He soon had all of us - including our parents - playing games such as 'Ring-a-Ring-a-

Rosie' and 'There was a Jolly Miller'. We had never done anything like that before. It turned out to be the only time such a thing ever happened. Soon after it there was a powerful earthquake but I don't think there was any connection between the two events.

A few days later, Jack and I were about to cross the road to play at our favourite place, the stream, when we saw two horses in harness galloping towards us in an apparent state of panic. We could see the harness but noticed that they were not towing anything. As they raced past we saw that they were very scared because behind them were the two front wheels of a buggy with nobody to control them.

What apparently had happened was that the owner had been sitting on the driver's seat ready to drive away, when the king pin bolt that attaches the front wheels to the body of the buggy must have broken. That caused the front of the buggy to fall to the ground, throwing the driver head first to the ground as the horses took fright and galloped away, taking the shaft and front wheels with them. Of course, it was not possible for anyone to stop them and we wondered what would happen. Blocking the road, about a mile further down was a solid gate, made out of galvanised iron piping, which the horses crashed into. We were told that they suffered bruises but were not seriously hurt because by the time they had reached there they had exhausted themselves and had slowed down. The event provided a lot of excitement for us of course.

One day, not long after I had my fifth birthday, I was in the vegetable garden with my mother watching her plant peas. When I asked her where I came from she told me that she had found me in a cabbage patch. When I asked which cabbage patch, she said it was a cabbage patch on a different farm that she did not remember. She said that God had left me there just for her. She also said that God sat up in Heaven with a big book and that whenever I did something wrong he wrote it down in the big book. I was concerned about that but I don't think it worried me unduly, because at that stage of my life I didn't think I had done anything that was very wrong. Later, as a teenager, I was less sure of that as a fact.

While we were in the vegetable garden I didn't feel very well and told my mother so. She told me to go inside and lie down for a while, which I did. When she came in I still felt unwell so I was put to bed. In the morning I felt worse and had a severe tummy pain.

There were two ways of curing whatever was wrong in those days. It was not practical to call a doctor because invariably the nearest doctor was miles away and that meant hours of travel in a horse and gig. So one cure was a dose of castor oil and the other cure was a dose of Epsom Salts. I was given a dose of castor oil. The next day the pain was worse. I felt a very sick little boy. It was then Christmas Eve. It was time to hang up our stockings for Santa Clause to leave a present. Our parents had bought a box of Meccano parts for each of us but since they would not fit into a stocking, we were told to hang up pillow cases.

I could not raise an interest, except to wonder if Santa Claus might think I was being greedy. In the morning I was not interested in whether or not Santa Claus had been and did not respond to the encouragement to see what Santa had brought me. Next day my parents decided that somehow they would have to get me to a doctor, so my father rode on horseback to a sheep station whose owner owned a motor car. In the afternoon the man with the car arrived. We all set off for the doctor at Rotherham, about twenty miles away. I was made as comfortable as possible in the back seat with my mother.

By that time I was in a great deal of pain. Of course, as there were no sealed roads in those days, the very bumpy road added to my misery. After about half an hour my pain suddenly eased off and I said I was alright and didn't need to go to the doctor. However, we carried on. I still remember the path into the doctor's surgery. In the surgery there was a high shelf containing a row of big bottles. I thought the doctor would reach for one of those big bottles, pour something into a glass, tell me to drink it and I would be alright. In fact, much to my disappointment, he did nothing. We went back to the car and set out to drive to Christchurch, over eighty miles away. By that time my problem was a burst appendix.

We arrived at Christchurch Hospital at midnight. The doctor at Rotherham possessed one of those magical appliances called a telephone, so he had been able to telephone ahead of us to tell the staff of the hospital that we were on our way. They were waiting for us when we arrived and what a blissful feeling it was for me when I was tucked into bed. Hardly had I had time to enjoy the feeling, when nurses arrived with what to me looked like a bed on wheels. I was taken out of bed and placed on the bed on wheels and wheeled away into a room with three very big, bright lights in the ceiling.

Several people in long white gowns were moving about. I was lifted off the bed on wheels and put on a table beneath those three big bright lights. I was lying on my back. A man in a white dress put something over my face and told me to breathe deeply. I did as I was told, although I didn't like the smell of something.

Then I began to dream. I don't know how I knew what an aircraft looked like, but I was flying a biplane. Looking down I could see the house where we lived, the woolshed and other familiar things, including a lone tree, which I knew wasn't there. From the wingtip of my aircraft a rope hung down, attached by its other end to the tree below. As I flew, the rope pulled my plane round in a circle and in doing so began to wind itself around the tree. As it wound round the tree the rope got shorter and the circles I was flying got smaller. Of course, when the rope became too short to allow me one more circle my plane swung round violently and plunged nose first into the base of the tree. A black sheet enveloped me and I knew no more until I awoke back in bed in the hospital ward. Years later I was to encounter that black sheet again.

I had rubber tubes inserted to drain the contents of my burst appendix, which had to remain in me for several weeks. Dr Ackland (later, Sir Hugh) did my operation and told my mother that another half hour later would have been too late. So I was almost the man who never was. Luck was with me from an early age it seems.

Chapter 3

Stubborn as a Mule

I was in hospital for eight weeks, during which time I almost forgot how to walk. Being in a children's ward, I was able to have some contact with other children - a nice change for me as my home location was so isolated. The draining tubes were in my operation incision for a few weeks. Stray nerves became caught in the wound and this caused it to remain very sensitive. Even now after more than eighty years I can't bring myself to touch the wound. When I was finally allowed out of bed I was taken to a table in the middle of the ward and told to practise walking while holding on to the table.

Out of hospital at last, I went back to a new home. At that time I did not know why but when I was older I learned that my father had decided that doing contract fencing in partnership with a friend would provide a better income. We had moved to a rented house on a different rural property not far from where we had been living previously. Nevertheless, there were new places to explore.

One day I saw snow on a hilltop nearby. I thought it was nearby because it didn't look far away. I had never seen snow close by so I decided to walk up the hill to see what it was like. I walked and walked, and walked, but still the snow was there on the hilltop. I had to return home without finding out what snow was like. On the way back I saw a notice on the top of a cliff, which said DANGER. Although I was only five, I was able to read the notice. Before marriage my mother was a school teacher. She was teaching us by using materials obtained from an organisation offering studies by correspondence. She taught Jack up to standard three and me up to primer three of primary schooling.

My mother introduced me to sex education under the influence of the taboos of the time. She was bathing me one night and noticed that my penis was stiff. She asked me why it was stiff and of course I had no idea. It was something that had always been there. I didn't know or notice what it was doing. She told me that I must never touch that part of my body, because if I did it might make me go blind. About that time a woman came to visit my mother and brought her three sons, all of whom were older than I. We were playing hide and seek among the pine trees when they grabbed me, pulled my trousers down and touched my penis. I wondered why, and it worried me. I began to think that there must be something special about that part of my anatomy.

One morning I heard that there was a horse in one of the paddocks which did not like children because at his previous place children used to tease him. About that time we had just learned how to make and use a bow and arrow. Jack shot an arrow into the paddock where the horse was. He asked me to get it for him. I looked to see where the horse was and saw him in the far corner of the paddock with his back turned to us. I quietly slipped through the fence and was bending down to pick up the arrow when I heard the pounding of hooves and looked up to find the horse almost on top of me. He knocked me to the ground and stood over me. Clearly he had made me disappear so suddenly that he could not see where I was, lying there on my back looking up at his big belly. I was wearing boots so I gave him the biggest kick on his penis that I could manage. The horse seemed to get a big fright as well as a sore penis because he charged away very fast while I got to my feet yelling my head off and running for home. I didn't even have a bruise to show for my encounter but had the horse known I was there he would have trampled me to death.

My mother did all her cooking on a wood burning stove. At the wood stack was a pile of blocks waiting to be cut into pieces small enough to be used on the stove. Before my father went to work one morning he told us to cut the blocks into pieces. He told Jack to use the axe and always to bring the axe blade down on the end of the block, not the side of it, because it could glance off dangerously. Jack was using the axe while I was gathering up the cut pieces and carrying them into the wood box. Jack tried to split a block while it was lying on its side. The axe glanced off and buried itself in my ankle. I had a very bad wound which kept me very quiet for months. My mother bathed it and dressed it every day but it did take a long time to heal. Like my appendix wound, a nerve apparently became caught up in a wrong place and even now I can't touch that wound either because it is so sensitive.

Rabbits had become a serious menace to farmers and I had learned how to set a trap. I was told that I could earn some money by catching rabbits, so I set out to do so. I also learned how to kill a rabbit quickly and painlessly. Eighty years later, while watching a T.V. survival programme, an instructor was explaining to a group of people how to kill a rabbit. He said "Having caught your rabbit, you will probably find that the easiest way to kill it is to find a good sized rock and smash its head in". I was very surprised because I felt that as an instructor he should have known his subject. The quick and easy way is to hold the rabbit up by its two hind legs. It will not struggle. While it is hanging in this position a blow to the back of its neck with the edge of the hand will kill it instantly and painlessly.

Although I dispatched quite a few rabbits, I did not earn any money. But in any case, if I had earned some there was nothing for me to do with it. I learned later that three rabbits would eat as much as one sheep and that if there were no predators around, one pair of rabbits could multiply to over one million in six months, hence the saying, "breeding like rabbits".

We had lived there for about two years when the farmer who owned the house apparently got into financial difficulties and needed the house in which we were living. To keep a roof over our heads, our mother took us to our grandparents on the West Coast.

There must have been much rearranging for my parents to do, such as the storage of furniture, but I knew nothing of that. I only remember leaving Christchurch by train, bound for the West Coast. Jack and I were keen to look out of the window so that we could see the engine puffing away and working hard to pull the long train. My mother said that it was not a good idea because we could get cinders from the engine in our eyes.

From Christchurch on the East Coast it is a steady rise all the way to Arthur's Pass at the foot of the Southern Alps in New Zealand's South Island, so the engine had to work hard. It did blow out a lot of cinders. We were anxious to reach the first of the sixteen tunnels through which we knew we were going to pass. We stopped at Springfield, where everyone got out of the train and bought refreshments. On boarding it again we knew we would soon be plunging into the first tunnel. We counted them all up to sixteen by which time we knew we were nearly at Arthur's Pass. Number seventeen tunnel, to be known as the Otira Tunnel, was in the process of being driven through the mountains. It was already over four miles long and would finally be a distance of five and a quarter miles in length when opened in 1923.

Arthur's Pass is named after Arthur Dudley Dobson who was given the credit for having discovered it in the early days of the arrival of white people, though the native Maori people had been using it for years. At Arthur's Pass, we boarded a Cobb and

Company stagecoach. Jack was allowed to sit up on top with other passengers. I had to sit inside with my mother - but I did so want to sit up on top.

There were different arrangements for the numbers of horses used, depending on the load they had to pull. We had a team of five horses, one each side of the pole, one in front of each of those horses, and a single horse in the lead. Originally, stagecoaches ran all the way from Christchurch but as the railway, which was in the process of being built, grew longer, the coach part of the journey grew shorter. With the completion of the Otira tunnel the stagecoaches were no longer used.

Our stagecoach journey on that occasion took a little under three hours. Gravel roads sometimes made it difficult for the horses to get a good grip, especially on the steeper parts. There were many ups and downs and some were steep. The view from the top of the pass was to some people quite frightening. We were looking down a very steep side of a mountain, into which a zigzag road had been cut. It was not possible for the horses to help to hold the coach back, so we were entirely dependent on the brakes. On the journey back up that road, able bodied people were asked to leave the coach and walk to lighten the load. The grade was so steep the horses had great difficulty in getting a grip. Six horses were needed when travelling in the easterly direction.

On reaching Otira, we again boarded a train. The carriages had one long seat along each side and at intervals along the floor for tobacco-chewing passengers to expectorate into were brass spittoons. As the daylight began to fade the guard came through and lit the gaslights along the ceiling. There were only two tunnels on the western side of the mountains, so it was not nearly so exciting, and by that time we were too tired to be interested in what was happening.

Our destination was Chesterfield, a small station ten miles north of Hokitika. It was dark when we arrived there. Our grandfather was waiting to meet us. He had brought his special wheelbarrow, which he used to take his can of cream to the station to be taken to Hokitika by train for the market. There was no road, just the railway line, so a well- used walking track existed along the side of the railway lines. Our luggage was loaded on to the wheelbarrow and we all walked in single file along the narrow track to our grandparents' home.

For the first time in our lives we were near a school. Three miles away at Awatuna there was a single teacher school. Arrangements were made for us to attend it. A train from Greymouth to Hokitika passed by at a suitable time so we were able to travel to school by train. There was no train home, however, so we had to walk. As we waited on the little station platform in the mornings, we could look along a straight railway line to a hill in the distance, around which the train would come.

When I saw the black engine in the distance I was always filled with feelings of trepidation because I knew I would soon be getting the strap. I was in primer three. Each night I had to learn from a standard one journal how to spell twenty words. All those in my class who had more than four mistakes had to join the queue waiting to get the strap. I think it taught me to spell reasonably well but I never did manage less than four mistakes. I also had to learn my 'times tables' and those along with the name Mary Hogan, my teacher there, became etched in my memory for all time.

Before we started to walk home after school, we used to lie down with an ear on the railway line to make sure that no train was coming. A long straight line in the direction of Hokitika allowed us to see that the line was clear in that direction. In the other direction we could not see because the line disappeared round a hill. It was in that direction that we had to walk. It was important to ascertain that no train was coming because we had to cross a river by the only means available, which was walking over the railway bridge.

For the first few times we were a little nervous because there were no sides to the bridge and also we could see the river below as we crossed the sleepers. The thought of being on the bridge when a train came was rather frightening. Once we gained a little confidence we did some practice at getting off the part where the lines were and on to the big bearers that sat on top of the piles. We convinced ourselves that if an emergency arose we would be able to deal with it effectively.

Once over the bridge, the railway line ran through a deep cutting with high banks on each side. Our mother had told us that if we should be in that cutting when a train came, we were to lie back against the bank and hold firmly to the ferns growing there, to avoid being drawn in by the speed of the train.

For many years since then, a good paved road has run alongside the railway, but in those days the road between Greymouth and Hokitika went inland through the old gold mining areas. It still offers so much of interest to someone who has time to explore, as we boys found when we were there all those years ago. In the nearby Kapitea stream was an abandoned gold dredge, which we loved to clamber over and which we pretended we were driving.

Fig. 3. Abandoned gold dredge (1923)

On the opposite side of the Kapitea stream were the remains of a timber mill, which used to mill the trees cut from the rainforest. To bring the logs to the mill from the forest, a tramline, using wooden rails, had been constructed. It ran deep into the forest. The tramlines and the trolleys that were used on them were still there, so we had much fun riding on them into the bush.

A large plateau above our grandparents' house, known as the Lamplow, was once a very rich gold mining area with a population of many thousands. It was strewn with old mining shafts. We were able to see the remains of old dwellings and streets. Although over thirty years had passed since the area had been abandoned for gold mining, there were still two old gold miners living there. Each lived in a little, single roomed hut with wooden sides and a canvas top. They both maintained nice gardens containing both flowers and vegetables. As a hobby one of them had beehives. He used to persuade the bees to create decorations out of bees' wax. We knew them as Bob and Jimmie. They were the only inhabitants on a large and desolate looking plateau. Both must have been living a lonely existence.

They never spoke to each other but our grandfather was on friendly terms with them both. While talking to Jimmie one day, he thought he might be able to solve what most people would have seen as an incredibly childish problem. Bob came walking by. Grandfather stepped out and stopped him, saying, "Bob, let me introduce you to a good friend of mine". Bob eyed him coldly and said in his odd way of speaking "Mustra Montagu, Jummie and me hold nor conversation - nor conversation" and walked on.

Our New Zealand whitebait probably ranks with oysters and crayfish as a delicacy but is nowadays too expensive for most people to buy. But at that time, in the season when they were running, I often went along to the Kapitea stream with a bucket with holes in the bottom, dipped it in the stream and went home with a meal for six. There were no refrigerators to freeze them and no aircraft to transport them quickly to market. Now that we have both those modern innovations the whitebait have been so thoroughly fished out that it is possible to spend a whole day whitebaiting and not catch more than a dozen.

Our grandfather had a few hundred acres of land, most of which was bush covered, but there was enough pasture to enable him to milk half a dozen cows and to send cream to a dairy factory in Hokitika. Having milked the cows in the morning, he would spend most of the rest of the day digging into a sandy bank to extract a little gold, which he sold to a bank in Hokitika.

At the nearby beach, he maintained a reserve of black sand. After a storm at sea, areas of black sand would be found along the high tide sea level. The sand was black because it contained many particles of iron that were heavy. So too were gold particles. He would gather up black sand into a heap. When the heap was big enough he would take his cradle down to the beach and sift out gold particles from amongst the sand.

When not at school I often helped him to do this. Apart from school, I have many happy memories of the time I spent on the West Coast. It was a fascinating place to have lived in, and even now, when I return there I feel those old feelings of pleasure within me.

We spent almost a year on the West Coast, by which time our father had been appointed manager of a sheep station in North Canterbury, so there was no longer a housing problem. For us it was a big change of environment and culture. No longer were relics of the gold mining era to be found around almost every corner. The rain forest that had become so much part of every day life was replaced by silver tussock and scrub covered hills where sheep roamed the open spaces. The myriads of birds filling the air with their wide variety of songs in the rain forest had given way to the plaintive bleating of sheep.

Our transport to school would now be by pony. Although we had more or less grown up with horses, neither of us had ever ridden one. We soon learnt. Jack was given a nice natured, willing pony, which stepped out freely without fuss, but I was not so lucky. My pony was exactly the opposite. Everything he did was under protest. He made life for me as difficult as could be imagined. He made me think for the first time that horses and some other animals could use logic in what they did. Until then I had believed that all creatures followed only their natural instincts in their behavioural patterns. I had been given a graphic lesson at an earlier age by the horse that had taken a dislike to children and had stood over me. The thought, however, didn't register at that time.

School was five miles away. On the farm next to us lived a girl who was two years older than I and a little younger than Jack. We used to meet and ride to school together. It took us just an hour to get there. It was a small country school consisting of one room and a porch. Between the porch and the school room was a door with two glass panels. We used to hang our school bags and rain coats in the porch. Most of the time I was there we had only twelve pupils and I was the only one in my class. It was a one teacher school. I saw many young children start school for the first time. We had pupils from the primers through to standard six, all in the one room. Most pupils arrived on ponies but there were two little girls who walked three miles each way. Several teachers came and went while I was there. They were always lady teachers and they were always nice ones who never used a strap

As time passed, Jack finished primary school and went to high school, where he had to board. I continued to meet up with the girl from the next farm and rode to school together as usual. Jack's pony was sold. I think my pony might have missed the company of Jack's pony, because from that time onwards he seemed to resent having to take me to school. For ever afterwards he behaved in a cantankerous way.

One morning he decided that he was not going to school and refused to budge. To impress upon him that I had a need to get to school, I armed myself with a stick and used it as a method of persuasion. He objected to that and did his best to buck me off. The more he bucked, the more I persuaded. Eventually he decided that he was achieving nothing, so he trotted away in fine style with spring in his step, which was most unusual. I felt very satisfied that I had been able to show him who was boss. Suddenly he jumped sideways up on to a narrow bank beside the road and scraped my leg along a barbed wire fence, damaging my leg considerably and making it necessary for me to return home to get my leg bandaged. After my wound had been attended to he took me to school without any further confrontation, doubtless feeling satisfied that he had won that round.

Fig. 4. Douglas on his recalcitrant pony (1928)

We had a special paddock at school where we left our ponies to graze until it was time to go home. One day my pony worked out how to open the gate, which he did, and allowed all the other ponies to go home, which they all did, while he stayed in the paddock, contentedly grazing. All the children without ponies had to walk home - all that is, except me. My pony did not go home - he went three miles in the opposite direction, so I had to walk a further three miles away from home and then ride eight miles home.

On the way home one day, with a strong wind blowing, my pony suddenly saw a small piece of corrugated iron that the wind had blown into the long grass on the roadside. He quite genuinely got a fright and shied violently. I was caught completely off guard and thrown out of the saddle. Next day, coming home from school, at the same place, he again shied violently. Knowing the tricks he was likely to play, I was not caught unaware. On the first occasion, on being thrown off, I was able to keep a hold on the reins, but I am sure that had I not been able to do so, he would have had much satisfaction in going home without me, leaving me to walk.

Except in the cities, all roads had a gravel surface and used to wind up and down the gullies. Since then, these roads have been sealed and the smaller gullies have been filled in, making travelling much faster. We used to stop at the bottom of one of those gullies to let our ponies have a drink at a clear pool. One day my pony sniffed the water at the edge of the pool, reacting with an obvious objection to what he smelt. I was not surprised, because the tractors working on nearby farms sometimes spilled oil or petrol, a small quantity of which could find its way into a stream. When this happened the oil or petrol always clung to the edge of the stream. My pony stepped into the water a little further from the edge, again sniffing the water. Still the water did not smell clear. He took a third step and checked before taking a fourth step, by which time he was in the middle of the pool. He then sat down - yet another round to my pony. Of course, I got thoroughly wet leaping off his back in the middle of the pool.

My pony was smart but not smart enough to realise that I too had a brain and was capable of thinking logically. Experience had taught me that when he found a new way to score against me, he would try the same move again at the first opportunity. Consequently, on the very next afternoon, before we came to the pool, I had armed myself with a stick. We stopped as usual to let the ponies drink. As expected, my pony repeated the performance of the previous afternoon in every detail. When I felt his legs folding up in the process of sitting down, I brought the stick down on his rump in a manner which was intended to convey the message that I did not wish to get half drowned again. He got the message and leapt out of the pool even faster than on the previous afternoon.

On rare occasions, particularly in the winter when the air was fresh, I would see my pony's ears turned to hear sounds that came from behind him. I would hear the sound of an approaching car and feel more spring than usual in his step. As the noise of the car got louder he would trot faster because he wanted to keep ahead of the car. Since he so rarely moved faster than the minimal speed, I always let him go as fast as he wanted to go. When the car was getting closer he would begin to canter. But with the car still gaining on him, he would break into a gallop. As the car drew level with us he would turn on an impressive bucking display at a full gallop because he didn't want the car to beat him.

Those were the days of service cars before buses became the method of travel. We usually got a friendly wave from the different drivers and learnt to recognise the different makes of cars. There were Hudson Super Sixes, Packards, and an occasional Stutz. These big cars could seat eight passengers, with their luggage tied somewhere on the car. They were all called touring cars, with hoods which folded down at the back. Usually the hood was down allowing the passengers the pleasure of plenty of fresh air and dust from the gravel roads. Closed-in cars with wind-up windows had not yet come on the market.

At school, because there were so few of us, everyone except the very youngest pupils joined in whatever games we were playing. We all knew each other just like a large family. We played our own versions of cricket, rounders, hockey and soccer. Girls and boys alike, big and little, all shared in the different games together. The bigger girls usually decided what we would do. From time to time also, the big girls would get together and decide whom they would have as boy friends. The respective boys would be advised accordingly. In standard four I had my first experience of being chosen as someone's boy friend.

One day, under some pine trees in the playground, I saw a small boy and a small girl standing together. The girl was holding her dress up. Her panties were down. The boy also had his pants down. I was very curious. Thinking that maybe they had a problem I went over to them and asked if they were alright. They quite innocently said they were showing each other what was different between boys and girls. I thought about my experiment with matches and felt I too would like to know the difference but wondered what God would write in his big book about me if I did so. Curiosity can have penalties.

In standard six my desk was beside the only window. That was nice for me because it was pleasant to be able to look out sometimes. I could see the row of young pine trees that were growing vigorously. They were about twenty feet tall, with their growing tips pointing to the sky. Since classes included children from primers to standard six, there were often many who needed individual attention from the teacher.

On one occasion our teacher was standing in front of us and addressing us all. Suddenly there was a strange rumble. Then the schoolroom began to creak and then to shake, gradually at first but then violently. Our teacher, standing in front of us, became petrified, gradually growing whiter and whiter. I looked out of the window and saw that the ground was shaking so violently that the growing tips of the young pine trees were at times pointing to the ground. It was an earthquake centred near Murchison on the West Coast. It subsequently became known as the Murchison Earthquake. It was very violent and repositioned a lot of local ground. It was not in a heavily populated place, so casualties were light.

By this time I had moved up to be the oldest pupil at the school and had seen quite a few pupils move on. My brother Jack was the only one who went on to high school. The economy was very depressed at that time. Many country children started work after leaving primary school. We had two good Prime Ministers in New Zealand, Sir Keith Holyoake and Norman Kirk, who never attended high school. As an ex-school teacher, my mother insisted that we must have at last two years' secondary schooling even though we had to board, which was expensive.

It was about this time that I first remember feeling a little apprehensive about what I read in the newspaper about Hitler and his Brownshirts, who seemed to be creating a lot of trouble in Germany. I was pleased that we were far enough away to feel that it was not our problem.

Since I was inevitably top of my class in standard six, being the only pupil in it, I could claim to be dux of my primary school (top pupil). Like my pony, however, my grandchildren were also capable of thinking logically. They reminded me that I was by the same token bottom of my class.

Chapter 4

Quantum Leap

Like many children of that era, I lacked confidence in myself. This was a deficiency made worse by the fact that no matter how hard I tried I was never able to satisfy my father's expectations over so many things. So on the advent of leaving home for the first time to go to boarding school, I was apprehensive about my ability to measure up to it and dreaded the thought of going there.

In the event it turned out to be no worse and no better than I had expected. All the other children were strangers to me and I became very homesick. There was a marked tendency for new pupils to be made the butt of practical jokes or even abuse - and for a boarder there was no escape. There was some consolation in the fact that there were others like me in the same boat. This helped to create new friendships. There were about fifteen boarders, four of whom were new.

I attended Rangiora High School. It was a mixed school, whose Head Teacher had progressive ideas about educating children. One of these was the need to learn to accept responsibility. Each class of pupils elected a committee, which held a meeting each Tuesday. Every Wednesday a representative from each class would then attend a council meeting to discuss the running of the school. I felt the idea was a good one because it created the feeling amongst pupils that they were part of their school and could influence how it was run. It did have an effect. In practice I sometimes saw a junior pupil reprimand a fellow pupil because he felt the image of the school was being tarnished.

Many years later I happened to tell a friend about the school council. He reminded me that it was a notable feature of the internationally famous Summerhill School in England, run by A. S. Neill, who, as its Head, had established himself as a progressive educationalist. His book on the school and his philosophy of education, which made a strong plea for the freedom and discretionary conduct of pupils at school, had been read in other countries, attracting the interest of parents who had reservations about the regular schooling provided for their offspring in their own countries.

Those who could afford the expense sent their children to Summerhill private school. Neill welcomed visitors to his school every Saturday afternoon. My friend undertook such a visit during the late 1960s, when Neill was elderly and near the end of his long career. In the hall reserved for Neill to meet visitors, my friend was standing at the front of the group near a small boy sitting cross-legged on the floor. When Neill came in he immediately spotted the boy. Within my friend's hearing the following conversation took place.

"Hello John, what are you doing here?" asked Neill. "I'm just watching", replied the boy. "But you know the council has decreed that boys were not to get involved at all on Saturday afternoons when visitors come, so run along immediately." My friend wryly remarked that the liberal principle of participation depended on having a policeman to ensure that people carried out the decisions that they themselves had made.

I was particularly interested to hear of my friend's experience, since it was the first time I had heard of any other instance at that time of a school run under that method. I had always assumed it to be the brainchild of the principal, J. E. Strachan. Perhaps it was not in fact unique. I felt bound to reply to my friend that we too had policemen to ensure compliance and that some of them as I knew from personal experience, were pretty proficient with the cane. But apparently that kind of constraint was strictly alien to A.S. Neill's philosophy and practice.

My school grounds were divided in half, separating the girls in one half and boys in the other. Even the school council must have accepted that it was imperative to keep the sexes apart. Unfortunately the boys' hostel was on the girls' side of the grounds, which meant that after school, boarders were not allowed to go to what was virtually their home until all the girls had left school. We were supposed to spend the intervening time in some of the class rooms doing homework, despite the fact that we would have an hour's 'prep' supervised by our housemaster, in our hostel, during the evening.

There was need for an initiative over that, because during late afternoons in the winter it was very cold in the classrooms. In the ceiling of our ablution facility was the lid of a trapdoor. An inspection of it revealed an area above the ceiling that could accommodate many refugees. By careful planning and organisation we devised a way of getting a dozen boys up there in less time than it took our housemaster to walk from the school to make sure that we were not in the hostel. It was warm up there and we discovered an added bonus. At the end of the building was a rectangular opening covered with bird netting to provide ventilation for the ceiling. As it overlooked the girls' bicycle shed, we could take station there to watch the girls arrive and depart.

Because I knew I was no good at doing anything, I did not participate in any sport, except a bit of rugby, which we were compelled to play anyway. I was surprised to find that I did as well scholastically as most of the other pupils, managing to pass all my examinations. I was able to go home only for the holidays at the end of each term and had no spending money.

On Sundays we were obliged to attend our respective churches. Having lived most of my life in fairly isolated circumstances, I think it was the first time I had been to Church. I was concerned to find myself standing with a prayer book in my hand stating that I believed various matters to be true. Since I had no way of knowing whether or not they were true - and had not even thought about them (although I had wondered if God really did have a big book to write things in) – I felt I was being obliged to stand in God's house and tell untruths. From then onwards I thought a lot about religion, asking myself lots of questions, but finally arriving at a solution that has continued to satisfy me. It is a subject on which there were many and varied thoughts. Each of us was entitled to have his own.

In retrospect, high school was mostly a non-event in my life. I no doubt learnt something from the experience. I made one very good friend, a fellow boarder, Cornwall Gray, who later joined the Royal New Zealand Air Force and was killed on his nineteenth operational sortie with Bomber Command.

On returning home after two years at high school, I became one of the staff on the sheep station that my father was managing. It was a big change for me to pass from sitting at a desk in school to the hard physical hurly-burly of the vast open spaces and thousands of sheep. I had a lot to learn. Reflecting in later life about how people learn and the value of formal training in commercial and industrial life, I realized that for me it was not so much a matter of being taught but what I had been able to learn by watching others. Accurate observation was and is clearly an indispensable element in the process of learning what to do in the realm of physical activity. But of course this in no way denigrates the importance of theory lying behind the physical action. It provides the keys to an understanding of the reasons for doing something in one particular way as opposed to another.

After paying my board, my disposable weekly income was five shillings – about fifty cents in today's New Zealand currency - but since I had nowhere to spend it, it had to be saved. The normal working week was six days and on the seventh day we did the odd jobs that we did not have time to do through the week. There was no provision for holidays. Working hours were mostly from eight in the morning until five at night, except during busy seasons when working hours were as long as daylight lasted. The hours were even longer again at the times that sheep needed to be mustered.

At those times we had to be out on the hilltops when the first tinge of a new day began to lighten the eastern sky. The reason for that was to take advantage of the known effects on sheep behaviour of the rises and falls of the air temperature. At dusk they made their way from the gullies, where the cold air was lying, up to the hilltops where the air was warmer. At daybreak they began to make their way down again into the nooks and crannies in search of tasty morsels. When they did this in the hill country they became so dispersed that it was impossible to gather them into a mob for treatment. While they were fairly congregated on the hilltops, it was usually a comparatively straightforward operation to gather them into a mob and drive them to where they were needed, with the aid of trusty sheepdogs. It was all part of a normal day's work. Overtime pay rates had not been heard of in those times.

On hill country, as all Welsh and Scottish shepherds well know, it could not have been possible to handle sheep without sheepdogs. They have a natural instinct that was probably antithetical to the interests of sheep in origin but which can be harnessed and enhanced by good training. They are intelligent animals. They, like humans, are able to learn by watching. A sheepdog learns a great deal from watching what the other dogs do. Of course, also like humans, they vary in intelligence, consequently varying in their ability and usefulness as sheepdogs.

They were controlled and instructed in their work with the sheep mainly by whistle commands. They could hear a high-pitched whistle at a great distance. On hills and mountains they were often required to work far away from their master, at distances up to a kilometre. Three types of sheep dogs were in use - Heading Dogs, which went out to bring the sheep back, Huntaways, which drove the sheep away, and Handy Dogs, which could do both tasks.

In time I had a good team of dogs, most of which I trained myself. They were my valued friends. We got to know each another very well during the years we were together. In turn they worked for me in mountainous country, hill country, and on flat land. During the winter months, when the pressure of work diminished, my father used to compete at sheepdog trials around the area. When I had gained sufficient proficiency, I also entered the various events.

There were some competitors, whom we called professionals, who used to attend most of the sheep dog trials throughout the whole of New Zealand. It made a nice holiday for them to go to such trials. The prize money helped to pay their expenses. Since both master and dog got lots of practice, those people won most of the prizes. The fact that I had a degree of success amongst all comers made me realize that perhaps I was not quite the country bumpkin I had sometimes imagined myself to be.

I spent much of my time on horseback on the hills, horses being the normal mode of transport in those times. If the hills were too steep for horses to retain a footing, we had to resort to 'shanks's pony'. When ewes were having their lambs I would spend eight hours of every day checking for ewes in trouble. Often I would disturb a group of wild pigs rooting up the ground in search of tasty grubs and plant roots. Their ancestors were released into the country by Captain James Cook on a visit to New Zealand in 1777. With ample food to eat and only human beings as predators, they flourished and multiplied, becoming a nuisance to hill country farmers. Not only did they root up good grass growing areas, they would sometimes develop a taste for new born lambs.

Meeting up with pigs brought memories of an experience I had when I was twelve that turned out to be more interesting than I had expected. A party of six had come from Christchurch for a recreational pig hunt. I say recreational because there were professional pig hunters who had appropriate rifles and dogs, trained especially to find and bail up wild pigs. Those men were just out for a day's shooting. Two of our staff took them to the best

Fig. 5. The Author in 1928 on the left on horseback with a friend.

places but I went along as well because I wanted to try out my rifle. So the party became nine strong. While our family had been living on the West Coast I was given a rusty old twenty-two rifle that had belonged to my uncle who was killed during the First World War. Having cleaned it up, and because it was my own rifle, I wanted to take it, even though I knew it was not powerful enough to harm a pig.

We had seven horses available, which meant that two of the nine would have to take turns at walking. While Bill, a staff member, and I were walking, the dogs bailed up a pig at the bottom of a gully. Those on horses had to ride to a place where they could get through the scrub but Bill and I were able to find a quick way through and arrived to find the pig bailed up in a small patch of scrub. Bill told me to keep out of the way because it was a boar. I knew that the tusks of a boar could be lethal. He called the dogs off so that he could shoot the pig without endangering the dogs. As soon as the dogs left, the pig charged Bill. He had a forty-four rifle, which made a very big noise. He quickly aimed and fired but the pig came on. Bill quickly reloaded, while taking a step backwards, and fired again. Still the pig came on and again Bill reloaded, while stepping backwards, and fired yet again. But still the pig came on.

From my position on the sideline I could see that if Bill took one more step backwards he would fall headlong down a bank in the middle of a gorse bush, so his life probably depended on the next shot. He fired for a fourth time but still the pig came on. That time in an instant Bill and the pig were in the middle of the gorse bush with the pig on top. They had both fallen on top of his rifle. Expecting to see blood spurting all around, I felt a desperate need to do something. But I knew that my little rifle was useless. I thought of poking the barrel in the pig's ear and pulling the trigger but since Bill and the boar were having a wrestling match I felt that it was too risky. I might easily shoot Bill. But I knew that under a pig's shoulder blade was a tender place, so I rushed over and poked the barrel under the shoulder and pulled the trigger. I had previously heard four times the roar of his forty-four. The puny little spit of my twenty-two sounded so pathetic but the effect of the damage it did to the animal was enough to distract him from his attack to allow Bill to slip out from underneath him. We both then ran over the bed of the stream with the pig after us.

The dogs had been for a drink at the stream and were now returning. The pig was wounded, so it soon left us and sought refuge in the scrub, where the dogs again bailed it up. Bill returned to the gorse bush and retrieved his rifle. His next shot – his fifth - killed the pig. I then found out what Bill had learned while wrestling with the pig in the middle of the gorse bush. The

Fig. 6. The pig that created much excitement. The two lead actors are on the left, and the star performer in on the ground! South Island. 1928.

pig was a sow, not a boar. Since sows did not have tusks, Bill survived unscathed. It did appear that my rifle was some use after all. Had I not taken it with me the situation might have been more desperate than it turned out to be.

Another interesting experience occurred during the times I was riding the range. It was not one that was fraught with danger or anxiety, at least not at first. A thick fog suddenly swept in from the sea. I was able to see only a few yards, but as I had been covering the same territory every day, I knew the country well, and knew my way home. Since I could no longer see the sheep I decided to do just that and go home. Occasionally I had to guide the horse in the direction I wanted to go, assuming he knew the route. A little later I realised that he did not know that I had decided to go home and that I was no longer following the usual route for that time of day. Quite abruptly, it dawned on me that I was not where I thought I was. In fact I did not know where I was. I stopped the horse and thought for a moment or two but remained uncertain as to which way to go. Then I got a big surprise. I thought the horse might know which direction to take better than I, so I dropped the reins on his neck. He instantly turned round and returned in the direction from which we had just come. Of course, he took me home, which did not surprise me, but what did surprise me was how he instantly knew what I meant when I dropped the reins on his neck.

There were many other activities in which I participated, apart from working with sheep. I learnt to drive and look after a team of six horses. That meant being out of bed at five o'clock in the morning, getting the horses into the stable, each in its own stall, and providing them with a feed of chaff for breakfast. Then each horse had to be groomed well with a currycomb, a special grooming brush, after which I went home for breakfast. With breakfast over I went back to the horses. I put the harness on each one before taking the team out to a paddock to work all day. Often we would be too far from home to return for lunch, so I used to take lunch with me, as well as a nose bag of chaff for each horse. When the horses decided it was lunch time they would stop. It was just the same at knock-off time. I did not need a watch.

With a day's work finished, the chains were unhooked from the horses. For me then it could have been a case of "A weary ploughman homeward plods his weary way", except that I typically sat on the back of one of the horses. On returning to the stable, each horse would go to his own individual stall where he would be provided with a feed of chaff, munched at his leisure, as a reward for an honest day's work. In the evening I used to go to the stable to let the horses out into a paddock. As the next morning required the usual early start, I had to get to bed early myself. We depended on kerosene lamps and candles for lighting. That form of lighting did not really provide sufficient illumination for reading. Wireless was still in the experimental stage. In any case since each day was always a fairly long and tiring day, bed never seemed a bad place to be.

We needed to grow winter feed for many sheep. Instead of buying petrol for a tractor, we grew oats to provide chaff for the horses. When the oats were ready for harvesting, it was usually my job to drive the reaper and binder, which at that time was a wonderfully innovative piece of machinery. The traditional method of harvesting was to cut the oats with a sickle and tie them into bundles by hand. It was a big step forward to cut the oats with a mower instead. As its name implied, the Reaper and Binder could cut the crop, bind it into bundles - called sheaves - and eject them on to the ground. The next step was to gather the sheaves into stooks in the paddock, where they stayed until they were thoroughly dry, when they were built into a stack.

A stack must be built in such a way that it will keep out the rain. It was crucial that the sheaves should remain dry. When more chaff was needed for the horses, a contractor would come in with a chaff cutter. The stack was then cut into bags of chaff. To do this a man would climb on to the top of the stack and fork the sheaves down to the man feeding the chaff cutter. Of course, during the winter the stack was a haven for field mice. Not only were there plenty of oats for mice to eat, but they had a ready made home that was warm and dry. Naturally, the mice were mostly near the bottom of the stack. When the bottom layer of sheaves was reached, field mice were running all over the place. I once had the uncomfortable experience of a mouse running up the leg of my trousers. Yes, it was on the inside of my trousers but I had the pleasure soon afterwards to report that no permanent damage had been done.

The age-old process of farming was as time consuming in my time as since time immemorial. From the time the ground was prepared for a crop and the seed had been sown to the time when the crop was harvested, the stack built and the chaff cut, a great deal of work was involved. For a farmer growing grain such as wheat or barley, the procedure was basically the same, except that for the final operation a mill was brought in to thresh the grain, instead of a chaff cutter to cut the chaff.

In these changed times the farmers pump petrol into their tractors and to harvest the grain a header threshes the heads of grain while it is still standing in the paddock. I had to learn to build stacks for grain and hay in the old-fashioned way that had been practiced for centuries. Hay stacks are no longer to be seen. The

Fig. 7. The author on the left building an oat sheaf stack in 1934

Fig. 8. Driving a reaping and binding machine in 1934

Fig. 9. On top of the hay in 1934

Fig. 10. Completed stack of oat sheaves

only grain stacks are oats for chaff. From my observations, however, it appears to me that stack building is clearly a lost art.

From the time I left high school until I was about twenty I rarely went anywhere. I was a home boy par excellence with scarcely any contact with my own age group, mainly because it was difficult to go anywhere. Since earning an income and being able to save much of it, I had bought myself a bicycle but as the nearest centre of any activity was eight miles away over hilly roads of gravel there was little incentive to venture forth. Metalled roads and a bicycle with gears might have been a greater inducement. I did however manage a couple of long trips during two periods of my life at that time.

The first of them was with my brother Jack, who was serving an apprenticeship at a foundry in Christchurch. During the Christmas break, he with two of his friends and I cycled about six hundred miles each way to see two of the world famous mountain glaciers, the Franz Josef and the Fox in the south-western part of the Great Divide of the South Island of New Zealand. We carried food, spare clothes and camping gear. It was hard going on the gravel roads, which were the norm in those days, and naturally there was a lot of hill work to do in assaulting the great mountain chain that forms the backbone of South Island. The total distance was so much further for me as I had to ride fifty miles to join up with them at the start of our adventure and another fifty to return home.

Two years later, during the Christmas break again, we did an even longer ride. That time it took us across to the West Coast at which point we turned northwards to the north coast of the South Island, eastwards along the north coast and then southwards back down the east coast. There were no tourist organisations operating in those times so if one wanted to travel, one made one's own arrangements.

I graduated from a bicycle to a motor cycle. I bought an old Harley Davidson when I was about twenty. It enabled me to make a little contact with the outside world. Sometimes I used it to go to rugby games for the local rugby team when they were short of a man and chose to call on me. I was far from being the stereotypical rugby figure of the New Zealand of today. To start with I knew little about rugby. I couldn't run fast. I was skinny and had little weight, so I had minimal value in the team, but I guess they

Fig. 11. A bike trip to the glaciers.

The author is on the left. His brother, Jack, is on the right.

Fig. 12. Setting out for the glaciers.

The author is second from the right.

Fig. 13. Puncture en route for the glaciers. Note the unsealed and traffic free main road.

Fig. 14. Stop en route for the glaciers at Chesterfield Railway Station where the author once caught the train to school.

Fig.15. Franz Josef Glacier in the early 1930's reached almost to the sea, but is now well inland.

Fig. 16. Franz Joseef Glacier.

The author on the left and his brother Jack on the right.

Fig. 17. Pancake Rocks at Punakiki during the trip to the glaciers (author standing)

Fig. 18. Queen Charlotte Sound Monument marks Captain Cook's stop for fresh water in 1777.

Fig. 19. The author on his Harley Davidson in 1936.

thought it was better to have me than nobody at all. From my point of view it did give me an opportunity to meet some of the locals. Ralph Gardner was in the team. He was also a boarder at high school at the same time as me, so it was good meeting up with him again. I also met his brothers, Alan, George and Eric, as well as his cousin Jim, all of whom were in the team. In due course I came to look upon George as my best friend.

Time came when I even ventured out to dances. I used to stand with the rest of the boys at the end of the hall, trying to pluck up enough courage to ask a girl to dance. All the girls were dressed for the occasion, and looked so nice in their ball gowns. The rhythm, melody and lyrics of the dance tunes created an atmosphere of enchantment that lingers still in my memory. Always we had an interesting variety of dances such as Maxina, Lambeth Walk, Veleta, Fox Trot, Waltz, Palais Glide and many others. As the band played a melody which had the appropriate rhythm for each particular dance, we tried to remember the melodies and words that went with them. Each had a story to tell, usually a love story. It was fun to be able to sing the words and the tune as well as to whistle the tune by itself - or better still, to be able to play it on an instrument of some sort. After finally making a supreme effort to approach a partner – usually when a dance had nearly come to an end – I would be dancing and wishing I had not wasted most of the evening just standing in the corner.

When my brother Jack had served his apprenticeship he went to England to gain further experience. Overseas experience in those times – as it is today - was justifiably regarded as a very useful stepping stone to a better job in New Zealand. It was my intention also to travel to England. I decided the best time to go there would be just as Jack was ready to return home. I thought I would see as much as possible of Britain and then travel round Europe with him by bicycle, before returning to New Zealand. As I had not been able to spend money in my isolated location, I had accumulated enough to enable me to see something of the world. I could travel by ship to England and back for a little over ninety six pounds sterling.

We were aware that travelling in Europe might have to be on a limited scale. There were many trouble spots. From 1936 to 1939 Spain was involved in civil war and Hitler had just reoccupied the Rhineland. It was expected that Jack would be ready to leave his work in two years. That fact gave rise to the hope that Europe would have settled down by then. In the event, by the time that the two years had elapsed, although the Spanish civil war had ended conditions in Europe were anything but settled. Hitler had made full use of the war in Spain to try out his war equipment, and was persistently nibbling at neighbouring countries with the pretext that he had to protect German citizens living there from exploitation and persecution. It was all very threatening in spite of his repeated assertions that he had no further territorial demands.

I left for Britain on the M.V. *Rangitata* at the beginning of 1939. I travelled steerage, which, in those times was the lowest class one could choose to travel. It was in the age before the advent of one class ships. At that time class distinction on board ship was rigid. Steerage was at the stern of the ship where most vibrations and propeller noises had to be experienced and endured to the full. However, we had good cabins. The food was excellent, as was the service, so I had no complaints. After the midday meal everyone went to their respective cabins for a siesta. Being young and active it was the last thing I wanted to do, but as nobody was on deck during that period to talk or play games with, I decided to lie on my bed and read. Soon I found it difficult to stay awake long enough to finish my lunch. Since then I have been able to go to sleep anywhere at any time.

We took two weeks to reach the Panama Canal. It was most interesting to watch the progress of our ship through the locks as it was raised to a higher level to pass through a lake, then lowered to the level of the Atlantic Ocean. Huge lizards ran along the banks as we sailed along. From Colon, on the eastern end of the canal, we sailed directly to Tilbury, the Port of London, where Jack met me. That part of the journey took three weeks, cruising at fourteen knots. There was plenty to do as we travelled. Ship travel appealed to me very much.

From London we travelled by train to Birmingham where Jack lived and worked. I spent a few days there with him before beginning my tour of Britain. He owned a motor cycle and side car which he had used to see a good deal of England. On discussing our plans and in the expectation that they would mature in the manner expected, Jack decided he would no longer need the motor cycle and side car so he sold it to me.

With such effective transport I was soon making my way north, with no rigid plans in mind. In the side car I had spare clothes, a

Fig. 20. On bord the MV *Rangitata, outward bound in 1939.*

Fig. 21. On Board the MV *Rangitata, outward bound in 1939.*

Fig. 22. Crossing the line on the MV *Rangitata, outward bound in 1939.*

Fig. 23. In the Gatan Locks of the Panama Canal, outward bound on the MV Rangitata in 1939.

Fig. 24. In the Gatan Locks of the Panama Canal, outward bound on the MV Rangitata in 1939.

small tent, sleeping bag, primus stove, a few tools and plenty of food. I was there to see the country, so it did not matter much where I went as long as I was going in a northerly direction, because I wanted to see Scotland.

Very soon I began to regret that I had not taken more interest in history while at school. I was finding myself in a country that was steeped in it. Everywhere I looked there was something of historic interest. If only I knew the history of it all I kept telling myself. Maybe an old castle or a township bore the name of an event in the distant past. I wondered from where it was that Dick Turpin had begun his ride to London. Little did I know on my ride north that, preserved beneath me, were precious relics from the years that Britain was occupied by the Romans.

In Nottingham I remembered something about Robin Hood and his merry men. I found the castle and grounds well maintained. I ventured as far as I could into the tunnel beneath the castle. I saw a bus displaying its destination as Sherwood, so I followed it because I thought it must lead me close to the remains of Sherwood Forest. Arriving at its terminus, I could see no sign of any trees. On the other side of the road a man was walking along the street, so I turned the motor cycle around and rode up beside him.

"Excuse me", I said, "are you a local man?" "I ought to be", he replied, "I was born here."

"That's good," I said, "you will be able to tell me what I want to know. I am a visitor from New Zealand and am looking for what is left of Sherwood Forest."

"Sherwood Forest," he queried, looking blankly at me.

"Yes", I prompted, "where Robin Hood used to be".

Again he looked at me blankly. "Robin Hood," he muttered to himself, as if he were trying to come to a decision about my sanity.

"No, I can't help. I'm sorry. I don't know him at all", he stated with an air of finality before hastily walking on as though he didn't want to be seen talking to me. I felt that perhaps I wasn't quite so historically ignorant after all. I believe there is an old oak tree that is reputed to be all that remains of Sherwood Forest but I never found it.

I continued to explore in a northerly direction, enjoying the sights as I travelled. I soon concluded that in my motor cycle I had the ideal method for seeing the country. There was little traffic to worry about. Most people did not have cars. The roads were all sealed, in stark contrast to the roads of New Zealand. I could cruise along at about twenty mph on a vehicle that balanced itself. Even the main roads took me through picturesque villages, which were such a captivating sight for me. I enjoyed everything I could see, but reflected how much more enjoyable the experience would have been if I could have shared it with someone.

Fig. 25. Camping en route to Scotland in 1939.

When I spotted a suitable place to pitch my tent, I stayed a day or two before moving on again, making my way gradually up the east coast of Scotland and planning ahead with the aid of a road map to ensure that I would always be able to fill the petrol tank at a convenient time. I planned to fill the tank at Thurso, near the north eastern tip of Scotland prior to making my way across the north coast. Arriving at Thurso, I saw no sign of a service station. Wary after my encounter with my informant in Nottingham, I accosted a passer by.

"Where should I go for petrol?" I asked politely.

He looked at me with a surprised expression on his face.

"Petrol", he said, "you won't find any petrol here."

That was an eventuality I hadn't counted on but decided that I would be able to fill the tank at Tongue, so on I went. At Tongue, however, the story was the same. No cars, therefore no petrol.

My plan was to travel across the north coast and down the west coast to Glasgow. Not knowing how isolated the northern parts of Scotland were, I made the foolish decision to carry on with half a tank of petrol. It was midsummer with almost constant daylight,

*Fig. 26. Sheep shearing as seen by the author in 1939
in Scotland.*

which may have made me feel a little over confident. On I went but soon found myself on a very rough, unpaved road. From time to time I had to stop and check the motorcycle for nuts that were working loose. My sidecar tyre went flat. I found that the tyre had worn completely through for about three inches. I mended the tube and covered the hole in the tyre with a spare tube. Continuing on and looking ahead I could see big, ominous looking black clouds building up. There was no sign of habitation of any sort, apart from birds and a rabbit or two. Rain drops were beginning to fall by the time I reached the north west tip of Scotland. It was time to call it a day and pitch my tent.

Next morning when I peeped outside I was greeted with a depressing scene. My motorcycle was looking very cold, wet and hungry, while still being drenched by heavy rain. I decided that worrying about the situation would change absolutely nothing, though a glance at my road map did suggest that there was cause for concern. I was able to console myself with the knowledge that I did have plenty of food with me, so I cooked myself a good breakfast, packed up camp and was ready for whatever lay ahead.

A peep into the petrol tank confirmed the worst of what I suspected. The tank was almost empty. When the engine spluttered I could switch to the reserve tank, which would take me about ten miles, after which it would be crunch time when I would have to decide what my next step would be to rescue myself.

Even though it was cold and wet, the old bike sprang into life in the usual way, and expressed no concern about having no breakfast. We were soon on the road, heading south into what looked like interesting countryside on the road map. I was surprised to have covered about fifteen miles before I heard the expected splutter from the engine. I was in bush country by then and was wondering whether the bush would make it better or worse for me when I became compelled to walk. I reached down and switched to the reserve tank. Crunch time was then just around the next corner. But around that next corner was a scene I could hardly believe. There was a road works camp with a petrol pump standing beside the road.

I had travelled all the previous day without seeing any signs of habitation, and certainly no signs of vehicles of any kind. A wise providence was certainly watching over me.

I asked a man standing nearby if I could buy petrol.

"Certainly you can", he replied in his delightful northern Scottish accent.

As I paid for it he said, "You look cold man, would you like a cup of tea? I live just across the road, and my wife would be happy to make you one."

It was a happy thought, and I accepted with gratitude. He took me across to his small dwelling and the three of us chatted for quite a while during which his wife provided me with a hot cup of tea and hot scones. They were both interested in what I was doing and asked lots of questions. Of course I told them about my previous day's travel, the problems involved and how pleased I was to see the petrol pump.

At one time during our conversation the man went outside for a while. I assumed that he had work to do and couldn't spend too much time talking, but in due course he reappeared and said to me, "I found a better tyre for your sidecar and have fitted it on."

What could I say to express my gratitude? Of course I would have been just as happy to pay for it as I was to pay for the petrol, but he refused to take any money. As a final gesture of kindness and generosity, as I was leaving, his wife thrust a bag into my hands and said, "Take these with you."

When I looked in the bag, I found six bananas. I left there feeling warm inside me and outside of me, concluding that the Scots themselves must make up the traditional stories about their being mean to hide the embarrassment of their generosity.

I had arranged to meet a Scottish friend at Eilean Donnon Castle, on the banks of Loch Duich where the Clan McRae Society pipe band was going to meet. At that time they were the world champions. I had the pleasure of spending the day with them. Dressed in all their regalia they marched along the banks of Loch Duich playing "The Road to the Isles." Even for those who, unlike me, did not appreciate bagpipes, the sights and sounds of that occasion must have been very stirring. They certainly were for me. I was able to appreciate by that event how adapted the bagpipe was to the Scottish environment. Afterwards I went into the castle and well remember the huge fire burning brightly – although it was the middle of summer - in a fireplace which must have been all of ten feet wide.

Fig. 27. The author goes native in Scotland (1939)

I slowly worked my way south until I reached the most south westerly tip of England, which, of course, was appropriately called Land's End. I enjoyed it all so much, and found it hard to single out anywhere in particular because it was all so beautiful. However, I feel I must make special mention of the quaint and beautiful villages in the Cotswold area. Today, I count myself fortunate to have seen Great Britain, especially England, at a dramatically different time, when physical movement around the country was an untold pleasure in itself, before it became spoiled by the torrent of road vehicles on ever more roads.

Fig. 28. In the Lake District in 1939.
Dry-stone walls were unknown in New Zealand

Fig. 29. At a slate quarry in Wales en route to Land's End
(1939).

*Fig. 30. Stonehenge as seen by the author in 1939, then
completely uncluttered*

Chapter 5

Take Off

By the time I reached Land's End in Cornwall I had spent nine months exploring England, Scotland and Wales. Continental Europe with Jack was the intended next item on the agenda. From Land's End I made my way back to Birmingham, said a sad farewell to my trusty old motorbike and bought a pedal bicycle. Jack and I kitted ourselves out with what we reckoned we would need for our journey and off we went on our bicycles, heading for London.

Fig. 31.An abandoned tin mine in Cornwall (1939).

In Europe the political situation looked very uncertain but we decided to press on with our plans. We considered that if there were a flare up of some sort, we would have time to scamper back to England. We took a few days to reach London, incorporating a lot more sightseeing on the way. Before we reached London, however, we learned that Germany had invaded Poland. It was 1 September 1939. But we took heart from an announcement by the Dutch Prime Minister that, as during the First World War, Holland would not be involved. His statement gave us hope that we could still see something of the Continent.

On arriving in London we learnt that all cross-Channel shipping had been cancelled, so the decision to venture or not to the Continent had been made for us. We also learnt that the ship on which we had booked our fares for the return voyage home to

New Zealand had been taken over for military purposes. We consoled ourselves in the Strand in London with a roast meat and vegetable dinner that we were able to buy for one shilling, which, in today's English money, would be ten pence.

We were obliged to report to the Foreign Office with our passports every few days, so it became impossible to venture far from Central London and we could not leave the country, of course. We cycled into Kent and stayed at a Youth Hostel to await further developments. During the night, there was a massive thunder and lightning storm that awakened me with enough alarm to wonder if war had already broken out. The next morning was calm and sunny, however, so we went for a walk in the hills. In the valley below, we watched a series of trains travelling in the direction of the Channel coast and through the windows we could see light glinting from the tin hats of the soldiers. We had a sense of being the observers of developments but no feeling of being involved either actually or potentially.

Next morning we went for a ride on our bicycles and came to a village where a group of people were standing, listening to a loud speaker in the square. We paused to listen too, and heard Prime Minister Neville Chamberlain announcing that since there had been no response from Germany to the demands of France and Britain that German troops be withdrawn from Poland, a state of war existed with Germany.

Very soon after that announcement came the dramatic sound of an air raid siren. Startled people all looked at each other, wondering what to do. It was a false alarm, apparently caused by an unidentified aircraft that flew across the Channel carrying a French general. We had heard the first air raid warning of the war to be sounded in England. At that moment the most improbable thought that could have crossed my mind was that I would also hear the last air raid warning of the war. In the event I actually did hear the last air raid warning of the war.

It was during those few hours that the final sentence of the writing on the wall that had been slowly but surely appearing - and had been of concern to me since my school days - was written. I was appalled at the thought that I should be personally involved in a war but it was clear that a menace was bearing down upon us. To deal with it we would have to fight. It would be a fight to preserve our freedom and the lifestyle we valued.

We spent two months filling in time as best we could before we were able to get a passage on a ship to take us home. During that time we saw or heard about the early events of the war. We witnessed the sad sight of small children, standing with their parents on a railway station platform, wearing their overcoats, a gas mask hanging from one shoulder and some precious possessions in one hand, waiting for a train to take them to some unknown destination, where they would be billeted with unknown foster parents. We heard how the newly developed skills of the Luftwaffe called Blitzkrieg had enabled the German army to overcome the Polish forces despite their desperate and heroic resistance in a matter of twenty-eight days.

At the same time in Britain, although war was the state that existed between Britain and Germany, strange assumptions were made about how it was to be conducted. In those early days they conceived warfare in terms that fell short of the practices that Germany had already adopted in Poland, that amounted to total warfare, but which ultimately became the norm for the war in all theatres where it was fought. It was thought, for example, to be important to avoid civilian casualties. Therefore, Air Force bombers could bomb military targets, but even then only as long as no civilians were killed or injured. A battleship constituted a legitimate military target if it were at sea, but when tied up at a dock side with civilians present in its vicinity it could not be bombed.

The theory was held that if bombers flew in close formation the combined firepower of their gun turrets would be sufficient protection against enemy fighters. On 4 September 1939, British Bomber Command despatched Bristol Blenheim bombers to bomb German shipping at Wilhelmshaven. Five were shot down. On 29 September five Handley Page Hampden bombers set out to bomb enemy shipping. None returned. On 18 December 24 Wellington bombers set out to bomb enemy shipping, nine being shot down. Two others were so badly damaged they had to be ditched in the North Sea off Cromer and a third one crash landed at Kingston Bagpuize, near Abingdon in Oxfordshire, making a loss of twelve in all – five from 9 Squadron, five from 37 Squadron and two from 149 Squadron.

At the outbreak of war Britain had fifty-five bomber squadrons with a total of 920 aircraft. The Fairey Battle force of 160 aircraft was quickly despatched to France. One squadron of Vickers

Armstrong Whitley bombers had not completed training up to operational standard. Of the rest based in the United Kingdom, no fewer than seventeen squadrons were converted into advanced training units. Consequently only twenty-five squadrons with 352 aircraft were available for operations. Since routine maintenance took a percentage of aircraft out of immediate availability, only some 280 bombers perhaps were actually available on any one day for operations. With the loss rate incurred by those early missions, it was quickly realised that the bomber force available would be eliminated in a short time. Theories and assumptions alike were being put to the test and found badly wanting.

At the same time obsolescent bombers were flying into Germany at night to deliver propaganda leaflets, warning the German population of the dire consequences for them if Hitler were not restrained. Losses of those aircraft were small. It soon became clear that the restrictions on bombing targets which put civilians at risk had to be lifted. The crucial importance of industrial targets in the Ruhr, for example, was recognised to the point of requiring the lifting of such constraints and also that bombers would have to fly at night to avoid an unsustainable loss rate.

We were eventually on our way to Australia via the Suez Canal on board the MV *Strathalan*, leaving Tilbury early in November 1939 and wondering if our passage for six weeks would be safely accomplished. At that early stage of the war at sea there was still respect for passenger ships on passage alone. It was not until 29 October 1939 in fact that German warships and U-boats were given permission to attack passenger ships travelling in convoy without warning. Until then surface raiders and U-boats had stopped enemy passenger ships to take prisoners or to afford the chance for their crews and passengers to take to their boats before sinking them.

The first hazard, however, turned out to be the weather rather than U-boats or surface raiders. The Bay of Biscay, notorious for its rough weather, certainly lived up to its reputation. We called briefly at Gibraltar but had just long enough ashore to see all we wanted to see. Once we were into the Mediterranean the sea was as smooth as a lake. Those of us who were willing to do so were allocated positions on the ship to maintain a look out. While I was on watch on the starboard side I was startled to see, protruding above the water about a hundred yards away, a projection which I thought could be a submarine periscope. I didn't want to give a false alarm, but I did want to give a warning, if one were necessary. Then I realised that whatever it was, it was rising and falling with the ripples of the water, and I felt relieved. In the event, at the time of our passage through the Mediterranean, there was no hostile enemy activity in progress.

We called at Malta and spent a day looking round Valetta, a very old and fascinating city, oblivious at that moment of the warfare that was about to assail it. I was particularly interested to see the milkman delivering the milk. He drove a herd of goats around the streets. Customers, who were mostly women, came forward with a jug, or billy, or any other suitable container. The milkman simply stopped a goat and delivered milk directly into the container. For me it imparted new meaning to the milk industry's claim to deliver fresh milk.

After leaving Malta we sailed through an incredibly calm sea. There was not a ripple on the water. It was as if the ship were sliding on a piece of glass. At Port Said we had another day ashore. Taking advantage of that duty free town, I bought myself a new camera.

On passing through the Suez Canal I was reminded of the Panama Canal. Suez by comparison was simply a channel cut through the sand. There were no complicated locks to negotiate. A

Fig. 32. Vendors accosting the passengers aboard the MV *Strathalan in the Suez Canal (1939).*

strange spectacle was provided for all aboard ship as we made our way slowly through the Canal. On the bank of the Canal on the starboard side along the edge of the eastern desert of Egypt appeared a large group of white-robed men, deliberately displaying their genitals. I found myself pondering the reason for it. If it were against the law there was no one there to administer the prohibition. Passengers on the ship as a captive audience dutifully continued to watch until distance neutralised the show. Was it a local custom to greet visitors, to ward off enemies or simply sexual compensation for endemic isolation? I have never discovered the explanation for it, nor whether we were uniquely privileged to see that display.

I had previously understood that the Suez Canal was wide enough only for one ship at a time to pass through it, so it was with some surprise that I spotted a ship heading towards us but glad to see that with care the two ships were able to pass each other safely. Soon after that the Canal was finally behind us and we were on our way through the Red Sea. From there until we left Bombay, the heat was oppressive. Air conditioning had yet to be invented, so there was no escape from the heat. It was always very tempting to go below deck to enjoy a cold shower. Whilst standing in the shower the decision to take it seemed thoroughly justified, but the act of drying oneself afterwards generated so much perspiration that nothing was gained by it.

We went ashore again for a day at Aden at the southern end of

the Red Sea before setting out to cross the Arabian Sea to Bombay, now called Mumbai, where we had three days to see and savour a little of India. Nearby on the waterfront there was always an assortment of vehicles of varying types and quality, with drivers who were willing to provide transport to wherever one wanted to go. Five of us from the ship hired a man to show us around the city. We saw a depressing number of poorly fed and housed people. Many people were lying on the streets, which were stained with the expectorations of beetle nut chewers,

Fig. 33. A street sleeper in Bombay (1939).

sleeping soundly and quite undisturbed by the noise and movement around them. Pedestrians stepped over them as they slept.

Our driver took us up Malibar Hill where he showed us grills across a gully on which human corpses were placed for vultures to feed. He said that the vultures had some special religious significance. We had a cup of tea at the top of the hill. Whilst drinking the tea I received an unexpected request from the girl who was sitting on the front seat between the driver and me. She asked me to change seats with her. The driver was apparently having difficulty in differentiating between the gear lever and her leg. I must have looked more trustworthy. To make it clear that he did not approve of the changed seating arrangement, the driver then returned us to our ship at high speed. With breathtaking nonchalance he negotiated the plethora of human, animal and vehicular contents in our path that left us in do doubt about the extent of his disappointment.

Our second day was spent taking a long trip out of the city into the countryside, which left me with no strong desire to return. We were not able to find out exactly what time our ship would sail, so spent most of the third day just walking around the city.

Two days out from Bombay, bound for Freemantle in Western Australia, rumour throughout the ship had it that a German pocket battleship had sunk a British freighter in close proximity to where we were. In fact it later emerged that the *Admiral Graf Spee* was on the loose in the South Atlantic and Indian Ocean, but far from our area. It sank the British steamer *Clement* of 5,051 tons off Pernambuco on 30 September 1939 and the tanker *Africa Shell* on 15 November 1939, south of Madagascar. Those two ships were followed by other victims, before the *Admiral Graf Spee* itself fell prey to the British cruisers *Exeter* and *Ajax*, and the New Zealand cruiser *Achilles* in the Battle of the River Plate, resulting in the inglorious scuttling of the ship and the death of its commander, Captain Langsdorff,

Our ship did not stop long enough at Freemantle to enable us to go ashore, so our next port of call was Melbourne, after a stormy trip through the Australian Bight. Looking around the Melbourne shops for a day was a pleasant change from being on board ship, and a relief from the rough crossing of the Bight. Hearing the familiar Australian accent made us feel that we were nearing home. From Melbourne the ship sailed up the East Coast of Australia to Sydney.

Approaching Sydney from the sea was a particularly interesting experience. We had been looking at the sheer cliffs of the coast line for some time. It was a little disconcerting when the ship turned and headed straight for them. At first there seemed to be no possible outcome other than a collision but as we got closer we could see the narrow gap in the cliff face. Beyond the gap, as we sailed through, we saw the spectacular sight of a magnificent harbour spread out before us, almost completely sheltered from the rough seas by the sheer cliffs. As we neared the huge Sydney Harbour Bridge I could see that it was not high enough for the masts of our ship to pass underneath, so concluded that we were heading for a mooring before the bridge. We drew ever closer to the bridge. I began to wonder who was in control of the ship as it did not slow down, even though it was heading straight for the bridge.

Fig. 34. The mast of the MV *Strathalan just passes under Sydney Harbour Bridge (1939).*

We got closer and closer and still were not slowing down. I looked again at the bridge and the masts. It was obvious that the masts would be broken off about half way up, if appropriate action were not taken immediately. But on the ship sailed. I stood, waiting for the disaster which clearly was unavoidable, but at the precise moment when the expected crash to shatter the hearing of everyone on board should have happened, the masts quietly slid under the bridge. I had much difficulty in believing what I had just seen but had to accept it as a fact.

Our ship was going no further than Sydney, so we had to await another ship. We spent a pleasant three days in Sydney, before Joining the M V *Awatea*, which was sunk later in the war during the North African landings, to cross the Tasman Sea to Wellington, New Zealand. From Wellington, we boarded the day-long ferry running down the

East Coast of the South Island to Lyttelton, Port of Christchurch, and at long last we were back home.

Of course a multitude of relatives and friends welcomed us home. As recognised world travellers we were made the target of questions from all sides. The talking went on for days. Soon, though, it was back to work and the memories began to fade into the past. War news became all-important. The war thrust itself into the forefront of our lives. Already, while we were away, our government had called for volunteers to join the armed forces. Among the members of the government it was noticed, were several key members who had been conscientious objectors during the First World War but apparently were able to join in the appeal without embarrassment.

My friend, George Gardner, had been to Australia to work for six months while I had been away but we both got back into the old routine at home, although becoming acquainted once again with our customary life did not stretch to the extent that we failed to notice the looming disequilibria. Many young men were already joining the armed forces. Both George and I felt it would be fairer if conscription were introduced, rather than leaving our defences only to those who were willing. However, after discussing the issues we decided to offer our services. We went together to Christchurch and joined the Army. I preferred to aim to be a pilot in the Air Force but lacked the necessary academic qualifications. Having signed on, we returned to work, to wait until the time to be called into camp.

Events from there on played a vital part in both our lives. Before I went to Britain, George used to tell me about a local girl whom he found extremely attractive. She was fourteen and still at boarding school. George was twenty, so he used to wonder if he ought to be so interested in a girl who was still at school. Her name was Nancy Stone. Nancy was by then in Christchurch, having left school. Having been unable to find suitable work in her own locality she had moved into the city where greater opportunities existed. She became friendly with a girl of her own age at her place of work, whose name was Margaret Shanks, known as Margie with a hard 'g' to her relatives and close friends.

From time to time, Nancy would go home to the country for a week-end, often inviting Margaret to accompany her. George lived near Nancy's home and would often tell me about the beautiful girl

Fig. 35. Nancy Stone and Margaret Shanks, the author's future wife (1940).

with whom Nancy had become friendly. Nancy had a brother, a sister and a cousin in the area who organised a camping trip at Easter with George and another local girl. Margie was invited and so was I, so for the first time I met the beautiful girl of whom George had so often spoken. She certainly was everything that George said she was. She was a beautiful person, not only in the way she looked, but also in her mannerisms and thoughts. Of course I felt most attracted to her but was very aware that a girl such as she could have all the boys in Christchurch knocking on her door and would be unlikely to be interested in a country bumpkin like me.

Fig. 36. Easter Camping in 1940. The author is seated on the front of the right hand car.

George and Nancy were married in the little country Church at Greta Valley. I was their best man, and Margie, who has a very nice singing voice, sang 'Because' as part of the ceremony in the

Fig. 37. The
author's Studebaker
in 1940, run on
Kerosene.

Fig. 38. Easter
camping in virgin
country of the
South Island in
1940.

Fig. 39. The
morning wash at
Easter camp in
the wilderness
mountain stream
(1940)

Fig. 40. Exercises at Easter camping (1940)

Fig. 41. The Easter camping group. The author is on the extreme right. (1940)

Fig. 42. The author and Margie in 1941.

Church. Nancy has survived to the present day but sadly my long standing friend George died in 1981. He survived life in the army during the Second World War, but at sixty-four his heart failed. He was a great loss. Nancy and the rest of us have had to make our way through life for over twenty years without him.

After a month, George and I both received letters saying that because we were helping to produce food we had been placed on the reserved occupation list. We could still be called upon at a future date, however. Meanwhile I learned that the Air Force had established a correspondence course, which could enable me to gain the necessary qualifications to train as a pilot. I had always had little faith in my scholastic ability but felt that there was nothing to lose by trying. Since the army did not want me, at least for a while, I decided to change to the Air Force. It took about six months to complete the correspondence course. There were times when I struggled. Private study like that, I found, was a good way to learn. You have to work things out for yourself. I learned, and having completed the course, I waited a further six months before being called upon to report for duty and told what to take with me.

My training began at Levin, in the North Island. About half way through the training the whole unit was moved to Rotorua, where we were billeted in hotels which had been taken over by the Air Force. No doubt the facilities at Levin were proving too small for the increased numbers needing to be accommodated. At that stage we were taking ground school, which exclusively involved classroom studies. There was no flying. Near the end of the course I became very ill with a high temperature. I was sent to hospital where I stayed beyond the time when the examinations were completed, so having been unable to complete the course I had to be relegated to a following course. I was disappointed at that because I had made a few friends by then and felt left behind when they moved on.

I began at the beginning again on the next course which I duly completed, making some new friends along the way. From Rotorua, we moved to Taieri, near Dunedin, in the South Island, where we learnt to fly. I had the feeling that flying would come naturally to me but such was not the case. I soon realised that as terrestrial beings we were used to accomplishing all our movements in the one plane. In the air, however, movements could be accomplished in any number of different planes, making it difficult to remain oriented.

Fig. 43. New recruits for air crew training in 1942 (author on extreme left)

I well remember the pleasure and excitement of my first solo flight. The De Haviland Tiger Moth training aircraft has two cockpits in tandem. The instructor sat in the front cockpit with the pupil in the rear cockpit. To see the front cockpit empty and to know that I was in control of the aircraft was a most satisfying - if slightly daunting – experience. Initially I had some trouble with air sickness, particularly generated by the obligatory aerobatics, but it did not persist.

On completing my initial flying training I moved to Wigram, on the outskirts of Christchurch. I had looked forward to the move as Margie lived in Christchurch, not very far from Wigram itself. Although we did not get leave very often, I did see her often enough to become engaged to her; which seemed to be an impossible dream come true.

I converted to twin engined Airspeed Oxford aircraft at Wigram. At that stage of my flying career it seemed a big step up to be flying an aircraft with two engines. Having gone solo, we each then teamed up with another trainee pilot, taking it in turns to do the particular exercises required of us. Harold Bruhns and I flew together and became good friends. Like birds of a feather, like minded people tended to associate with one another. As well as Harold Bruhns, my particular friends were, Bob Garbutt, Alan Frampton, Joe Lennon, and Arthur Jones, who was the son of a

Fig. 44. The author training with an Airspeed Oxford in 1942

Minister of Defence in the New Zealand cabinet during the Second World War years.

It was at this stage of my training that we were introduced to the possibility of accidents. Two members of our course were killed while flying together when control of the aircraft was lost as they were indulgently waving to friends on the ground. In another incident an aircraft crashed during night flying and caught fire but fortunately the pilot was thrown clear of the fire, though he was knocked unconscious.

As had happened to me near the end of the first course, I fell ill again. I developed measles and went into hospital. Fortunately I had passed all ground subject examinations but had not undertaken the required night flying. It was at that stage that we became qualified to wear our wings so I was acutely conscious of the fact that if I did not complete the course by doing the night flying, I would not get my wings. My friends would once again move on without me, while I waited to join the next course.

Fortunately, I was able to talk my way out of hospital a little earlier than had been planned for me. I went to Margie's home, where I thought I saw two blackbirds on the back lawn. As Margie and I walked together down the street, I saw two street names on a post on the other side of the street. My eyes had not yet recovered from the measles.

At Wigram, the chief flying instructor told me I did not have to complete my night flying, if I did not feel up to it. I knew I was not fit to fly but I also knew that if I did not fly I would have to be relegated to the next course, while my friends left the country without me. When darkness came, the goose necked lamps were placed in line for the runway and their wicks were lit. My instructor and I climbed into an Oxford. He told me to show him what I could do. At best, my confidence left much to be desired but since the instruments looked decidedly fuzzy my confidence was at an even lower ebb than usual.

We took off and did a circuit of the aerodrome. On the landing approach I found it very difficult to judge whether or not I was too high, since it was the first time I had seen an airfield that appeared as just a row of flames from goose necked containers marking the runway. I was having much difficulty in seeing the instruments because they were fuzzy. To make matters worse, there were occasional heavy rain squalls. When each rain droplet hit the windscreen it splattered, making it difficult to see outside. I was very dependent on my instructor for guidance and even when he said nothing I knew he was there to put things right as needs be.

In the event we did land safely. I hoped to hear my instructor say "That was alright, now let me see you do that again". But instead of that he said "OK, now do that by yourself and that will do". I took off again. On the approach to land I was more scared than I had ever been before. My lack of experience made it difficult to make the necessary judgements. With adverse weather conditions still prevailing, it was difficult to see anything. However, again I landed safely. Much later, when I was flying a Lancaster and tired after a sortie which may have taken eight or ten hours but feeling relaxed about the landing process, I used to reflect on the difference in life that experience makes.

On the completion of the course, a wings parade was laid on. All qualifying pilots were lined up. Our Commanding Officer shook the hand of each individual and pinned on his wings, while an official photographer stood by to record the event. It was a proud moment for us all. Altogether, it had been an especially long period of time in training for me, owing to my indispositions. I began it on 11 January 1942 and completed it on 19 December at the end of the year, the day I received my wings and was promoted to the rank of Sergeant.

It seemed to me to be a strange policy that pilots should be differentially ranked as either commissioned officers or as

Fig. 45. The author receiving his wings from the Commanding Officer of Wigram. (1942)

non-commissioned officers. In ascending order the former included Pilot Officer, Flying Officer and Flight Lieutenant, covering the ranks of regular operational pilots. The latter in ascending order included Sergeant, Flight Sergeant, Warrant Officer 2 and Warrant Officer 1. As in a university, we had all reached the required standard in all the set subjects, but we did not all receive the same 'degree'. If there had to be a difference, one would have thought that the best pilots or the best leaders would have been the ones to receive a commission - but clearly that was not the case, as practical experience had already demonstrated.

The dichotomy had been formally raised as an issue for the first time at the United Nations' Air Training Conference in Ottawa in May 1942. The Canadians wanted all aircrew members to be commissioned. All the anomalies and inconsistencies of the longstanding policy were recapitulated at the Conference, reflecting the widespread concerns being voiced throughout the Air Force. The British argued that "a commission is granted in recognition of character, intelligence....and capacity to lead, command and set a worthy example". They argued that the Canadian proposal would depreciate the standing of a commission if implemented. Rear gunners, for example had to undertake a personally onerous job but they were not called upon to perform the leadership and command duties expected of an officer in the discharge of that job. The issue was eventually resolved by the commissioning of all pilots automatically. Other members of aircrew were commissioned according to the existing criteria.

It was, however, in no way strange that in New Zealand as a remote part of the world and the then British Empire that there should be such a flowering of interest in flying and such a strong voluntary response to the call for flyers to go to war. In the First World War in 1916 steps were taken to train pilots for the Army Air Corps, creating the foundation for what was to become the Royal New Zealand Air Force. But there had been an important antecedent to all the interests and achievements of flying in New Zealand during the twentieth century, about which there has been world-wide ignorance. A New Zealander was a founder member among those who took the first initiatives to fly. Richard Pearse was a South Canterbury farmer, not a trained mechanic. In 1902 he built a petrol engine from scratch that was light enough for an aircraft. He was not a trained engineer yet in the same year as the Wright brothers succeeded in flying, he designed and built an aircraft looking very like a modern micro-light which he got off the ground.

His formal education was slight yet he invented many other things. It is generally conceded that Pearse actually achieved powered flight over a gully but it was not the controlled flight which the Wrights demonstrated with their machine. It was nevertheless a remarkable accomplishment to build the whole aircraft with its engine from scrap by himself. He later invented controls for an aircraft which were in fact conceptually in advance of those adopted by the Wrights and Bleriot. He was a man ahead of his time. The strain on family income prevented him from attending university in favour of his brother. Had he been able to attend the University of Canterbury it is thought most likely he would have come into contact with Ernest Rutherford, New Zealand's greatest scientist. It is tempting to speculate what the outcome would have been from such an eventuality. Coming from a humble family he had no education beyond rudimentary primary schooling. He lived an isolated life as a subsistence farmer but had an irrepressible desire for enquiry with an inventive mind. It is known that he subscribed to the magazine Scientific American or something similar, from which it is probable that he picked up the interest then being shown in the possibility of powered flight following the widespread use of balloons, especially in the United States.

It was with satisfaction therefore that I found myself with so many impressive fellow flyers and had finally achieved a pilot's qualification in accordance with a long tradition. We were all then eligible for final leave before being sent overseas. Because of the danger from submarines, all shipping movements had to be top secret, so we did not know when we would sail. Arrangements were in hand for Margie and me to be married on the completion of the wings course but we could make no positive arrangements for our honeymoon. We were unable to be certain that we would actually have a honeymoon. Harold Bruhns agreed to be my best man and we were married on 29 December 1942. It was a truly lovely wedding, arranged under very difficult conditions. Margie looked so beautiful I felt I must treat her like a piece of precious Dresden china.

Margie and I were very conscious of the fact that our married life could be a very short one. We were both well aware that the survival rate was low. I told her that I felt I was not being fair to her to marry under those conditions and that she should remain free. She was adamant that she wanted to marry. Since I did too, of course, our wedding was arranged. It was our own joint decision. I did not discuss it with my parents. As Margie was living at home, no doubt she discussed it with her parents. Luck was kind to me. Late in 2002 Margie and I celebrated our 60th wedding anniversary. She still looks beautiful with all the added advantages that maturity and age can bestow. She has gained the aura of wisdom and good judgement that have accrued from her long and productive life. Her looks, mannerisms and thoughts retain all the appeal to me now that they did those many years ago, reinforced for good measure by the realisation that they generate the same assessment and appreciation in others.

After our wedding, Margie and I were able to travel to the West Coast of the South Island, then north to Nelson, on to Picton, then south to Kaikoura, where we stayed until the fateful telegram arrived to report to Wigram. After reporting back to Wigram, I joined our group of newly trained pilots to find that we were under orders to travel to Wellington on the ferry from Lyttelton, the port of Christchurch. Margie travelled with me. We had had so little time together. In Wellington she stayed with friends, while I was obliged to report to the Air Force. We spent the next day together, after which I had to return. We said good-bye in the late afternoon. I expected to see Margie again next day but first thing in the morning we boarded the ship and left port in the afternoon. I was not to see Margie again for almost three years.

In that late afternoon, a group of us assembled on deck. It was 11 January 1943. We were without an escort, at sea, sailing alone, on board the *MV Akaroa*, a New Zealand ship, with the distant horizon that was New Zealand, slowly sinking from our view. We watched in complete silence.

When there was only a wide expanse of ocean left to see, I turned and looked at the group standing there, and wondered how many of us would see New Zealand shores again. As I watched New Zealand slowly sink from view, I hoped I would survive, but felt at that point that there was nothing I could do to improve my chances. It was just a matter of luck. But what was luck?

Fig. 46 & 47. The author and Margie marry on 29th December 1942.

Fig. 48. The author and Margie on their honeymoon in January 1943.

Chapter 6

Perilous Voyage

In 1939 I had been on board a ship on my way to Britain for pleasure and exploration. Four years later and deeply into the Second World War, early in 1943, I was again on board a ship, this time the *MV Akaroa*, heading for Britain but for a very different purpose. Any pleasure in it was to be entirely subjective and the exploratory aspects of it would be of an invariably lethal kind. On my previous trip I had seen much of Britain but Hitler had prevented my crossing the English Channel to Europe. This time, I would again see much of Britain but this time Hitler would help me to cross the Channel to visit Europe, albeit with a bird's eye view of it.

As before, we were making for the Panama Canal. For two weeks there was nothing to see but sea. It wasn't difficult to fill in time, as I enjoyed travelling by ship. I always found the engine room an interesting place to be. The ship's crew members there always made us welcome. There were games to play on deck and there was a good library on board. It was rather pleasant to have nothing to do but indulge in some quiet reading. As in the case of my return passage to New Zealand from Britain in November and December 1939, we had to take turns on watch. It was not a matter of finding volunteers, as it was on the former occasion. There were plenty of available personnel to cover the watches as required.

We were travelling on a passenger ship as passengers, but since we were in the Air Force the officer in charge told us what to volunteer to do. As a group of newly trained pilots, we made up only a small percentage of the total number of passengers, the rest being a mixture of mostly men and women, but some children. I was surprised that so many people were travelling, in view of the current wartime circumstances.

We had a day ashore in Panama, which allowed us just enough time to look around a little. Some of us hired a taxi to see as much as possible in the time available. We also had a day in Colon, at the Atlantic end of the canal. Many local people tried to sell us various things, but it seemed pointless to buy anything. To me, the process of making our way through the locks, through first the Gatun Lake and then through the other locks down to the Atlantic Ocean level, was just as interesting as it had been four years previously.

Once clear of the Canal, the ship turned northwards along the east coast of the United States. We were told to be extra vigilant on watch at all times because German submarines had been very active along that coast. We happily arrived without incident in New York, after a voyage of some twenty-four days. We stayed in the city for ten days while a convoy was being assembled to cross the Atlantic.

Our New Zealand shoulder flashes opened the way to an amazing amount of hospitality and generosity in New York. Our uniforms looking a little different from American uniforms, they attracted more attention. Although most people had no idea where New Zealand was, they realised that we had to be far from home, so they wanted to make us feel welcome in a strange country. It was a common experience, while walking along a street, to be grabbed by the shoulder by someone who insisted on buying you a drink.

While walking the streets of New York it was intriguing to look up at the sky to try to see the state of the weather. For us New Zealanders it felt strange to be cut off from the vast expanse of sky to which we were accustomed back home. It was not easy to tell whether the sky was clear or cloudy by looking straight upwards between the incredibly tall buildings.

We made the acquaintance of Nola Luxford, whose name had been familiar to us all in advance of our arrival in New York. She was a New Zealander living in the city who created a group to welcome, to entertain, and to assist New Zealand servicemen in transit. She was a wonderful person. She must have brightened the lives of hundreds of far-from-home Kiwis.

With her help, we sent home a gramophone record, on which we were each able to send a spoken message to someone special. In those times to send a record was a splendid novelty. Of course I sent records to my parents and to Margie. I also sent a couple of frocks and what I thought were some silk stockings to Margie but I was in unfamiliar territory when buying the silk stockings. They turned out to be made of nylon.

It was a great opportunity for us all to be in a big city like New York. We did our best to make the most of it. We familiarised ourselves with names like Radio City, Grand Central Park, and

Times Square - and of course we went to the top of the Empire State Building. From up there we had a great view across the city. To get to the top there were two elevators, a fast one and a medium speed one. It was the same coming down. We came down in the fast one but having arrived at the ground floor, we had to wait for our stomachs to catch up with us.

Having travelled in the London Underground system, which was always very clean, I was not favourably impressed by the rubbish in New York's subways but attributed it to wartime conditions that prevented normal standards of maintenance. New York was a city that never slept. By the time the planned convoy had assembled and we were ready to sail, to sleep was the only thing we wanted to do. It had been a stimulating experience for us, and we left feeling that we had made the most of our opportunities. It was on or about 14 February 1943.

Dusk was bringing the day to a close as we quietly made our way down the ice-covered Hudson River past the Statue of Liberty. It seemed that its light of liberty was being held aloft defiantly with a clear a message for us as we set out to make our contribution to the war effort.

In spite of having to do routine watch keeping, we soon caught up on the sleep we had lost in New York. When we looked over the ship's railings we saw all around us other ships of all shapes and sizes. Our ship, still the *MV Akaroa*, was not a fast ship, but was capable of a lot more speed than it was actually doing, having to conform to the necessity in convoy for all ships to travel at the speed of the slowest ship in the convoy. On the outskirts of the convoy we could see several naval ships, which we thought were destroyers, on which we depended for protection from enemy submarines.

The 'Battle of the Atlantic' as it had become known, was a desperate fight for survival between ships bringing vital supplies to Britain and their escorts, and German submarines endeavouring to cut off those supplies. Germany's huge fleet of U-boats was skilfully deployed in the Atlantic, being notably effective by way of the enormous losses of shipping they inflicted on the Allies during the period 1941 to 1943. Naval protection for convoys and anti-submarine capabilities were stretched to the limit, whilst hundreds of ships were being sent to the bottom. Merchant Navy personnel in large numbers were losing their lives, being obliged to live for twenty-four hours every day with the knowledge that at any moment they could be struggling to survive in the freezing water, amid burning oil, often in mountainous seas.

Theirs was only a slowly recognised and under sung but vital contribution to the outcome of the Second World War. Their casualty total was huge, comparing with that of Bomber Command in making their significant guarantee of open shipping lanes.

As Britain's aircraft manufacturing industry expanded, more aircraft were allocated to Royal Air Force Coastal Command squadrons to help the Royal Navy to turn the tide of battle against the U-boats. In addition, Royal Air Force Bomber Command was able to affect the war at sea by interrupting the production capacity of Germany, inflicting specific damage on shipyards, engine plants, ball-bearing factories and transportation systems to impede the orderly production of U-boats and maritime aircraft. Its bombing campaign was also maintained against the ports and pens where operational U-boats were being repaired and prepared for their voyages.

Bomber aircraft were also of direct use against the U-boat. An aircraft could keep watch over a large expanse of ocean. The water disturbed by a submarine on or near the surface could be seen from a great distance in daylight, making an attack possible. Aircraft were of limited use at night however when submarines came to the surface to recharge their batteries and were at their most vulnerable. The use of radar and flares was of some assistance to the aircraft but a real break-through came with the invention of the Leigh Light.

In 1941, Squadron Leader H. de V Leigh suggested to the Air Ministry that a powerful, short-range searchlight would enable a bomber aircraft to be effective against a U-boat at night. Tests were carried out using a Wellington bomber that had already been equipped with a generator for magnetic mine-sweeping. However, the Air Ministry preferred to develop a device known as Turbinlite, which ultimately proved unsatisfactory. Tests thereafter resumed with what became known as the Leigh Light, proving the soundness of the concept. A twenty-two million candle power, twenty-four inch retractable searchlight was fitted to most Coastal Command aircraft by mid 1942, enabling them to attack a U-boat without warning at night. In so doing however attacking aircraft were exposed to spirited resistance from the submarine's 40 mm deck armament, when the boat was unable to dive in time. U-boats were sunk in this way but aircraft were also shot down by them.

In the first five months of 1942, aircraft operating in the Bay of Biscay area had not sunk a single U-boat but had lost six aircraft. The Leigh Lights that were installed in most Coastal Command aircraft became an important factor in reducing shipping losses thereafter from 600,000 tons per month to 200,000 tons per month.

My own technical knowledge and general knowledge about the horrors and loss rates of the war at sea combined to give me mixed feelings as we began our voyage to England. It was interesting to experience how the war at sea was being handled but a chilling thought that well over one hundred ships had been sunk in a single month. We were all intrigued when our ship, being only three days out from New York, suddenly left the convoy and sailed alone to Halifax in Nova Scotia, Canada. We learnt that the convoy controllers had been informed that a U-boat pack was assembling to attack the convoy, which consisted of ninety-six ships, and from which in fact many were lost. It was decided that our ship, full as it was of servicemen and many women and children, would be safer by sailing under different arrangements.

At that time the apotheosis of U-boat success against cross-Atlantic Allied shipping had been reached. The tonnage sunk by U-boats was from March 1943 onwards about to be dramatically reduced after reaching phenomenal heights. Numerous U-boat packs, such as the Burggraf (13 boats), Wildfang (8 boats), Westmark (17 boats), and Neptun (9 boats) Groups were operating in the Northern Atlantic and deployed in various locations in the paths of the convoy we had left after New York and our own convoy out of Halifax.

Our convoy got through totally unscathed as others did. There were two probable explanations for the achievement of crossing without loss. The first was that effective use was being made of the intercepted command signals being sent to U-boats from their shore headquarters. The German naval codes had been cracked by the 'Ultra' organisation at Bletchley in Britain, to the extent that when information of the assembly of a U-boat Group had been received, a convoy could be accordingly rerouted. Alternatively, as happened to a convoy during the period of our own crossing, when a U-boat unaccountably foundered or was fortuitously sunk, a gap in the long chain of U-boats on watch was created through which a convoy could pass undetected.

In Halifax, the harbour was completely frozen over. On going ashore we found that the streets were also covered in ice. Cars driving along the roads had icicles hanging down under their mudguards to the roadway, which had broken off their tips. It was so cold there that we were only too glad to return to the ship, where we could keep warm. We spent a week in Halifax while a new convoy was assembling but we didn't go ashore again. It was such a contrast with New York.

Waiting in harbour during that week our ship slowly acquired a coating of hoar frost, which grew rapidly once we were at sea again. Having left harbour in Halifax on or about 24 February to join a new convoy, I think we must have travelled even further north, because soon it seemed that the whole sea was frozen over. Frost on the ship's rigging had become about two inches thick and on the railings round the deck it looked about four inches thick.

Above my cabin was a steam winch, which had some very loose joints. To prevent it from freezing up, it was kept running for twenty-four hours each day. Its clonk, clank, clonk, clank noise immediately above my head was not conducive to sound sleeping, yet I became so accustomed to it that I no longer heard it. Early one morning, towards the end of the voyage when we were approaching the coast of Ireland, the winch was stopped. The sudden silence of that was deafening enough to awaken me as though a bomb had exploded.

As usual we had to maintain the watches – a mighty cold experience while they lasted. Fortunately a watch was for only two hours, after which, if it were late at night or early in the morning, we would make for the galley to make some hot toast in a warm atmosphere. I felt that the watches were superfluous as I couldn't imagine that a submarine would try to push its periscope up through the ice but wiser heads than mine were making the decisions.

One night I saw a ship flashing a message with its Aldis lamp. The ship had buckled some plates and was leaking. I didn't see any action as a result, so concluded the leak was under control.

About half way across the Atlantic one of our escort vessels broke down. Our ship had to take it in tow. Some of us were standing by the rail at the stern, watching the process of getting the tow line attached. During it I had a coughing fit in a way that I had never coughed before. My top denture shot out and gracefully floated down to the ice below. There they were. My teeth were actually lying on ice in the middle of the Atlantic. I could see them lying there, so near and yet so far. I was paralysed with frustration. They would end up in Davy Jones' Locker for ever and I would have to be condemned to soup for breakfast, lunch, and dinner.

One morning, having left the ice behind for warmer waters, we saw a flurry of activity. Three escort vessels began rushing around at speed while sounding their hooters. We never knew the reason for their sudden activity but we were left to speculate that a U-boat had been detected. Once within the range of Coastal Command aircraft, we felt much more secure. They gave invaluable help to the Navy. One morning, near the end of my watch, a Boeing Flying Fortress appeared and proceeded to circle the convoy. It was a very pleasant feeling, just watching and knowing that we were under the protection of friends who had the ability to see danger and protect us from it.

On watch, if an emergency arose, we were supposed to blow hard on a whistle given to us for the purpose and to ring the bridge from a nearby telephone to advise the nature of the emergency. As I watched the Flying Fortress, my relief arrived - an army officer returning from India - to take over the watch. He asked me if everything was alright. I assured him that it was. To make him conversant with the current situation, I pointed out the Flying Fortress that was circling the convoy, whereupon he immediately grabbed his whistle and blew furiously. I looked anxiously up to the bridge and was relieved to see that no action was being taken. The uncharitable thought passed through my mind that with officers of that calibre in the army, the prospects of winning the war could be in jeopardy.

The remainder of the voyage was plain sailing into the port of Cardiff, in South Wales. Our group of pilots boarded a train for Bournemouth via London. In Bournemouth we became just another small bunch of Air Force personnel to add to many other similar groups from various parts of the world. We were billeted in hotels in the seaside town with weather that welcomed us with sunny days. It seemed a pleasant place to be. At last we had arrived. My friends Harold, Bob, Joe, Alan and I had all managed to stay together, but another friend, Arthur, had stayed in New

Zealand. The time of parting for all of us was looming, however. Soon we would be taking our different pathways into war.

It was about the middle of March 1943. To be greeted with brilliant sunshine, after spending ten days and nights sailing through a frozen sea, was indeed an elevating experience. As a popular seaside resort with many hotels, Bournemouth was a very suitable reception centre for Air Force personnel arriving from other parts of the world. I had a room in a hotel from which I could look down on an attractive park, located centrally in the town. I remember seeing many Air Force men sitting on the ground, surrounded by mail that had recently arrived from home. It took up to three months for letters to come from Australia or New Zealand. I was impressed by the efficient organisation of the catering there for two thousand men at each sitting. Altogether it seemed to be a salubrious way to spend time in the middle of war.

One day in particular was a little different from all the others, threatening to take the shine off our fortuitous vacation. It gave me cause to remember it well. I had just had lunch and was reading the newspaper in my room. I heard a very loud and unfamiliar noise outside. On going to the window, I saw four Focke-Wulf FW 190 fighters, their cannons blazing, seemingly heading straight for me. Moving very fast, I put two brick walls between me and the cannon shells. The earlier marks of the Focke-Wulf FW 190 carried one 1,100 lb (500 kg) bomb mounted centreline. A later mark was actually able to carry one 3,968 lb (1800 kg) bomb mounted centreline. The fire-power they were able to release between them was therefore considerable, resulting in the deaths of servicemen in the park, the demolition of several buildings, and some fires. As they had skimmed the sea on the way in, there was no air raid warning. They just disappeared as quickly as they had arrived. That was my introduction to enemy action.

That attack was evidently one of many similar hit and run raids carried out along the south coast and south-east of England for a while from the end of 1942. A verbal order direct from Hitler for 'vengeance' attacks on Southern England stipulated that purely civilian targets were to be attacked. The campaign became known as 'Jabo' raids, the word in German standing for the strong affirmative response with which Hitler's order was to be executed. The mastermind of Jabo raids was Oberstleutnant Pelz, later to be also responsible for the 'Steinbock' operation against Britain in 1944. The first Jabo raid was carried out by one 5th Staffel Rotte on

27 November 1942 on the Dungeness peninsula, in which the locomotive of a train that they raked with canon fire exploded, causing one of the attacking Focke-Wulf fighters to crash, killing its pilot. German pilots recorded subsequently strafing hotels on beach fronts and firing at anything that moved, whether people, animals or vehicles.

At the earliest possible opportunity I arranged to have some new teeth made. I could have obtained them from the Air Force, but that would have taken much too long, as we were going on leave in a few days' time. So I managed to get a replacement set through a private dentist. I was intending to visit friends in Nottingham. As the crow flew, Nottingham was not so far from Bournemouth, but I soon discovered that railway travel in war-time Britain left much to be desired. I suppose it was mainly because of the sheer volume of service people who had to move around on a railway system that also had to transport so much war material and was subject to bombing and disruption. Conditions were certainly in stark contrast with those I had experienced on my previous visit to England. However, I finally reached my friends in Nottingham, where a warm welcome awaited me and where I was able to give my new denture a trial run. It fortunately performed satisfactorily.

Reporting back after a week's leave, I was sent to an airfield called Desford, in Leicestershire, where, on hearing that I had to fly Tiger Moths again, I immediately thought that I had to prove that I could fly an aircraft. The reason given to me, however, was that I needed to learn to navigate in England. Experience had shown that pilots who were used to the wide, open spaces of Australia, Africa, Canada and New Zealand, tended to get lost when confronted with the many apparently identical villages so close together in the English countryside.

In the air a Tiger Moth was very manoeuvrable but was not so easily handled on the ground. It had no brakes. The only way it could be steered was by using the slipstream from the propeller that was blowing on the fin and rudder. If a wind from behind were stronger than the slipstream from the propeller, the aircraft became impossible to steer. I was ordered to do an exercise on a day when a strong wind was blowing. As I taxied out on the grass airfield, a gust of wind from behind pointed my aircraft towards a sudden drop in the ground at the edge of the airfield, over which I could have toppled. I was faced with a dilemma. Should I close the throttle and hope that the aircraft would stop before toppling over it? Was there enough space to give a burst of power to the engine to cause the aircraft to leap towards it but at the same time enough slipstream over the rudder to turn the aircraft away from the danger?

I chose the latter option. The manoeuvre worked perfectly. I completed the flying exercise as ordered. On return – and knowing the difficulty I had had in steering the aircraft on the way out — I landed in a position that allowed me to taxi into wind all the way to my dispersal point. Much to my disappointment, no sooner had I landed than another aircraft came out from the very place I was aiming at. We were taxying head on towards each other. One or the other of us had to give way. From my experience of being pointed by the wind towards the dangerous drop, I knew that I was the only one who could give way. I also knew that if I didn't give the other pilot a wide berth, we could chop each other into small pieces as the wind might suddenly point him straight at me. I turned about forty degrees. But that was a mistake. Immediately the wind lifted my port wing gradually higher and higher until my aircraft fell forward on to its nose, then on to its back, and broke its back. I suddenly found myself in a most undignified position, hanging in my straps, with my world upside down.

I was aware that to release my straps and drop head first to the ground would risk breaking my neck. I really needed to take some weight on my hands but I needed one hand to release my straps. In fact, I did land fairly heavily on my head but took some of the fall with one hand. Having released my parachute, I then forlornly set about the long walk across the airfield to the flight office. Since I had just broken a perfectly good aircraft, my Flight Commander was not pleased. Clearly, from the questions he asked, he was doing his best to find a good reason to blame me. My conscience was clear, however. It was soon obvious to me that he realised that it was foolish to allow flying to continue under such windy conditions. Flying was promptly discontinued and with it a certain degree of exoneration for me.

Having mastered to some extent the art of map reading in England, I then had to take a navigator aloft and teach him all I knew. Having covered a lot of territory during my pre-war travels around Britain, enjoying the quaint beauty of so many of those villages at close range, I was interested to have a completely different, all-encompassing perspective from the air. Had I been flying in the basket of a balloon, I would have had time to enjoy the picture below, but even a Tiger Moth travelled too fast to permit such a luxury.

I spent six days at Desford and then returned to Bournemouth for a week, before being sent to South Cerney, a few miles north of Swindon on the edge of the Cotswolds area, where I renewed acquaintance with Airspeed Oxford aircraft, which I thought I had left behind for good at Wigram in New Zealand. I was delighted to have been sent there because it was a part of England that I had enjoyed so much before the war. I thought it was the most beautiful area of the country and justifiably deserved to feature so frequently in magazines and calendars. I was pleased there to meet up again with Bob Garbutt. He had preceded me to South Cerney by a week. I hadn't seen or heard anything of Harold Bruhns or Alan Frampton, neither had he. During our stay there we managed to visit a few of those famous Cotswold villages.

To reach those villages, I was able to overcome the ingrained absence or difficulty of war-time public transport as a result of the following incident. An engine maintenance Sergeant at South Cerney was very keen to fly. He seemed particularly keen to fly with me, no doubt because I used to let him handle the controls. On one occasion I let him land the aircraft. He did the landing approach but as we neared the ground - and after he had positioned the aircraft perfectly - he said to me "You take it now". His nerve failed at the last minute. However, since he had done so well up to that point I thought that he should carry on with the landing. I felt that if he got the last bit wrong, I would be able to put it right. I told him that he was going to land the aircraft and I would close the throttles. He made a complete success of it and was afterwards justifiably ecstatic to realise that he had actually landed the aircraft. From that moment onwards, transport away from the aerodrome was never a problem for me, as he owned an old car, for which, somehow, he seemed to be able to get some petrol. Sometimes in addition we were able to make use of an Air Force vehicle that was going in the right direction.

A picture remaining clearly in my memory from those forays was of Bob and me walking back to the airfield, along a country road, with a field of corn on our right. In New Zealand we would have called it a paddock of wheat, which didn't sound nearly so expressive. In that part of the world, red poppy seed had become mixed in with wheat grain, so that in the Autumn, when harvest time approached, fields of wheat were bright with colourful red poppies. On the roadside, we could see many red poppies amongst the wheat. When we were flying, we could look down on masses of red poppy flowers. As we walked, Bob began whistling " When the Poppies Bloom Again". In those days the 'pop' tunes had a melody which one could whistle or play on an instrument. Their lyrics had a little story to tell, usually a love story, and it was possible to hear the story because the vocalist was not drowned out by the backing group. When we were young we used to strive to learn the melodies and the words of the songs, and loved to listen to them over and over again and, if possible, to play them on an instrument of one kind or another. Particularly during the war period, they caught the mood of the moment, and reflected heartache and sadness, and the hopes and aspirations of everyone. Sadly, they only expressed the hopes that were duly dashed for so many.

While at South Cerney, I was sent to Cranage in Cheshire to take the course offered by No.1531 Beam Approach Flight. The technology of the Beam Approach enabled a pilot, when flying blind, to locate the airfield and land safely by using a directional beam. I spent a week there and returned to South Cerney. Bob had moved on by the time I returned. I was never to see him again.

My night flying experience - which had been limited to a single but memorable flight in an Airspeed Oxford at Wigram - being woefully short of requirement, meant that I had to spend the next five weeks practicing night flying. I knew I needed to do a lot of night flying and expected to have to learn about many other aspects of flying when I arrived in England, assuming that it would all be part of operational training. However, with hindsight, I felt that I had much to learn but did not need a crew with me for most of it. It could also have been done on a smaller aircraft.

One night I got a very big fright. I was tense and oversensitive to negative possibilities. It passed over quickly but not before the shock wave that flashed through me delivered first the fear and then the relief as it evaporated. I was mainly watching the instruments of course but glanced ahead and saw the navigation lights of an aircraft with which I was going to collide within the next split second. I had no time to react in any way but the crash never came. The source of it was actually two lights on the ground, a red one and a green one, spaced in such a way that they appeared like the navigation lights of an aircraft about to meet me head on. Night flying could be scary at times.

I had almost completed my flying at South Cerney when I developed a very high temperature. It was the third time that illness had intervened in my pilot training. That time it turned out to be mumps. Off I went into hospital, yet again. I was glad to be there because I felt very sick but before long I began to feel like an impostor. There were so many genuinely battle scarred patients there. I was told that mumps could have serious implications for an adult but after a month I was discharged, sound in body and soul.

My next posting was back to Leicestershire, to Number 28 Operational Training Unit at Wymeswold. Pilots, navigators, bomb aimers, wireless operators and gunners were gathered there to learn how to put into practice what they had learnt up to that stage of their training. It was there that they all came together for the first time to work as a crew. We were all put into a big hall and told to sort ourselves into crews. Since we were all strangers to one another, it was a somewhat intimidating but interesting exercise. The brevet each person was wearing enabled everyone else to identify the trade of its wearer but there was no way of knowing how good he was at his job. Just what criteria could one use to choose each other?

Previously, I had met Roy Griffin, a fellow New Zealander and bomb aimer. We agreed to fly together. Next I wanted a good navigator but how could I tell what a good navigator looked like? Many others were looking around and thinking they wanted to team up with a good pilot but what did a good pilot look like? I saw two navigators talking together, both of whom looked promising to me. I approached them and asked if they had crewed up yet. One had joined Bill Green, a fellow New Zealand pilot, but the other was available, so Jack Warwick accepted my invitation to join.

At that stage of the proceedings, I was approached by a wireless operator, who asked if I could use him in my crew. I was happy to say yes, so Alf Dawson became the fourth crew-member. Years later, I learnt that Alf had had a good friend with him at that meeting. They both liked the look of Bill Green as a pilot so they tossed a coin to see who would go with Bill. Alf lost the toss but got me. Little was he to know that losing the toss saved his life. Bill Green and his crew joined 625 Squadron and were shot down on their seventh operational mission on 11 April 1944, only the bomb aimer surviving the crash.

Fifty years later Alf conceded the reservations he had had about joining my crew. He put it this way. "By that date of my time in the Royal Air Force I had seen and met many pilots. I suppose I had unconsciously formed an impression of what pilots looked like and ought to look like. The two pilots who were left with incomplete crews were both looking for a Wireless Operator/Air Gunner. As soon as I saw Doug my first reaction to myself was that he didn't look like a pilot. On looking at them my pal Colin and I remarked that Doug was very tall and thin, whilst Bill Green looked the part. We didn't look at them facially so much as physically. Doug was someone you couldn't help noticing but not someone you thought of as a pilot. My pal and I were in a quandary as we both fancied joining up with Bill Green, who conformed in my mind with what a pilot ought to look like. Colin said we should decide with the toss of a coin. He won, but I have been the winner. I was dismayed to lose the toss. But how could anyone ever know in advance the significance of such an act of chance?"

"I can only say that I was lucky. Doug turned out to be such a good pilot – to the extent that he saved our lives dramatically at least once, and probably routinely by his constant attention to technical matters regarding the aircraft itself and the tactical measures he built into his regular flying against the night fighters, coping with adverse weather conditions, and taking the best opportunities to survive the defensive efforts put up by the enemy around target areas. He was cool, patient and determined. If we failed to bomb on our first run up to the target he would take us around again in spite of the enveloping battle. Of course, we should have gone at Brunswick. He was never the same after that. It was as if he had looked into the jaws of hell and decided he wasn't going in. I would go with Doug anywhere, the best pilot in the RAF. So much for stereotyping".

I still needed a rear gunner, but all the gunners present were spoken for, except for one who was away having treatment for a skin complaint. He had no option but to join our crew when his treatment was completed. We were happy eventually to have John Miller in our team as our rear gunner.

There were then five of us. That composition constituted the aircrew for a Vickers Wellington bomber but to form a crew for an Avro Lancaster bomber we would have to be complemented by an engineer and a mid-upper gunner at a later date. For the following seven weeks our five-man crew would spend the time working together to master the routines we needed before setting about the ultimate job for which we had spent many months - for some of us nearly two years - in training. Any further training would be mainly to fly different and bigger aircraft. We were all aware that the ultimate test was creeping closer.

Chapter 7

Making the Grade

Being a member of an aircrew was a new and unfamiliar experience for each of us. Until then, as far as I was concerned, training instructions and exposure to learning had always been directed towards me personally, acting by myself, and requiring an individualised response. It had been the same for each other member of the newly formed aircrew. But the time had come for us to learn to act as members of a team, not as individuals. We had to practice how to act and learn together. In the process we would have to get to know each other, to discover our respective strengths and weaknesses, and to work out an interpersonal modus vivendi.

Until we began our training flying as a crew, there was little more knowledge that most of the new crew members would be able to acquire. Our objective when in the air would be to put what we had already learnt into practice. The navigator already knew all he needed to know about navigation, except that from then on he would have to become familiar with an electronic navigation aid known as Gee. He had learnt the basics on the ground, but needed to put his knowledge into practice in the air.

I had to learn to fly a Vickers Wellington 1C with Pegasus motors. Until that had been accomplished there was little the rest of the crew could do. There were lectures on topics of common concern, which we were obliged to attend and which we worked in between flights.

Affectionately known as a 'Wimpie', the Wellington was generally regarded as a reliable old work-horse, which could take lots of punishment and still fly on. Its geodetic construction of magnesium alloy made it a robust aircraft but in the event of a crash resulting in a fire, the crew could be easily trapped in a flammable cage. Much depended on the Wellingtons in the early days of the war, when Britain had so little with which to take the war to the enemy. They continued to shoulder their share of the burden of delivering bombs on enemy targets through until 1943.

In today's world, my introduction to flying a Wellington would be very different from what happened to me in 1943. Today I would climb into a Simulator that inside looked exactly the same as the cockpit of a Wellington 1C. I would be able to go through the motions of starting the engines as if for real and hear the appropriate noises. I could go through the process of taxying out to the runway and taking off. I would be able to see the ground disappearing beneath me as I retracted the undercarriage and when I had done a circuit I would be able to see the runway ahead on which I was preparing to land. I could do that over and over again until I was thoroughly familiar with flying a Wellington 1C. I would then know where all the appropriate switches and levers were and what they all did, knowledge acquired without leaving the ground, such is the power of modern technology embodied in the Simulator.

Reality then was far removed from such technology. I simply sat in the remains of a recovered crashed Wellington 1C that still had all its necessary levers and switches intact. There I pretended to start up the motors and taxi out to the runway. I pretended to push open the throttles to take off and pretended to retract the undercarriage. I pretended to go through the cockpit drill for landing and pretended that there was a runway ahead for me to land. But I was able to do that over and over again until I was thoroughly familiar with a Wellington 1C and knew where all the appropriate switches and levers were.

In those days we did have the forerunner of the Simulator. It was called a Link Trainer, in which pilots sat with a closed hood over themselves. In the darkness, a pilot was confronted with the basic blind flying instruments and a joystick with which to steer the horrible thing. In his ear-phones he heard the instructor's voice telling him what he wanted him to do. At every step along the way during our training we were obliged to practice the various exercises in the Link Trainer. Mainly because the appropriate feelings of flying did not accompany the manoeuvres we did in it, we did not like the Link Trainer. It did enable us, however, to practise flying blind without having to use an aircraft. Since we would be flying in the dark on operations, it was essential to be completely competent when flying by instruments.

A Wellington 1C was not a big aircraft by the standards of the later bombers of Bomber Command but it was a lot bigger and heavier than anything I had previously flown. For my first flight in one I had an instructor with me of course, but I was surprised to find that my crew also had to come along. I felt sorry for them. They must have been anxious as I came in to land for the first time. The flight at least gave them the chance to become familiar with their new surroundings and to learn where things were and how they worked.

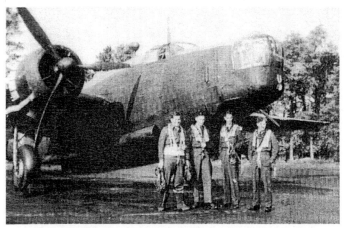

Fig. 49. The author, second from right with three members of crew with Wellington 1C. (1943)

After about three hours I was deemed competent to fly without an instructor and then spent about five hours doing circuits and landings. From that point onwards we operated as a crew, practising all the things we were likely to have to do over enemy territory. Bombing practice featured largely, as did cross country flying, which also incorporated practice bombing of several targets along the way.

Before I had a crew to fly with, including a navigator to tell me what course to steer, I had always needed to depend on myself to find my way to where I wanted to go. Early exercises we had to do as a crew included flying to various points, giving Jack Warwick our navigator some practice in using the Gee set as a means of finding our positions. On one of them, being so used to doing my own navigating and not yet having proof of Jack's ability, I had been keeping track of where we were. When Jack said over the intercom system that he had completed his exercises and gave me a course to steer for home, I decided that he had made a mistake. I said "Jack, for the first time I have found you wrong. You have given me the wrong course". Jack replied "Sorry about that, steer your course for home". I did as he said and followed my own course for home but had not gone far before I realised that we were not where I thought we ought to be. In fact I then did not know where we were. I was obliged to apologise and to tell him that he was right and that I was wrong. He just said "OK" and gave me a new course to steer.

Never again did I query information which Jack provided for me. If I had a question to ask, he always had a ready answer and there were many times when he had to work under extreme difficulties. I could not have wished for a better navigator. I'm sure one could not have been found.

About six hours of our operational training were spent in practicing how to evade fighters. With a Spitfire or Hurricane diving to attack us, I would carry out the appropriate evasive manoeuvre while John Miller (Dusty) in the rear turret would aim his guns at the attacking aircraft and press his triggers. Instead of firing bullets, a cine camera would record the action, which, when projected on a screen, revealed the right and wrong deflections he had made.

The wartime double daylight saving of two hours gave us long evenings of daylight. So it was very late one evening as dusk was approaching and our training for the day had been completed, that on walking back to our digs we saw smoke rising from the area where our hut was. We slept in long huts, each of which accommodated a dozen personnel. The sound of the siren of a fire engine made us quicken our steps in the direction of our hut. We grew more concerned with every step we took, fearing that the smoke we were watching was from the remains of our worldly possessions.

Feelings of relief were mixed with concern for others when we found that the hut next to ours was on fire. By the time we arrived the fire brigade had managed to get the situation under control. Half the hut had been saved. It transpired that one of the occupants of the incinerated hut had had a special reason for wanting to look smart before going into town. He had used his own electric iron to press his shirt. He removed one of the light bulbs and plugged in his iron. When the iron had cooled, he put it back into his kit bag and went to town. Unfortunately, he forgot to unplug it and replace the light bulb. Someone else came into the hut, switched on the lights, did what he came to do, and went out, leaving the lights switched on. No one else came into the hut before the iron became hot enough to set fire to the contents of the kit bag, and ultimately the hut.

It was soon possible to undertake our cross-country flights and bombing practice at night time. For each we would typically be airborne for four to six hours. To prove our efficiency we had to make a practice bombing run over several different targets during the cross country flight. At each target there was an infrared beam projected skywards, its precise location unknown to us and of course invisible to us anyway. If we made our bombing run over the correct target our camera would record the infrared beam on its film, thus showing which targets we had found and bombed accurately.

One of those flights was especially noteworthy. Our instructions were to fly out to sea from the coast of Wales, reduce height, practice air to sea firing and finally put in some bombing practice on Cardiff, Bristol and other towns. Information from the Met office told us that a wind of 30 mph from due north was forecast. Jack made out his flight plan accordingly. We took off at dusk and climbed to our operating height of ten thousand feet. We were above a 9/10 layer of cloud and could see nothing of the ground. Having no Gee set, our only navigational aid was radio fixes from Alf's loop aerial. We had no Gee set because we were on a simulated operational sortie. When on actual operations, we would be able to use Gee only a short distance into France before the Germans jammed it. So we had to get used to managing without Gee.

The numerous loop fixes that Alf provided for Jack didn't seem to make sense to Jack. It was common knowledge that loop fixes tended to be unreliable when over mountainous country - and we were in the area of Wales. I told Jack that I would probably be able to pick up a pinpoint, as a check, somewhere on the coast of Wales. When the elapsed time indicated that we should have been over the coast of Wales, I could not see the coast of Wales. In fact I could see nothing. Knowing that clouds tended to hang lower over high hills and mountains, I did not want to risk coming down through the clouds to ascertain our position.

We had to abandon the firing of our guns over the sea in favour of heading for Bristol, using DR navigation. To our surprise there was no sign of Bristol, so we went yet further south but could still see nothing. By that time we reluctantly came to the conclusion that we had no idea where we were but since our general direction had been southerly I decided to head north. After about half an hour through a small break in the clouds I suddenly saw sea beneath us with land on our left. In the discussion that followed, I suggested that maybe we had inadvertently crossed the Atlantic and were flying up the coast of America. My suggestion did not appeal to the rest of the crew. We did agree though, that logically the East Coast of Ireland seemed the most likely location.

Soon after that through another break in the clouds, I saw a red flashing beacon, known as a Pundit. Pundits were spread all around Britain and provided a wonderful aid in times of need such as ours. Each one flashed a letter of the alphabet in Morse Code that was changed daily to deny help to the enemy. I read the letter and we discovered that we were flying up the Bristol Channel. The land on our port side was the Cardiff area of Wales. On our starboard side was the coast of Cornwall, Devon and Somerset, but I could not see it owing to the amount of cloud.

We were a long way from home. The atmosphere was very cold. Our heating system was not working and we were all feeling a little on the miserable side. It would have done nothing to raise our spirits if we had known in addition the fact that we were flying in a gale of 120 mph coming from the north. Jack had made his navigational calculations allowing for a wind of 30 mph. When I decided to fly north, we must have been almost over France. That was the first occasion on which I had to realise how wrong the Meteorological forecasts could be. Many more such occasions of sharp differences between forecasts and reality were to follow in even more difficult conditions. The technology for weather forecasting available during the war years was used to the full but in retrospect it may be seen how ludicrously simple it was when compared with what can be deployed for contemporary aircraft operations. Meteorology may never become an exact science, but the contrast between the capability of the RAF meteorologists during the Second World War and the technology at their disposal on the one hand and the performance of contemporary meteorologists on the other hand is great enough to create an impression that the forecasters of today by comparison are near to the possession of it.

At least we knew at last where we were. That helped our morale. We expected to find our way home. I viewed the petrol gauges with a small degree of concern but was not unduly worried about the readings. Cloud cover had begun to break a little and we were able to sight a few more pundits. We knew that we were probably flying into a head wind. But the slow progress we were making soon made us realise that the wind had to be very much stronger than the forecast had indicated. Loop bearings that Alf provided began to make some sense.

Our progress was so slow that finally I did begin to feel serious concern about the quantities showing on the petrol gauges. I kept my thoughts to myself. For all of us to become worried would not change anything. We were making progress in the right direction and the engines were not showing other than normal function. Without expressing any concern, I just gave myself over to being patient.

Eventually, as the needles on the gauges pointed to empty, I knew that we were close enough to home to make it. My relief was palpable. It was premature, however, because on arriving it was a shock for me to look down on an airfield completely obscured by fog. My first thoughts were to ask Jack where an alternative airfield that was clear of fog might be but realised that it was a question he could not answer. If he had given me a course to an alternative airfield, the flight there would almost certainly have exhausted our petrol. There could have been no guarantee, furthermore, that it was actually free of fog.

At that point, the wise Providence that watched over me must have taken control. Incredibly, my conscious mind seemed to close up. I had absolutely no awareness of what I did until I stopped the aircraft in the middle of the runway, called control and asked "Where are we?" I knew we were on the main runway but I could not see where to go from there. Control said "Wait there". In due course a van arrived with 'Follow Me' written in lights on the rear panel. We were led to a dispersal where I parked the aircraft and shut down the motors. With much relief we all got out, only to find that we still did not know where we were, except that we were at our own airfield. We were not at our own dispersal and we had no idea which way we should walk to get to the Mess and our digs. With our parachutes over our shoulders, we groped our way across the airfield, gradually finding little things we could recognise. It was about three o'clock in the morning so there was not a great deal of activity around. We were hungry, having had no food for nearly eight hours. A meal and a good bed was a thought that made a great appeal. It was with relief that we put that flight behind us.

Life at that station consisted of flying, attending to domestic matters and seeking diversions in the nearby towns. Usually in the evenings, a transport would run into the nearest township for the benefit of those who wished to escape for a brief period of relaxation. Some of our crew often went there but for me there were other things to do. My first priority was to write to Margie. If possible, I wrote a little each day and posted a letter each week. Each letter was numbered so that Margie would know if any went missing. Letters usually arrived in batches so by looking at the numbers, Margie would know which one to read first. I benefited from the same device since Margie numbered her letters to me too. Many other letters demanded my attention. My mail seemed to be from people who wrote because they felt that they should, so I felt it was only right to send them a reply.

I also gave a lot of my time becoming familiar with what other crew members had to do. My training had taught me the basics of how to navigate, the principles of engines, radios, guns and bomb-sights but I wanted to obtain a working knowledge and understanding of the operational problems and difficulties each crew member was likely to encounter. Our crew awaited an engineer and a mid upper gunner. They would join us when we reached the point of transferring to four-engined aircraft. Then the seven man aircrew would be entering upon the most interdependent relationships of their lives – if only for a brief continuation of life. As it happened, for those like us who were lucky enough to survive, the bond that in those times developed between us was to last for the rest of our lives.

Our time on an Operational Training Unit station made us very aware of the important contribution women were making to the war effort. Members of the Women's Auxiliary Air Force (WAAF) cooked, packed parachutes, worked in clerical jobs of all kinds, drove transports, calibrated instruments, and worked in intelligence, amongst many other duties. They above all provided the voice we loved to hear from the Watch Tower, confirming our safe return to our home base.

WAAF girls were accommodated in the 'Waffery' under the control of a more mature woman known as the Queen Bee. Liaisons between airmen and WAAFs were officially frowned upon but often flourished, although an Australian was heard to say "A man can't make much progress with a girl in this bloody country. In summer it never gets dark and in winter it's too damned cold".

At Wymeswold we made the acquaintance of a small magazine which from then on we would find in every mess we visited. It was a humorous training magazine, known as T M. In the T M, Pilot Officer Prune, a slightly dishevelled, vacuous looking fellow always featured prominently. He epitomised someone who, because of a self-righteous attitude, was capable of making the most stupid mistakes for which he was awarded the Most Highly Derogatory Order of the Irremovable Finger. Each publication contained anonymous awards that we knew were for a stupid and probably dangerous action on someone's part. Because it was written in a light and comical nature we found it easy to read but at the same time we were conscious of the importance of the message and were sometimes reminded of something equally stupid that we ourselves may have done. So it often carried messages from which we could learn valuable lessons, if we had the wit to take notice and heeded the implications.

On 16 November 1943, the day before my twenty-seventh birthday, we finished our operational training. Our next posting would be to Winthorpe in Leicestershire. On that station I would have to learn to fly a Stirling four-engined aircraft. Before that transfer, however, we were due for some leave. To spend my leave I planned to return to the Highlands of Scotland. My journey into the Highlands of Scotland was a long but interesting one. Alf Dawson (Digger), our wireless operator, came from Carlisle in the North of England and was going home for his leave. He invited me to break my journey, spend a night there, and meet his parents and sisters, which I was very pleased to do. It was winter by then. In the darkness of a winter's morning in Carlisle I awoke to the sound of wooden clogs on cobbled streets as factory workers made their way to work. By train from Carlisle I travelled via Edinburgh and Inverness to a small village called Rogart near Golspie, not very far from the northern tip of Scotland. Heavy snow fell during the latter part of the journey. I well remember a mantle of snow covering the country with the railway line showing in dark contrast, snaking its way through a completely white world.

In Rogart I was welcomed by my wife's relatives. They were farming folk. During my stay there they took me to see the little cottage, standing alone on a hillside, where Margie's grandmother was born. After the war I was able to visit the area again, taking Margie with me. It was a great thrill to be able to take her to see

Fig. 50. A complete crew at last in front of a Stirling at Winthorpe in 1943.

Fig. 51. Shortie by the wheel of a Stirling. (1943)

Fig. 52. Winter at Winthorpe, March 1944.

that little cottage. During the First World War, Margie's father had spent some of his army leave in Rogart.

His hosts as a family consisted of the parents, a son, and two daughters. At the time of my visit the son and two daughters had grown up. The son was running the farm. At a later date I was to spend leave with the daughters, who by then had families of their own.

Each morning I awoke to the sound of a nearby stream trickling over rocks accompanied by the twittering of birds in the trees. It was an idyllic setting. In contrast to the continuous roar of aircraft engines to which I had become accustomed, I found the atmosphere unbelievably peaceful, recalling poignantly for me the rural scenes of home among which I had grown up.

It seemed so unreal to remember that a war was being savagely fought somewhere else. There would be all too soon the moment when I would be introduced into it. Perhaps when I reached that point, I reflected, the memory of so quiet and peaceful a spot would assume an additional dimension of perfection for me. I resolved to make the most of the opportunity to relate to the charm and restorative qualities that offered themselves at every turn in the surrounding area. I derived much pleasure from climbing the hill at the back of the house, from where I could look down on the village of Rogart and the countryside forming its context. I felt as an escapee from prison must feel. There was the experience of exultation from the brief period of freedom, quickly followed by knowing that all would come to an end. It did end all too soon of course. I had to board the train back to England and the roar of aircraft.

The purpose of being at Winthorpe was to convert to four-engined aircraft. We were allocated an engineer and a mid upper gunner to complete our crew. Les Meace, a lad of nineteen years from Yorkshire became our engineer. Ron Adams from Norfolk became our gunner for the mid upper turret. We then had a crew of seven, which was the requirement for a four-engined bomber.

Much of our first few weeks in Heavy Conversion Unit Number 1661 was spent either at lectures or shovelling snow off the runways. One of our lecturers told us "When you get on to operations, forget about this weaving business. You will have a high performance aircraft. Fly straight and level. Show the enemy who is boss. Fight it out with them". I often wondered later on whether that was official advice, or just his personal opinion. Whatever the origin and purpose of it I can say from my own subsequent experience that it must have cost the lives of many of those who followed it.

There was a substantial amount of technical information that I had to learn about a Short Brothers Stirling bomber. We had to learn about the new navigational aid, which Jack and Griff (our bomb aimer) would need to be thoroughly conversant with. It was airborne radar, code named H2S, which projected a signal below and ahead of an aircraft. It was reflected back to the aircraft giving a picture of what it had struck on a cathode ray tube. Even when flying in cloud, it clearly showed coast lines, rivers and lakes, and a fairly well defined shape of cities. Since it could not be jammed by the enemy, it was a very valuable navigational aid, usable anywhere. Later on, during our tour of operations, we sometimes used it to deposit our bombs on a target we could not see.

About that time, in a letter to Margie, I wrote "This war is not only a battle between armed service personnel, it is also a battle between scientists. First one side devises something new, then the other side finds a counter measure, and vice versa". In 1942 enemy night fighters were fitted with 'Lichtenstein', an airborne radar device with a range of five miles, which enabled them to home on to our bombers. From then on there were two types of night fighters, namely 'Wild Boars' (single-engined) and 'Tame Boars' (twin-engined). Twin-engined night fighters carried a crew of two, the navigator using 'Lichtenstein' to guide the pilot to his quarry - the bomber flying to or from its target. Single-engined night fighters, having a pilot only, normally attacked only over the target, where the pilot could see the bomber silhouetted against the lights and fires below, although in addition they sometimes managed to find bombers in the dark away from their target areas.

From July 1943 onwards RAF bombers dropped strips of tinfoil (code named Window), causing a blip to appear on enemy radar screens that was indistinguishable from a blip made by a bomber, rendering most enemy radar ineffective.

German ground operators were able to pick up emissions from H2S and 'Monica' sets in our bombers. Monica projected a signal behind a bomber to give early warning of an approaching enemy fighter. Although our bombers were all equipped with devices to blow up all secret equipment in the event of a crash, Germany soon discovered our innovations by the examination of crashed aircraft and deduction from the facts of operational realities. They constantly created measures to counter those important technical advances. In the autumn of 1943, SN2 radar with a longer wavelength and a range of four miles was fitted to their night fighters, making them immune to our Windows.

The enemy soon developed a method of enabling their fighters to find our bombers by homing in on the signals emitted by our H2S and Monica. It was quite some time before that fact was realised by our commanders and officials and given the attention it deserved. However, H2S remained a very valuable aid to navigation. It could be switched on for a brief period when needed, then switched off until needed again. The wireless operator could look at a screen in front of him, code named 'Fishpond', while H2S was switched on. He was able to see reflected signals in the form of a blip from each of the bombers around him. Since the bombers were all travelling at a similar speed he would know that no enemy fighters were in the vicinity. However, if he saw a blip that was travelling faster than the others, it could be inferred that an enemy night fighter had joined the bomber stream, although an allowance had to be made for the possibility that it was a Mosquito which sometimes flew with us as a counter to enemy night fighters.

Arising from information derived in that manner, as a crew we developed our own system of evasion that could be followed as a precautionary measure or as an actual deflection of an attack. If the faster moving signal appeared to be following us, we would first change course a positive amount - say thirty degrees - and hold steady on that course. If the 'suspect' signal did the same the inference had to be drawn that we were being stalked by an enemy night fighter. Digger would then keep a close eye on it, telling me when it had closed to 200 yards. I would then carry out a standard manoeuvre known as a corkscrew. Suffice it to say that one complete sequence of the corkscrew was usually sufficient to lose the fighter. From the point of view of the pilot or crew of a night fighter, it was much easier to find and deal with a bomber that was holding a steady course, straight and level, than to try to follow one that was gyrating around a dark sky. Such gyrations, however, on occasion ran a greater risk of collision with other bombers.

Snow was all around us at Winthorpe. It was a case of all hands to the shovel handles. Nearly all hands, that is, as Jack and Griff thought that they really did need to learn all about H2S to the point that they felt they would be wasting precious time fiddling around with shovels, with or without handles. That was the way they saw their future responsibilities. I was not inclined to discourage such conscientious initiative. Most of us were unable to conjure up excuses that were plausible enough to avoid the obligation so we had to join the snow clearing teams.

Clearing snow on an airfield was a frustrating occupation. Just what does one do when standing in the middle of a runway that was forty metres wide with a shovel full of snow? Did one walk twenty metres either way to empty the shovel, or did one throw the snow as far as possible – say about six metres - for someone else to pick it up and pass to the next man? Confusion could reign. Dumping snow on a patch that had just been cleared excited vociferous protests. It did not quite come to blows but it was always a muddled use of labour, bordering on the chaotic. Apparently the Americans had a better solution. They simply drove a snow plough down the runway a couple of times. But it gave us some physical exercise.

One way or another, we finally had one runway cleared of snow, with a two metre high snow wall along each edge of it. In a few days, those walls had settled into a metre high wall of solid ice along each edge, prohibiting all flying. Nearly all flying, that is. Three top brass persons had important business elsewhere and decided to fly to wherever they needed to be in spite of the conditions. Next morning the airfield displayed three Stirling bombers with no undercarriages. I'm sure that had the ice walls not been there all three would have made normal landings but all three aircraft swung on landing, leaving their wheels embedded in the ice walls.

Soon Griff would have to release bombs on enemy targets by using the RAF Mk XIV bomb sight, which was used on all RAF operational bombers. Until then we had not encountered that device, so he had to spend time familiarising himself with its technicalities before putting his skills to a practical test. That bomb sight was a very sophisticated piece of equipment, designed to compensate for the unstable platform from which the bomb aimer had to aim his bombs. Obviously, to drop bombs on a target the pilot had to fly the aircraft accurately over the target and the bomb aimer needed to release the bombs at the critical moment. If the aircraft were bouncing around, as a result of exploding anti-aircraft shells or rough weather conditions, the bomb aimer could find himself looking at many places other than the target. Whilst the pilot struggled to hold the aircraft as steady as possible, the Mk XIV bomb sight corrected most of the irregularities that the pilot couldn't manage to deal with.

It was at that period of our conversion training that Jack developed a high temperature, necessitating going into hospital. After a few days, it looked as though he would be there for quite a while. Since there was little the rest of us could do without Jack, the remaining members of the crew wanted me to ask for leave. I told them that if I did that, we might be provided with a new navigator and told to get on with our training. However, they persisted in wanting me to ask for leave. Fortunately, the Flight Commander could see the picture and was understanding. He advised me to keep quiet and out of sight as much as possible or we would be likely to get a replacement navigator. The weather came to our rescue. Since conditions prevented flying anyway, we were able to await Jack's return.

By the time that Jack was well again, the weather had improved, and it was my turn to start learning something new. I had already familiarised myself with the various switches and levers, and where they all were in the cockpit of a Stirling. I memorised various technical details about the aircraft and had done all my imaginary simulation in the remains of a crashed aircraft.

During my first attempt at taxying a Stirling for real, I felt that I would never manage the art. It was strange to be so high off the ground. I was sitting nearly twenty-three feet up. But the disconcerting thing was that when I started the aircraft into a turn, it didn't want to stop turning. When I finally managed to persuade it to stop and tried to turn the other way, it repeated the process in the opposite direction. I was surprised though how soon I did manage to control it and was soon confidently able to drive around a curvy perimeter track. I had found the Wellington very much bigger than any aircraft I had flown before. With four propellers instead of two spinning round outside the windows and a big fin and rudder following along such a long way behind, the Stirling seemed massive. Every new step was intimidating at first but soon familiarity made everything seem normal. After six hours I had the controls to myself.

Chapter 8
Taste of Action

Having completed all our training, we were ready to commence operations and could have done so immediately if we had been operating with Wellington aircraft but from 1941 onwards Wellingtons had given way to the four engined bombers, the Stirlings, followed by the Halifaxes, and finally by the Lancasters. These aircraft had a much greater bomb carrying capacity and eventually superseded two-engined aircraft for night operations completely. The purpose of our next stage of training was therefore mainly to enable us to familiarise ourselves as a crew with the different working environment of a four-engined aircraft and for me to learn to fly it. It entailed many of the things we had practiced on Wellingtons but with different and additional equipment.

Much of our time was spent doing cross-country flights, both by day and night. Bombing practice was also high on the priority list, as was astro navigation practice. During this period, sadly, Digger received news that his mother was seriously ill and was not expected to live. A week later he sent me a telegram, telling me that she had died. There wasn't anything new that Digger had to learn, so we were able to continue our training without him.

Atrocious weather, as it happened, made for very little flying and a lot of time attending lectures. When Digger returned we spent many hours practising dinghy drill, in case we had to ditch in the sea and escape drill in case we had to abandon our aircraft. Parachute landings had to be practised to ensure that we actually survived the impact with the ground in the event of having to bale out. Landing by parachute was about equivalent to jumping off a ten feet high wall. The trick was to learn to bend our knees and roll immediately on impact with the ground.

We also spent much time practising seeing in the dark. We were told that our eyes had about 100 million rods and about 7 million cones, the rods being concerned with night vision.

Rods were very sensitive to outline and movement, but did not help with detail or colour, rapidly losing their sensitivity in the case of Vitamin A deficiency. Cones were concerned with daylight vision during which we discerned colour and detail. When we saw something out of the corner of our eyes, the natural reflex action was to look straight at it, focusing on it by using the cones of the eye. If, in the dark, we saw an object with our peripheral vision, and chose then to succumb to an uncontrolled natural reaction to look straight at it, the object probably disappeared. The teaching included the projection of moving objects onto a dimly lit screen in a dark room, which we had to learn to watch without looking straight at them. During my tour of operations, I was at times surprised by how much I could see in the dark.

Because of the bad weather, we weren't as busy as otherwise would have been the case, so I was able to catch up on my correspondence. As well as my usual letter to Margie, No 69, at that time, amongst others I wrote to Bob Garbutt, Alan Frampton, Joe Lennon, and Harold Bruhns. In my diary, I recorded on 16 January 1944 that it was one year to the day since I had sailed away from New Zealand's shores for the second time. We also managed to find time for a little social activity, spending a night on the town in Nottingham and on another night going to a dance in Newark, where we met Jack's friend Reg, and Digger's friend Colin, both of whom had joined Bill Green's crew.

We were in the Midlands of England, surrounded by all types of industry. Consequently, sometimes it was almost dark in the middle of the day owing to the murky industrial pollution, so flying conditions were not good. After three weeks we had finished all the things we needed to practise both in the air and on the ground, so were ready for our next assignment, which was to take place at the Lancaster Flying School at Syerston. The Lancaster was to be the aircraft to which I was assigned to go to war.

At the outbreak of the Second World War the main types of aircraft forming the heavy long-range bombing capability of Bomber Command of the Royal Air Force were the Hampdens, Whitleys and Wellingtons. They were all twin-engined, all-metal monoplanes which had replaced the severely obsolescent types which had served in the inter-war years. Their limitations, however, were soon brought to light during the first two years of the war. The potential need for greater speeds, higher cruising altitudes, heavier bomb loads, heavier self-defence armaments, and even longer ranges was quickly realized.

As early as 1941 the first of a trio of new types designed to realize some or all of these enhanced characteristics came into service and with continuing improvements and adaptation of their functions they served Bomber Command for the remainder of the war. They were the Short Brothers Stirling, Handley Page Halifax and the Avro Lancaster.

The emergence of the Lancaster bomber was the result of a twist of fate. Its progenitor was originally built as a twin engined aircraft known as the Manchester, with Rolls Royce Vulture engines. It operated from February 1941 to June 1942 but it was said that more of those aircraft were lost through engine failure than through enemy action. The inner cylinders of the H configuration overheated and no solution to the problem could be found, so the fuselage was lengthened and the wing span increased to take four well proven Rolls Royce Merlin engines. Its first operational flight as a Lancaster took place in June 1942. It gained the reputation of being the best of the British heavy bombers of the Second World War, some being modified to carry the bouncing bombs as used on the Dam Busting raid in May 1943.

The first Lancasters - three of them – to be delivered to Bomber Command arrived on Christmas Eve in 1941 at Waddington, making it the first Lancaster station. They were delivered to 44 (Rhodesia) Squadron to replace its ageing Hampdens. Numbers were built up during the weeks which followed, sufficiently for a force of twelve to be sent on the first operational mission carried out by Lancasters. On 17 April 1942 a low level attack on Augsburg was mounted, costing the loss of seven aircraft.

The Lancaster proved in turn to be adaptable for attack on all types of target, including strategic high level carpet bombing of cities and towns, attacks on pin-pointed targets such as ships at anchor, rocket launching sites or particular factories, low level assaults on specialized targets such as dams, minelaying, and tactical support for ground forces. In 1944 when plentiful aircraft existed they were also used in Conversion Units for final training purposes.

With its four Rolls Royce Merlin engines, the Lancaster was a large aircraft for its day. It had a crew of seven, the same number as that of the Stirling (Marks1 and 3) and Halifax (Marks1 and 3). Its wingspan at 102 feet was just two feet short of that of the Halifax 3 and Boeing Flying Fortress (Mark 1). In gross wing area it came third behind the Fortress and Stirling. It was a long aircraft at 68.9 feet but fell just short of the length of the Whitley (Mark 5) which it helped to replace and also that of the Halifax but it fell well short of that of the Stirling, which reached a length of eighty-seven feet.

When parked on the ground, the Lancaster towered over anyone standing beneath its nose at 19.5 feet - in marked contrast to the relatively low heights of the Whitley and Hampden - but a little less than the height of both the Halifax and the Stirling and about the same as that of the Wellington, which in its day had been a very tall aircraft. At 68,000 pounds maximum weight it was heavier than all other Bomber Command types used in the Second World War with the exception of the Stirling.

Its other important characteristics were a relatively fast top speed for British bombers at that time of 459 kilometres per hour or 275 miles per hour at 15,000 feet, a maximum altitude of 7,467 metres or 25,000 feet and a range of 2,350 miles. Those capabilities enabled the Lancaster to be suitable for return flights to all important European targets, bearing in mind that the distance from London to Vienna is about 900 miles.

But the foremost characteristic of the Lancaster was its phenomenal bomb load capacity. This was continually adapted to take armaments of increasing tonnage such as the 'Tall Boy' of 12,000 pounds. They ranged up to a total capacity of 22,000 pounds which was the weight of the 'Grand Slam' – that at 7.7 metres long and 1.2 metres in diameter was the biggest bomb produced in the war, the Lancaster being the only aircraft that could carry it. Smaller bombs of 2,000 pounds and the 'Cookie' of 4,000 pounds were the common payload. The first production of both these bombs for the Lancasters was made in the Great Western Railway Works in Swindon. This bomb payload of the Lancaster was sharply in excess of that of all other types of bomber in use, including the Boeing Flying Fortress and the Consolidated Liberator of the American Air Force.

British bombers were generally armed with .303 guns - two each in the front and mid upper turrets and four in the rear turret. American bombers were much more heavily armed with consequently larger aircrews and smaller bomb loads. It was expected thet they would then be adapted for successful daylight bombing but in the event German fighters overcame them to the extent that their daylight operations had to be curtailed until the arrival of the Mustang fighters fitted with Rolls Royce Merlin engines and drop fuel tanks. The Mustang provided a long-range and effective escort.

Frankland's verdict on the Lancaster was that it was "the best of its class which appeared in the Second World War. It had the capacity to lift a ten ton bomb. It was robust and reliable in action, and on targets of equal risk, suffered a lower casualty rate than its equivalent versions, the Halifax and Stirling. Like them, it had not the capacity however, to survive in combat with opposing fighters".

Altogether 7, 414 Lancasters of all marks were built during the war, including 430 in Canada. Of this number 3,349 were lost in action while serving with great distinction as the most effective bomber aircraft of both the Allied and Axis forces. It became the mainstay of Bomber Command's campaign right up to the end of hostilities and had a distinct claim to be one of the most critical tools of warfare to serve the Allies. One measure of this is the fact that ten Victoria Crosses were won by members of Lancaster aircrews.

After the cessation of hostilities in 1945 and the completion of the job for which it had been designed, in modified form the Lancaster lived on for many years through the Cold War period as the Avro Lincoln, a long-range aircraft adapted for maritime surveillance. Some of the original Lancaster aircraft still exist as museum exhibits – for example, in the Australian National Museum in Canberra, in the Aeronautical Museum in Perth, Australia, in the Aeronautical Museum in Auckland, New Zealand, and in the Royal Air Force Museum in Hendon, north of London. In addition a Lancaster exists at East Kirkby, one of the old wartime Lancaster airfields in Lincolnshire, England. It is capable of flying but is restricted to giving rides on the ground owing to the cost of maintaining it in airworthy condition which its private owners, as a voluntary group of enthusiasts, are unable to afford.

Of the two original Lancasters known to be still flying, one is in Canada supported by enthusiasts, the other being owned and flown by the Royal Air Force. Together with a Hawker Hurricane and a Supermarine Spitfire, this latter aircraft forms the celebrated 'Battle of Britain Memorial Flight' which has regularly featured in Air Displays and national historical and celebratory events in Britain for many years. By this means the Lancaster has flown on into the twenty-first century. It was designed by Roy

Chadwick who was decorated with the CBE for his remarkable achievement.

The Lancaster was justifiably regarded as the most significant heavy bomber of the Second World War. However, it must be noted that it was not without its peer in every dimension. The later models of the Handley Page Halifax - its main rival on the British side – were superior in some. The Halifax was a more comfortable aircraft for its crew and it could bomb with greater accuracy. Halifax aircraft dropped more bombs than all the other types of bombers employed by Bomber Command put together, with the exception of the Lancaster. Furthermore, the Halifax Marks 3, 6 and 7 suffered lower loss rates than the Lancaster, a fact qualifying Frankland's claim. A substantial 29% of Halifax crew members were able to bale out successfully as opposed to 11% from Lancasters. But on the basis of the calculated logistics of the time, Harris pressed home his policy for Bomber Command mainly with the Lancaster. It was cheaper to produce, it had superb handling qualities and could carry the greater bomb load – half as much again as the Halifax. A total of 6,176 Halifaxes of all marks were produced compared with the total of 7,414 Lancasters.. The Halifax assumed a variety of disparate tasks as the war continued – such as glider towing, supplying the needs of Resistance organisations, carrying paratroops, and Coastal Command work – in addition to its work as a heavy bomber and for which it proved very versatile - whereas the Lancaster remained firmly confined as a heavy bomber.

During those three weeks and once I had grown accustomed to a larger aircraft, I found the Stirling a nice aircraft to fly, but it lacked the performance required for current bombing operations. It had become the 'Ugly Duckling' of the four engined bombers. Designed in 1938 with a wing span of 112 feet, it encountered its first setback when the Air Ministry stipulated that it must have a wing span of no more than 100 feet so that if could fit into a standard RAF hangar. Flight tested in 1938, with a wing span of 98.1 feet, its take off and landing runs were too long, so its undercarriage was lengthened to increase the wing angle of attack. The prototype flew in May 1939 but the undercarriage had collapsed on landing. A second prototype with a strengthened undercarriage flew in December 1939.

The Stirling's first operational flight took place in February 1941. As a symbol of Britain's growing offensive power, the

Stirling became a morale booster for the general public. As wars were not won by being defensive, it helped Bomber Command to keep the offensive flame burning. However, possibly because of the modifications that had to be made to it, it was unable on operations to climb higher than 17,000 feet. That limitation, of course, made it more vulnerable to anti-aircraft fire and exposed it to bombs falling from friendly aircraft flying at higher altitudes. Those vulnerabilities resulted in higher loss rates than those suffered by the Halifax and Lancaster. Early in 1944 Stirlings were replaced by Lancasters. New Zealand's 75 Squadron was the last to fly Stirlings on bombing operations. The Stirling, however, continued to make a useful contribution to the war effort as a glider tow, by delivering provisions and personnel to the Resistance Movements in enemy occupied countries and as a transport aircraft.

Perhaps 'Fate' decided that it was time for us to be 'blooded' for what was to come, because our time at Winthorpe certainly had its ups and downs apart from the problems that the weather created. For one thing Jack had to go into hospital but Digger had his 21st birthday and I was promoted to Pilot Officer during our stay at Winthorpe. However, in reply to my letters to Bob Garbutt, Harold Bruhns and Alan Frampton, I received an official letter from the Royal New Zealand Air Force Headquarters, advising me that Bob had been shot down and killed on his first operation to Berlin, Harold had failed to return from a mine laying operation in Kiel Bay on his fifth operation, and Alan had been shot down and killed on his sixth operation, which was to Frankfurt. Of the five friends together during initial training at Wigram in New Zealand, only Arthur Jones and I were still alive. I wasn't sure about Arthur because he had stayed behind in New Zealand.

We left Winthorpe on 14 March 1944, travelling by train about twenty miles to Syerston. On arrival there I was startled to see a Lancaster bomber comfortably settled on top of one of the buildings and assumed that Pilot Officer Prune had been training there. I had recently been surprised to learn that a high percentage of deaths in Bomber Command were the result of accidents. The reason was not difficult to understand. Much of the flying in Bomber Command was blind flying by instruments. Since natural instincts seemed to be in conflict with the demands of flying blind, many accidents must have been the result. To become proficient at flying by instruments alone did require an immense amount of practice, during which many hazards had to be faced.

We spent the first eight days at Syerston attending lectures, practicing further dinghy and parachute drill, and learning about the internal workings of a Lancaster. All of it had to substitute for actual flying which the continuing bad weather still prevented. When we did finally take off for our first flight, we were unable to land back at our base because visibility had deteriorated so much. We found somewhere else to land and returned to base by courtesy of RAF transport.

Our second flight was my first solo on a Lancaster. It went well until I wanted to return home only to find that someone had crashed on the runway. I was told to wait. We circled the airfield until after dark but finally had to land at another airfield. Again we returned home by RAF transport. I got into bed at 0215 hours.

Our next day was a busy one. We practiced circuits and landings during daylight but because the atmosphere was too murky over our own base we had to practise them at a different airfield. We arrived back at our home base at 2100 hours and set off on my night solo flight at 0030 hours to do circuits and landings at a different airfield. The aircraft suffered a flat tyre there, so yet again we returned home by RAF transport, arriving at 0800 hours. A five-hour night cross-country flight completed our time at Syerston. Since it was the end of a week, we were given week-end leave, which I spent with friends in Nottingham.

On Monday morning, 3 April 1944, RAF transport took us to Newark railway station, where we caught a train to Spilsby in Lincolnshire. There we waited for a very long time. We were not impressed with the delay and thought jokingly about tendering our resignations but eventually transport arrived and delivered us to our next home, which was home with a difference. It was to be the base from which we would go to war. It was East Kirkby RAF Station No 55, the home base of 57 Squadron and 630 Squadron in the southern wolds of Lincolnshire, where we were to join 'B' Flight of 630 Squadron in Five Group of Bomber Command – one of the eleven groups in the Command , each of which had the same objective of taking the war to the enemy but each specialising in a particular aspect of operations. Until then, each airfield we had been on during our various training programmes had been physically a fairly compact unit, but the buildings and facilities of East Kirkby, comprising as they did an operational station, were widely dispersed, making the station less vulnerable if attacked by the enemy. On the heavy two-squadron bomber stations there were generally about 1,000 ground crew members and other members of staff plus about 200 members of aircrews.

630 Squadron, whose Motto was 'Death by Night', was formed on 15 November 1943 at East Kirkby near Spilsby, Lincolnshire and remained there for its entire existence until it was disbanded on 18 July 1945. Equipped with Avro Lancaster aircraft, its first operational mission was on 18/19 November 1943, when nine of its aircraft were dispatched to bomb Berlin. It subsequently took part in all the major attacks mounted against the German capital. Its last bombing mission was on 25 April 1945, when five of its aircraft bombed Berchtesgaden. In all the squadron dropped just over 10,347 tons of bombs. Its last operational mission was on the night of 25/26 April 1945, when four of its aircraft laid mines in the Onions area of Oslo Fjord off Horten but its last mission before the German surrender was on 4 May 1945, when thirteen of its aircraft were engaged in ferrying liberated prisoners of war back to Britain from the Continent. The Squadron's personnel aggregated the following awards: 1 DSO, 1 bar to DSO, 1 BEM, 42 DFCs, 4 bars to DFCs, 11 DFMs, and 1 AFM.

On arrival we noticed that aircraft were parked at various dispersal points around the airfield as a precaution against an enemy attack. We ourselves were dispersed and accommodated in Nissan huts spread around the countryside. Commissioned and non-commissioned aircrew members were separated in different quarters. Since I was the only officer in our aircrew, I was separated from the rest of my crew. I was told where to find my hut, which accommodated six. With my kitbag on my shoulder I trudged across the wide open spaces, eventually finding what would prove to be my home for the next five months.

Three officers were sitting on one of the beds talking as I walked in. A quick look around indicated to me that a bed in a convenient place in a corner was vacant, so I dropped my kit bag there. One of the three looked at me and said "You are not going to sleep in that bed are you"? I said "I thought it looked unoccupied, so it would do me". He said. "No, don't sleep there, that is the 'Jinx' bed. Everyone who sleeps in that bed goes for a 'burton'". As I had already made a point of doing everything that superstition said I shouldn't do during my career in the Air Force to date, I said "It's probably time for some changes to be made". Many indeed went for a 'burton' while I was living in that hut. Every bed except mine had a new tenant, some more than once, their occupants variously going missing, killed in action or becoming prisoners of war.

Next day we met our Flight Commander, Squadron Leader Roy Calvert, a fellow New Zealander. I also met many of the 'B' Flight crews, individuals from all parts of the world. After that we were mostly preoccupied with getting settled in and attending a few lectures. The weather was unsuitable for flying but I had to do a quick circuit to show that I knew how to do it. Because of the dispersed nature of our workplace, we all needed bicycles. Plenty of them were available because each time a crew failed to return, seven bicycles were looking for new owners. We were all given one. They remained ours for as long as we needed them. When we no longer needed them, for whatever reason, they went back into the bicycle pool.

On the third night operations were laid on. Much to my surprise and concern, I was listed as dispatching officer. As I had no idea what the duties of a dispatching officer were, I had to make some quick inquiries. All went according to plan so there was actually little for me to do.

The next day was doubly glorious. The sun shone and the crews on the night's operation had all returned safely. We ourselves were listed to do a six-hour cross country flight in the afternoon, so we spent the rest of the morning getting organised. We were airborne at 1500 hours and landed back at 2100 hours after a pleasant and uneventful trip.

Each morning, on notice boards around the station, Daily Routine Orders (DROs) were posted, as well as the names of the crews on the Battle Order, when 'ops' were on. All personnel were expected to familiarise themselves with the details. Having done that, we ground tested an aircraft in readiness for a night cross-country flight.

On Easter Sunday after an early tea, we took off as the sun was getting low in the sky, climbing to twenty thousand feet. From a cloudless sky, we gazed down upon England, spread like a topographical map beneath us, the low rays from the setting sun creating a panorama of light and shade which was a joy to behold. Never before had we seen such a strikingly beautiful scene. I was fascinated to listen to the expressions of delight from the rest of the crew. With our microphones left switched on, of course, we were able to talk to each other quite naturally, though we couldn't see each other.

When the sun disappeared beyond the horizon and the scene below quietly faded into the dusk we flew on, apparently alone in the dark but starry sky. Soon a full moon began to appear as though to prove that anything the sun could do, it could do better. Again we gazed down on an incredibly beautiful scene of England, this time bathed in moonlight enhanced by small fleecy white cumulus clouds fringing the picture. We landed back home at seven o'clock next morning and we all agreed that it had been the most interesting cross-country flight we had ever done.

I think a large part of our satisfaction stemmed from the pleasure we derived from the aircraft in which we were flying. From my point of view, it was clear that much thought had gone into the planning of the pilot's cockpit layout, making it so convenient for the pilot, and so different from the Stirling. Other crew members expressed similar thoughts with respect to their own stations in the aircraft. Also, it was the first time I had flown an aircraft with inline engines. I found that I derived pleasure from watching them seemingly nonchalantly sitting there, spinning their propellers. Unlike radial engines which I had grown accustomed to and which looked only like engines, each of the Lancaster's inline engines seemed to have its own individual personality and a smiling facial expression.

Next day I slept until 1230 hours. On reporting to our flight office, I found that operations were on that night and again I was listed as the dispatching officer. I seem to have discharged my duties as dispatcher in a competent manner. Happily I recorded that all our aircraft returned safely.

The following day was Tuesday 11 April 1944. Along with the DROs, the battle order for the night's operation to Aachen, was the statement that I would be flying as 'second dickie' - the term used for a pilot who went for observational purposes on his first operational flight as a passenger with another crew - with Flight Lieutenant Robbie Roberts and crew. There were anxious comments from the rest of my crew, as well as anxious feelings in my stomach. That night as an observer with another crew I had to go to learn what I would have to do with my own crew on undertaking our first operational mission. I realised at last that I would very soon be doing what I had set about learning to do nearly two years previously.

Then came the briefing for the forthcoming night's operation. Navigators had an earlier special briefing to give them time to make the many calculations needed regarding wind speeds at various heights, courses to steer on the different legs to be flown on the way to the target, and other calculations, data which would all come together on their flight plan. They then attended the final briefing that included all crew members.

With Robbie Roberts and the other crews allocated for the night's operation I ate a very special meal - special because it consisted of bacon and eggs, the latter being a luxury for the general public. That was standard practice for aircrews going on operations, and with good reason. It was often referred to as 'the last supper'. Usually after such meals there was a little time to spare during which we could do a few final jobs before getting ready for take off. We were always told to clear our pockets of all items that weren't essential, because enemy interrogators were very clever at using personal items to break the spirit of prisoners of war, and thus gain useful information.

I had agreed to meet Robbie and his crew at their aircraft dispersal point at a pre-arranged time. We were all appropriately dressed for the occasion and climbed the little ladder on the starboard side, each crew member making his way to his particular station in the aircraft.

Robbie started the motors and checked that everything for which he was responsible was as it should be. All the rest of the crew respectively followed suit. When all were satisfied that all equipment was in good working order and ready for the night's operation, Robbie shut down the motors. We all climbed out and sat around on the grass. Most men lit a final cigarette.

In order to reap the maximum benefit from each operation, as well as giving aircrews the best chance of survival, each operation was carefully planned and ran strictly to time. Each aircraft was allocated a take off time. We did not fly straight to our target but along the way made several false feints, with the object of making it as difficult as possible for the enemy to organise his night fighters to be in the right place at the right time. Also, by staying close together, we could swamp the defences, making it difficult for them to concentrate on individual aircraft. To keep close together in the dark where we could not see each other we had to make sure we were on time at each turning point along the way.

Depending on wind direction, it sometimes took longer to taxi to the take off point than at other times. When the time was right, we all climbed back into the aircraft. Robbie started the motors and we taxied to the end of the runway in use. Radio silence applied throughout, of course, because the enemy could learn much from listening to our radio conversations. At the take off point at the end of the runway was a black and white chequered caravan, from which would be flashed either a red or green light. We got a green light telling us that we were free to take off. Robbie had already positioned his aircraft facing down the runway. Releasing the brakes, he pushed open the throttles. The responsive roar from the four Rolls Royce Merlin engines caused the heavily laden aircraft to quiver from end to end. When I felt the vibrations of the wheels on the runway cease and felt the little thump as the wheels locked in the up position, I knew I was heading for enemy territory and combat for the first time.

For the first five hundred feet of altitude the engines had to work hard, lifting the weight of the aircraft itself, its seven crew members and 1.75 tons of bombs into the air. If any engine part were going to fail, the most likely time for it to do so was when it was under maximum load, so as soon as we had reasonable clearance from the ground, Robbie eased back a little on the throttles. Almost as soon as we were airborne, the ground seemed to be slipping into darkness but as we climbed we crept back into daylight and even had a glimpse of the setting sun for the second time that day.

All around us as we climbed for height were other bombers, all heading in the same direction, making for a rendezvous point from which to set course for the target area. Seeing them in all directions seemed to provide a little feeling of security, even though I knew that such security was illusory. The fact that I was with a crew who had already survived twenty-three operations added a little comfort, though as yet I did not know the true value of their experience. I was sitting where the engineer normally sat. No provision was made for passengers so Robbie's engineer had a night off and I took his place. As captain of the aircraft, a pilot needed a working knowledge of the duties and difficulties of each member of the crew, although it remained most unlikely that he would ever be able to leave his post to help anyone. Being familiar with the engineer's duties therefore made me eligible to replace him.

By the time we reached the coast of France darkness had descended upon the world. It seemed inconceivable that the Continent below could appear to be so devoid of signs of life even though the atmosphere was clear. After a while a layer of cloud developed beneath us. Robbie expressed to me his concern that the target would be difficult to see. I felt that his remarks were designed to make me feel that I was part of the team, because no other conversation was taking place. We had been taught to avoid all unnecessary talk.

I began to feel relieved that we had attracted so little opposition from the enemy. In the distance there were numerous bursts of flak, and there were searchlights weaving about but we were keeping out of trouble. Things looked very different, however, when we arrived at the target area. The cloud had cleared and we had a good run up on the target but there were lots of searchlights and flak. But our luck held and we had no problems. We were well on our way home before I saw seven aircraft shot down some distance behind us. Since we were supposed to try to keep together to make it difficult for the enemy to concentrate on individual aircraft, I wondered why they were so far behind.

Later I learnt that Bomber Command had also bombed a target at Culne in France and there had been much night fighter activity. The enemy's preoccupation there had no doubt made it easier for us. Sadly, we were to learn later, that Bill Green and crew were shot down on that target, all except the bomb aimer being killed. Jack's friend Reg and Digger's friend Colin were in Bill's crew. Digger's life had depended on the toss of the coin that brought him into my aircrew.

It was with some degree of relief that I saw the water of the English Channel merging with the coastline of England. I had just watched the last of the seven aircraft I had seen shot down plunging like a fiery torch into the darkness below. In fact, a total of nine aircraft of those tasked to Aachen on the night of 11/12 April 1944 failed to return. A Lancaster Mark 1 of 49 Squadron, LL 899 EA-P which took off from Fiskerton at 2031 hours, piloted by Flight Lieutenant D J B Bacon BA DFC was intercepted at a height of 5388 metres at 2326 hours by a night fighter piloted by Oberleutnant Heinz-Wolfgang Schnaufer of Stab 1V/NJG 1, two kilometres north of Sint-Lenaarts, twenty-five kilometres north of Antwerp, near the hamlet of Henxbroek Antwerpen. All seven of the crew, two of whom were members of the Royal Canadian Air Force, were killed and buried in the Antwerp Deurne Cemetery but their remains were later transferred to Schoonselhof Cemetery.

There was never any trace of Lancaster Mark 1 ME 572 VN-2 of 50 Squadron, piloted by Pilot Officer E A Skillen of the Royal Australian Air Force, which took off from Skellingthorpe at 2054 hours. The names of the crew are commemorated on the Runnymede Memorial. One member of the crew successfully baled out and was made a prisoner of war when Lancaster Mark 3 JA 695 QR-W of 61 Squadron which took off from Coningsby at 2048 hours, with Flying Officer E A Williams DFC as its pilot, was brought down, the six members of its crew being buried at the Antwerpen Deurne Cemetery but later at Schoonselhof Cemetery.

It was believed that a night fighter brought down Lancaster Mark 3 ND 389 OL-A of 83 Squadron piloted by Pilot Officer V McConnell which took off from Wyton at 2045 hours. At 2205 hours a radio message from the aircraft was received on 2765 kcs as "SLY V MCYA 2342 56603". Nothing further was received from the aircraft. It crashed at Beerse Antwerpen, six kilometres west south west of Turnhout. All members of its crew were buried at Schoonselhof Cemetery. A second aircraft from 83 Squadron lost on the attack on Aachen was that of Lancaster Mark 3 ND 395 OL-E which took off from Wyton at 2044 hours piloted by Flight Lieutenant P F Denny. Flak at 13,000 feet over Aachen brought it down. It crashed near the Postamt in the Schützenstrasse, all the crew being buried in the Rheinberg War Cemetery. Pilot Officer N W F Thackray was the pilot of Lancaster Mark 3, LL639 JI-R of 514 Squadron from Waterbeach which took off at 2101 hours but was shot down. The pilot and two others of the aircrew were members of the Royal Australian Air Force. A funeral service for the six members of the crew who were killed was held on 15 April 1944 at St Truiden in Belgium. Their bodies were eventually buried in 1945 at Heverlee War Cemetery.

When LL784 PG-W, a Lancaster Mark 1 of 619 Squadron which had taken off from Coningsby at 2043 hours and piloted by Squadron Leader J W E D McGilvray DFC reached Holland it was either hit by flak or attacked by a night fighter and blew up. The explosion expelled two of the aircrew from the aircraft. They both landed safely and were made prisoners of war. Among those killed was Warrant Officer A A Munro DFM who had already completed a tour in 61 Squadron. A second loss for 619 Squadron at Coningsby that night was that of a Lancaster Mark 3, EE 116 PG-Q, piloted by Flight Lieutenant H J Moore, which took off at 2040 hours. It was abandoned on fire at 16,000 feet over Holland near Tilburg, Noord-Brabant. It fell to ground at Waarde, Zeeland. Two members of the aircrew, including the pilot, Flight Lieutenant H J Moore successfully landed and were made prisoners of war. The other five crew members were all killed and were buried at Bergen op Zoom War Cemetery.

The ninth loss on the Aachen mission was that of JB 470 F2-M, a Lancaster Mark 3 of 635 Squadron which took off at 2043 hours from Downham Market. Attacked by a night fighter, it crashed two kilometres east of Roosendaal, Noord-Brabant. All seven crew members were buried in the Roosendaal-en-Nispen General Cemetery but the remains of the pilot, Pilot Officer R A Leader of the Royal Canadian Air Force, was moved after 1945 to Bergen op Zoom Canadian War Cemetery.

A warm welcome from my crew greeted me on my arrival back. They had stayed up specially to make sure I came home. The last step on our long training journey had been taken. My mixed up emotions made it difficult to answer their questions, but I tried to appear positive. Preparations had been fully accomplished. Action was the next step for us all together.

Six days passed before we made our first operational trip as a crew. Twice we were on the battle order, which helped us to learn to live with the anxiety that haunted us whenever we were so listed. Twice the weather granted us a reprieve and allowed us to feel that all encompassing feeling of relief, even though we knew it could be only temporary. There was plenty to do during that welcome interval. Getting to know our aircraft was one of them.

We had been allocated our own aircraft and ground crew. Our aircraft was Lancaster N D 527 with the 630 Squadron identification letters LE. The identifying letter for our aircraft was 'O', for Oboe, so on the sides of our aircraft was painted ND 527 LE-O. We completed our first twenty-eight operations in this aircraft before it foundered. On its next trip with another crew it collided over Nevers with ME 796 LE-S, another Lancaster from our station that was on its twenty-second mission. Our radio call sign for 630 Squadron was GAUNTLEY and the call sign for East

Kirkby airfield was SILKSHEEN. At all times, both in our aircraft between ourselves and between our aircraft and ground control, words were kept to a minimum in order to keep the means of communication freely available for emergencies.

LE-O had been Flight Lieutenant Cab Kalloway's aircraft in which he and his crew had just completed a tour of thirty

Fig. 53. Jack and Shortie on top of lancaster LE-O with the author between them (1944)

operations before leaving the squadron to lead a safer life. There was some encouragement for us in the proof thereby offered that it was possible to stay alive long enough to complete thirty operations Twenty five of those thirty operations had been done in LE-O. To us it seemed that it was a good omen to be taking over an aircraft in which a crew had completed a tour. We felt the need to find something to feel positive about because we had just heard the news about Bill Green's having been shot down. Jack, Digger and I had lost good friends even before we had made our first venture into enemy territory.

When the weather made flying impossible, we had an opportunity to meet our ground crew and others on the squadron but those occasions were all too rare. We never really got to know our ground crew, which saddened me because they were so important to us. Any work that had to be done on our aircraft was done outside, so often under conditions that were extremely cold and miserable. Neither did we get to know many other members of the squadron. When we couldn't fly there was always much to do as a crew, such as escape practice or lectures or swotting up on technical information. There was also the fact that life was so short on the squadron that there wasn't the opportunity to get to know people.

In the earlier days of the war the little village of East Kirkby had played host to a ghost airfield which was designed to fool the enemy into thinking it was a real airfield worthy of dropping bombs on. As the war progressed, however, the growing demand for more and more real airfields resulted in the change of status for East Kirkby to become a real airfield. It was pleasantly situated relative to a few other small villages and was located not far from Boston where the Boston Stump was an ever present land mark. Sometimes, as a crew, we would visit a pub in another village but those occasions didn't happen as often as we would have liked. As my quarters were in a different area of the base from the rest of my crew, there was a tendency to neglect social contact between us.

On a low hill on the outskirts of our airfield was a wind driven flour mill owned by Mr and Mrs Ely, which was still in operation and attracted a lot of interest, particularly from men from other countries where such things did not exist. We went for a walk up there one day and watched the operation of grinding wheat into flour. Mr and Mrs Ely were most friendly and made us very welcome. From there we walked on to the little village of Old Bolingbroke, where we stopped for a few ales. We were served our drinks in jam jars. As a result of the war there was a shortage of

Fig. 54. Crew Transport at East Kirkby - Dusty's car and Shortie's motorbike

glasses but in no way did the jam jars detract from the taste of the ale.

Dusty's brother owned an old Standard car which he did not use, so he kindly lent it to Dusty. Shortie owned a motorbike, and since we were now permanently settled in one place for a while, he brought it on to the station. Thus, with our own private transport we were able to visit villages further afield. Usually, Dusty, Griff, Digger, Les and I would squeeze into the Standard, while Jack would sit on the pillion seat behind Shortie. After an evening at a pub somewhere we would head for home with Shortie and Jack leading the way. Jack would sometimes flap his arms like an albatross endeavouring to get airborne from a choppy sea and Shortie would zoom round the corners like a Spitfire pilot lining up on an ME 109, while I watched from behind, concerned that a few too many beers might cause me to loose two valuable members of my crew.

By that stage of the war in May 1944 it was clear that the perverted system that had taken control of the German nation and had duped the people into thinking they were fighting for a necessary and worthy cause, would eventually collapse. Fighting would cease, peace would be restored and our loved ones would return to living normal lives. Aircrew loss statistics clearly showed that we as a crew were unlikely to survive to see those times but as Cab Kelloway had just demonstrated in the aircraft that we had taken over, there was always hope.

Chapter 9

First Encounters

Tuesday 18 April 1944 was a lovely sunny day, reminding me of New Zealand and giving me a touch of nostalgia. In the morning we took our aircraft up for a flying check to make certain that everything was in working order exactly as it should be for the night's operation. Once again we were on the battle order but this time we knew by the weather that there was no chance of its being cancelled. At last, after so much training, so many delays and so many preparations it looked as if we were about to go into action for the first time as a bomber crew.

In the afternoon we attended our first briefing as a crew. Along with other navigators, Jack had already attended a special navigators' briefing to receive the specific information that was necessary for each sortie. Always our route to the target consisted of a series of diverse legs designed to confuse the German defences and make it as difficult as possible for the Germans to decide on the best deployment for their night fighters. In addition, by keeping strictly to set times we were able to concentrate all the aircraft involved together to allow insufficient time for enemy defences to concentrate on any one particular aircraft.

All crews sat together in the 'ops' room at the far end of which was a dais, behind which on the wall was a large map of Europe covered by a screen. When all crews were assembled the leaders of various sections entered and took up their positions on the dais. We were welcomed by a Wing Commander who drew back the screen over the map of Europe and told us that our target for that night was the Jervisy railway marshalling yards on the outskirts of Paris. The route we would take there and back was marked on the map by tapes showing the various legs. Pilots were given a small map on which only the legs were shown, which I found easy to memorise. It was a device that I always found helpful.

An audible murmur of approval swept through the assembled crews because although the target was right in the middle of the German fighter belt, it was only a short trip. With luck we would soon be back home. A civilian meteorologist told us what weather we could expect over the target and what to expect on arrival back home. In turn, if there was something in particular they wished to say, information and advice were then provided by the Intelligence Officer, the Bombing Leader, the Engineering Leader and Flight Commanders. This became the standard procedure at all our subsequent briefings. Finally, the Wing Commander impressed upon us that we must be very careful to make sure that no bombs went astray because tenement buildings bordered the railway lines. It was important to avoid French civilian casualties. He then gave us the 'basic QFE' for the night, told us to synchronise our watches on his signal to do so and wished us good luck.

The 'basic QFE' was just any number, say, for example, 950, which enabled us to set our altimeters to read the correct height above our airfield when we returned home. During the time we were away, which was sometimes ten hours or more, the barometric pressure at our airfield may have changed considerably. Since our altimeter depended on the barometric pressure to tell us what height we were flying at, we needed to be able to set the current barometric pressure at our airfield on our altimeters, without providing the enemy with that information. On our return, as the estimated time of our arrival approached, base would radio us a message, say, "QFE plus sixteen". By adding the sixteen to our 'basic QFE' of 950 I would set 966 on my altimeter that would then tell me our correct height above our airfield.

Briefing over, the die had now been cast. Whatever we chose to do from that moment onwards, the thought continuously lurked around, "I wonder if I will be doing this to-morrow". Apart from being concerned about the actions of the enemy, I was concerned about my ability to deal with the swing that takes place when full power is applied to a bomb-laden aircraft. A few weeks previously, a pilot taking off for the first time with a bomb load had lost control. He ran off the runway, tore through a hedge, shot across the road to Stickney and into the next field where the bombs exploded. The blast was so powerful that windows in Skegness, fifteen miles away, were broken The only part of the aircraft remaining after the explosion was the rear turret which was blown a considerable distance away - amazingly with the rear gunner still inside it. He was taken out with no more physical effects than a few bruises.

No mention was made by any of my crew members about the anxious feelings which I know must have been churning around in the pits of their stomachs, just as they were in mine. We now made our way to our respective messes for our special 'ops' meal of bacon and eggs. Eggs were always in short supply, so to have them was a special privilege. The last meals before take off were always quiet occasions with little conversation. Even the few experienced members seemed to want to be alone with their thoughts.

As each person finished his meal he left the mess and made his way to the crew room and proceeded to dress for flying. It was a twenty-minute walk from our mess to the crew room. It was a journey I normally I did on my bicycle but after the 'ops' meal I always liked to walk it alone along the narrow, oak tree lined road, sharing my thoughts with Margie, so far away in New Zealand, yet seemingly so close.

In the crew room there was always a lot of chatter. The action of dressing for flying provided an opportunity for making jocular comments and a means of releasing pent up anxiety. Gunners had most work to do while dressing. As they could not be provided with hot air in their turrets, they had to wear electrically heated suits. They sometimes needed a little help to fit them on. For the rest of us in the aircraft hot air from the engines was available. I always flew dressed normally in my battledress and ordinary shoes, except for a heavy white issued pullover which I wore in case I had a broken windscreen. Usually the outside air temperature was over fifty degrees centigrade below zero but even if I brought the aircraft down to warmer temperatures as quickly as possible, it would become lethally cold during the interim.

Outside the crew room members of the WAAF were gathering crews together and delivering them to their respective aircraft, often with tear stained cheeks and sad eyes. We found our 'O' for Oboe Lancaster waiting patiently on its dispersal site ready to do what we might ask of it. Each member of the ground crew had completed the maintenance and any repair work on the aircraft for which he was responsible and certified it by initialling the appropriate place on the Form 700, which I had to sign if I was satisfied with everything. I could always sign with confidence. Flight Sergeant Dalrimple was in charge of the ground crew for our aircraft and I knew I could rely on him absolutely. There was never enough time or opportunity to spend with the ground crew, something I always regretted. Our lives were dependent on them.

We climbed into our aircraft as soon as we arrived at the dispersal. Having checked that everything seemed to be as it should be, I started the motors and activated all related equipment to ensure that everything was functioning correctly. The other members of the crew were doing likewise in their respective stations in the aircraft. Once all had been confirmed as being in operational order I then shut down the motors. Following custom we all got out of the aircraft and sat around on the grass until it was time to start taxying to our take off point. We followed this procedure for take off because we operated on a fairly rigid time schedule. When it was our time to take off we needed to be ready and waiting as we certainly didn't want any last minute hold ups to upset the operation.

Variations in wind direction caused variations in the position on the airfield from which we took off, making it necessary to estimate how long it would take to taxi from our dispersal to the take off point. A little practice was a big help but since this was our first 'op' I had to make a calculated guess. Of course, strict radio silence had been observed since the briefing. I kept a close eye on my watch. When I decided it was time to move, we all climbed the little ladder at the rear end of the aircraft on the starboard side and made our way to our respective stations. As I entered the doorway and looked towards my seat away up front, the thought as to whether or not I would be able to walk back down the aircraft flashed through my mind. I felt I had to run to my seat to get that part of entering the aircraft over quickly. Once in my seat I was alright as I had to be busy. Since we had already checked that everything was in working order, I needed only to restart the motors and join the line of aircraft taxing round the perimeter track.

At 2052 hours we got the green light from the control caravan at the end of the runway in use. Having already checked that all crew were ready for take off, I quickly advanced the throttles to about three quarters power. Knowing that the aircraft would have a strong tendency to swing to the left until it had gathered sufficient speed, I applied more power to the port motors and a lot of right rudder. This tendency was endemic, being created by the combined effect of the four propellers rotating in the same direction. Ideally, it would have been better for the two engines on one side to rotate in a contra direction to those on the other wing to neutralise the bias. From the manufacturing mass production point of view, however, it meant a reduction in the benefits of scale since 50% of engine production had to be different from the other 50%. By the time the airspeed indicator showed 60 mph I felt I had adequate control and advanced the throttles to full power. At 115 mph I lifted off, retracted the wheels and climbed away on our first operation as a crew into enemy territory.

We climbed to ten thousand feet above our airfield, before setting course for France. At that height it was still daylight and we were able to see other aircraft around us, which gave a degree of comfort. I had the feeling that all the German night fighters were out looking for us. As we crossed the English Channel with the enemy coast looming ahead it looked so very ominous. I was scared. By the time we reached the French coast darkness had descended and I felt very alone.

It was important to avoid casual conversation in case an emergency arose, so nobody spoke until Jack's voice came over the intercom, telling me that a course alteration was coming up in two minutes. Hearing his voice seemed to relieve the tension to some degree. I kept a constant roving lookout from the tail on the port side round the nose of the aircraft to the tail on the starboard side, with a quick glance at the instrument panel in between. "Next course 184 Doug", came from Jack. "Roger" was my simple reply in using the standard word for meaning message received and understood. Jack had a compass and altimeter so was able to confirm that I was steering the correct course. There were a few more course alterations before reaching the target but no frightening incidents.

On arriving at the target, our master bomber told us by VHF radio that the target was effectively marked and we were to go straight in to bomb. We had reduced height to five thousand feet but there wasn't a lot of anti-aircraft fire, or flak as we called it, but fighters were fairly active. We achieved an adequate run up on the target, which was the most scary part because I had to hold a steady course for quite a long run to give Griff the chance to make a good aim. Griff directed me which way to steer, by saying either "a little to the right" or "a little to the left", but fortunately never asked me to back up a little. During the run up to the target in this way we in turn became exposed as a good target for the opposition. I knew that the moment I heard Griff say "bombs gone" the aircraft would leap up considerably with the release of all that weight, so I needed to be ready to correct the attitude of the aircraft so that the camera would still be looking at the point where the bombs were going to land.

A one million candlepower photoflash was released with the bombs, timed to light the area where the bombs were landing, so that if all went according to plan, we could bring back a photograph of our bombs landing on the target. Obviously there were many reasons why things didn't always go according to plan but enough good photographs were always brought back to enable a good assessment of the exercise to be made.

In order to have the camera pointing at the area where the bombs were going to land I needed to keep the aircraft flying on the bombing run for as long as it took for the bombs on being released to reach the ground. Once we were relieved of our bombs the aircraft felt so light and manoeuvrable. Naturally I didn't want to make a target of ourselves any longer than was necessary and felt the need to take evasive action but I still had to hold the steady course until a red light on my instrument panel flashed, telling me that the camera had taken its photograph. That was the part I found hardest of all to bear.

We left the target area unscathed and set course for home. After about half an hour, in the blackness of the night, we saw a radial engined fighter sitting on our port beam. It was the glow from his engine that made him visible to us. He made no effort to attack. He just sat there, flying in formation with us. I thought he might be acting as a decoy while another aircraft attacked us from a different angle. I told Dusty in the rear turret to watch carefully elsewhere and Shortie to watch the one we could see. Of course I also watched the one we could see very carefully. After a while I saw his starboard wing go down as he came in to attack. I reacted so violently by going in the opposite direction that I shot Jack's navigating equipment all around his office, some of which he never found again, which was very puzzling. From that moment onwards both fighter and bomber lost track of each other so we went on our respective ways.

Later on I offered Jack my apologies for scattering his equipment all around his office but he assured me that no apology was necessary since he was all in favour of my action. Thinking about the episode later in the light of experience I concluded that the enemy pilot was probably just as inexperienced as we were, which probably made us both lucky. Had he been experienced he would not have given us such a good opportunity to see him and if I had had the experience that I later gathered, I would have quickly slid underneath him and let our mid upper gunner blast him out of the sky. Luck can be good as well as bad.

Soon after that incident I found myself flying a little behind and a little below another bomber. It felt comforting to know we were with friends. I could clearly see the rear gunner sitting in his turret and felt like giving him a wave but knew that as he was looking down against the dark earth he probably could not see me. Then the horrifying thought struck me. If he could not see a big bomber just behind and below him, how could he hope to see a smaller aircraft like an enemy fighter.

During our training we had been told that it was not safe even to trust our own bombers. Those that had crashed landed in enemy territory and were not too badly damaged were sometimes repaired, given more guns and sent up to mingle with our bombers. If that rear gunner could see us he should have reported the fact to his skipper who would undoubtedly have moved elsewhere. My next thought was whether Dusty would have been able to see a bomber flying just behind and below us. To feel more secure I moved elsewhere and I felt that perhaps a useful lesson was there to keep in mind.

Even in the dark we could see the difference between earth and water and we could see the welcome sight of the English Channel beneath us as we crossed back into home territory. Suddenly, however, on the starboard beam searchlights pierced the sky and backpack shells began exploding over a wide area. It seemed that while we had been away there was an enemy air raid on London. We were in a prime position to see the action. Although at that stage we were not accustomed to participate personally in air raids, we felt that our experience in being so well placed as spectators was unique. It was spectacular to watch. Only Jack and Digger could not easily see the action. Since we were on course for our home base Jack was able to leave his desk and look out, while Digger looked from the astrodome. There were many comments from crew members and I felt a little concern about the unnecessary chatter on the intercom but since we were now back in friendly territory I did not interfere. At an instant, on our port side, at a distance of about four hundred yards, a brief stream of cannon shells went skywards, followed about ten seconds later by a big explosion. The flaming remains of one of our own bombers fluttered down to earth. We all saw it happen but nobody spoke. It was another harsh lesson for us on our very first trip. Silence reigned on the intercom.

There were feelings of relief for all of us when we felt our wheels back on terra firma. We had survived our debut and had been fortunate enough to have some important lessons demonstrated to us. Altogether 202 Lancasters and four Mosquitoes of 5 Group and three Oboe Mosquitoes of 8 Group took part in the attack. Fourteen Lancasters were despatched from our station. The one aircraft lost from the raid on Jurvisy from the station that night crashed on return at Chapelbridge, near Whittlesey in Cambridgeshire. ND 475 DX of 57 Squadron was a Lancaster Mark 3 which had taken off at 0100 hours, piloted by Pilot Officer A E Oberg of the Royal Australian Air Force. There were no survivors. One of the aircrew, Pilot Officer Adams at forty was one of the oldest members of Bomber Command aircrews to be killed during 1944. Two other members of this aircrew were in their thirties, well above the average age.

On 19 April 1944, the front page of the daily newspapers in Britain flourished a photograph under the title, "A Tribute To The Bombing Accuracy Of The RAF". It was a photograph of the Jervisy railway marshalling yards after we had visited them the night before. It was a remarkable photograph. Standing, apparently unscathed, beside what remained of the marshalling yards were the tenement buildings, while the marshalling yards themselves were a mass of twisted railway lines and bomb craters. We learnt later that one aircraft did overshoot slightly. Its bombs demolished a building which happened to be the regional headquarters of the Germany Army. The French gave the RAF credit for more skill than it really deserved.

At this stage of the war the invasion of Europe by the Allies was getting close. The techniques employed by Bomber Command had become very suitable for demolishing small areas to make it difficult for the Germans to move their troops and equipment around quickly. Leonard Cheshire of Five Group, in conjunction with Micky Martin had evolved an excellent system of marking targets, which enabled the main force bombers to place their bombs mostly very accurately. Each aircraft was required to aim in turn at the same point as clearly marked.

In contrast, American bombers flew in daylight in formation. When the lead plane dropped its bombs it was the signal for all the rest to do likewise. Consequently, the bombs were spread over a wide area – a technique that was not conducive to the accurate bombing of small targets.

From our point of view, there seemed little doubt that we were going to be on the winning side. We hoped to be still alive to see the victory but as the war was about killing people and destroying their valuable property and means for making war, the process for doing that had to go on until the bitter end. We in particular had to get on with the process of killing and destroying and risk being killed ourselves in the course of doing that to make our contribution towards the final outcome.

I got to bed about 0300 hours and slept until mid-day. After lunch I went down to our flight office but there was nothing specific to do so I walked to our aircraft and had a talk with our ground crew. Some were busy patching shrapnel holes in our aircraft. They were all so busy going about their duties that I felt I was an intruder. However I was able to spend a while with Flight Sergeant Dalrimple. After that I made my way back to our Mess where I was amazed and delighted to meet Joe Lennon. He was equally surprised to meet me. Not only had he joined our squadron about a week previously, but he was also in "B" Flight, the same as me. Joe and his crew had been on the same night's operation to Jurvisy. Needless to say, we had lots to talk about. So much had happened since we last saw each other. Joe said he was the world's worst letter writer and apologised for not writing. There didn't seem to be anyone back in New Zealand with whom he kept in contact. We talked until it was time for the evening meal after which I retired to my Nissan hut to write three letters and an aerograph before getting into bed.

The fact that he had been with our flight for a week and I had not seen him was typical of life on a bomber station. Most crews survived on the average for about a fortnight, so there was no chance to get to know them. Those who were lucky to stay alive longer than that were busy working together as crews, away on bombing practice, keeping familiar with various forms of escape practice for emergencies, doing air tests, flying on operations or sleeping, so there was little chance to get to know each other.

10 April 1944 dawned fine but with a very cold wind. Our crew found itself on the battle order again which triggered that ominous feeling in the gut that ceaselessly churned away, no matter what we did or where we went. I met up with the rest of the crew and we walked down to our aircraft to take it up for an air test but the ground crew were still busy working on it so we had to wait until after lunch to carry out the test.

East Kirkby bomber station had been farm land before becoming an airfield. From the dispersal site where we had parked 'O' for Oboe we could look across to a little old brick house which had once been a farm cottage. It was not far from the middle of the airfield so that no matter which runway was in use four-engined bombers were constantly roaring past it. There were still a few shrubs growing where once a garden had been. I often looked at that little cottage looking so lonely as it did near the middle of a busy airfield. I mused about what stories it would be able to tell in the future if ever it could talk.

Further away on the outskirts of the airfield was a low hill topped by a clump of trees. Although it was a low hill it was high enough to be a nuisance on a dark night when visibility was bad. It was something we always had to keep in mind because it was on the circuit we followed when making our preparations to land.

Looking a little to the left was another hill on which stood the wind driven flour mill owned by the Ely family. This hill was far enough away not to provide any major concerns. When we looked in that direction and saw the sails revolving, Digger would often jokingly say that a warning was being sent to the enemy to say that we were coming over that night.

Behind our 'O' for Oboe, as it sat being groomed on the dispersal pad, was a dilapidated wire fence beyond which was an old, uncared for orchard, to the right of which, a short distance away was the village of East Kirkby. On the occasions when we went directly from the Mess to our aircraft, we usually climbed through a hole in that fence, as it gave us direct access to our dispersal.

Meeting the rest of the crew after lunch, we went together down the road to the hole in the fence, climbed through and took 'O' for Oboe up for an air test. All systems worked satisfactorily. It was very pleasant being able to enjoy the pleasure of flying a fine aircraft. By the time we had finished all we needed to do, it was time for our special bacon and eggs meal, after which we went to the briefing for the night's operation.

Briefing followed the same procedure as the first one we had attended. The target also was almost identical. It was the railway marshalling yards at La Chapelle in France. At the conclusion of the briefing, the CO complemented us on such a good performance at Jervisy and told us to repeat it at La Chapelle. We synchronised our watches. As we prepared ourselves for flying and drew our parachutes from the store we were conscious of the fact that we had survived one sortie into enemy territory and hoped that fate would smile on us enough to enable us to survive again.

After arriving at 'O' for Oboe's dispersal, the procedure was the same as before. After I had started the motors we all checked that our particular equipment was functioning as it should. I then shut down the motors and all seven of us sat around on the grass, most of us having a final cigarette. We were in reality close to being terrified but preferred to describe it simply as anxious. When I decided it was time to prepare to start taxying, we again climbed on board and took up our respective positions. Again, as I climbed the little ladder and looked to my seat up front, the thought flashed into my mind, "I wonder if I will walk back down here". I had to run up to my seat to get that intimidating part of preparing to take off over as quickly as possible.

With motors running, all checks completed and all crew members ready to taxi, we slipped into the snake like line of aircraft on the perimeter track, to the steady roar of Rolls Royce Merlin engines and the hiss of braking operations. At night time the perimeter track was lined with little blue lights with a cover over the top so that they could be seen from ground level but not from the air, to avoid giving aid to marauding enemy aircraft intent on attacking the airfield.

The contours of the ground could make it difficult for taxying. Sometimes there were quite sharp corners to negotiate. On some occasions it was difficult to decide exactly where the track was. It was vitally important to stay on the perimeter track because if one wheel went on to the grass, with such a heavily laden aircraft, the wheel would sink into the ground and the aircraft would become bogged down, creating a hold up for following aircraft and possibly putting the whole schedule of the operation in chaos. Steering was done by applying a little brake to one wheel or the other and sometimes, if necessary, a little extra power to one of the outboard motors.

We made our way to the take off position without incident. I had 'O' for Oboe lined up looking along the runway ready to go. Having already completed one take off with a bomb load and knowing how it felt, I was a little more confident the second time round. I watched the aircraft in front of us nearing the end of the runway and knowing that I was about to get the green light as well, with the brakes firmly on I advanced the throttles to three quarters power. The green light pointed in my direction and flashed. I released the brakes and let the aircraft gather speed. While pushing the control column forward to get the tail up, I advanced the throttles to full power on the port side while applying right rudder, then full power on all throttles when I felt I had the aircraft's tendency to swing left under control. Once clear of the runway I retracted the undercarriage and at 500 feet slowly reduced the flaps.

Again we climbed above the airfield to gain height before setting course for La Chapelle. Darkness had enveloped the earth just before take off but as we climbed we went back into daylight. The sun was already dipping below the horizon so by the time we reached the French coast it was again dark. From time to time as we flew on course we were hit by the slipstream of another bomber. This meant that we were in the middle of a swirling mass of air created by the four propellers of the aircraft ahead – an aerial torrent that was strong enough to tip us upside down if no corrective action were taken. Getting into slipstreams always provided a bumpy ride for a brief period but also a good feeling as the experience reminded us that we were amongst friends.

It wasn't long before, as on our first trip, I found myself looking up to a rear gunner sitting in the turret of a bomber in front. I felt that he should have been traversing his turret from side to side, watching for enemy night fighters, but he was just sitting there. I wondered if I was being hypercritical and over sensitive to think that his apparent passivity could be the undoing of himself and his entire crew. I felt that I could have shot him down so easily. He seemed to be so vulnerable. It made me realise that we could be equally vulnerable, if we were equally guilty of such nonchalance.

Suddenly, just as I had seen over England while we watched the air raid on London, at a distance of a few hundred yards on our port side I saw a stream of cannon shells going skywards, followed a few seconds later by a big explosion and the flaming remains of one of our bombers plunging earthwards, along with seven bodies which a minute ago had been seven live human beings. It was a startling sight to witness, spawning as it did a wave of different emotions, not least an injection of fear as well as the immediate corrective realisation that it wasn't us – we were still alive and flying onwards.

We flew on in the dark, feeling the odd thump from the slipstream of another bomber. My roving eyes - covering the sky from the tail on the port side past the nose to the tail on the starboard side - were ever more vigilant. Sometimes I paused to look at the engines. They had a pleasing fascination for me because they seemed to have a personality of their own - they always looked complacent no matter how anxious I was feeling. The spinner on the front of the propeller looked like a nose thrust willingly forward, seeking to do what was being asked of it. The exhaust stubs looked like eyes and ears. Below and behind the propeller was the bulge of the oil cooler which was easy to interpret as a shapely breast. I grew to look upon them all as my friends.

Before we reached the target I saw two more aircraft shot down, each of which I reported to Jack because we were expected to record the area in which we saw such occurrences. As before, the target was nicely marked when we arrived. Although the flak was much heavier than that of our first trip, we managed a good run up and bombed successfully without any damage to ourselves. On our way home two more aircraft were shot down close to us as well as several too far away for me to see in any detail.

From seeing the two shot down nearby, I learnt something which probably did much to keep us alive for the remainder of our tour of operations. As before, I saw a stream of cannon shells go skywards, followed by the explosion. In each case I was able to count the number of cannon shells. Each time there were fifteen shells going skywards at the same angle. Thinking back to the previous aircraft I had seen shot down, I realized that the sequence had always been exactly the same - always the same number of cannon shells, always going upwards at the same angle and never with any return fire from the bomber. Clearly, the enemy fighters were creeping underneath our bombers where they could not be seen by our gunners who had to look down into the dark earth. In contrast the enemy night fighter pilots were looking up to big bombers silhouetted against the lighter sky. Since the shells always went up at the same angle, I deduced that the guns must have been fixed to the fighter in an upward firing position, making it possible for the fighter to fly straight and level underneath the bomber to a position where his cannon shells could be fired into the bomber's petrol tanks, causing them to explode.

My thoughts on this subject returned to the period of our training when our lecturer told us to fly straight and level and fight it out with the night fighters. In view of the facts I was discovering in action I reflected on how misguided that advice seemed to be. I wondered how many lives that advice had cost unnecessarily and if the bombers I had already flown underneath were following that advice. Obviously it was not possible to fight it out with an enemy you cannot see but the answer must surely have been to make it as difficult as possible for the enemy to sight on to you. From that time onwards I never stayed in one place for more than a minute.

After the war I learnt that at that particular time the German night fighter force was at its peak of efficiency. The technique of the tame boar fighters was as I had concluded, except that they had been flying under our bombers at a much lower level than I had assumed was the effective range - in fact between fifty and one hundred metres. They had also used an infrared beam to position themselves correctly below the bomber. There had been a logical development in German thinking. In 1917, during the First World War, British bombers had begun to bomb German targets at night. German fighter pilots, in diving from above to attack, were often dazzled by searchlights so a certain Feldwebel Theid mounted two upward firing machine guns on his aircraft. In 1941 German night fighter pilots usually crept under the British bombers, pulled the nose of their aircraft up, and raked the fuselage from nose to tail. Later on in doing so, they could hit the sensitive 4,000 pound 'Cookie', if one were aboard, which exploded and blew up the bomber and often the fighter as well. Hauptman Schoehert experimented with a similar gun arrangement on a Dornier 217. In the summer of 1942 General Kammhuber authorised slanting guns to be fitted to three Dorniers for experiments. Field tests in early 1943 were very successful and became standard equipment by June. Known as R 22, they were fitted to Junkers 88s, Dornier 217s and Messerchmitt 110s with Schrage Music cannons.

Using Lichtenstein Radar to approach fifty metres below the bomber and infrared light to match the speed of the bomber, the night fighter moved one metre ahead. It then put a two seconds burst of fifteen cannon shells into the petrol tanks of the bomber before quickly moving a safe distance away. If the bomber had full petrol tanks, as on its outward flight, within eight to ten seconds the whole aircraft became a flaming torch. If the petrol tanks were getting low, as on its return flight, within the same time span, the bomber would blow up, resulting from the explosion of the petrol vapour filling the near empty tanks.

In February 1943, the Operational Research Committee (ORC) of the Royal Air Force discussed whether or not German night fighters were using upward firing guns. In March Dr. Dickins stated that some damage which crews thought were from light flak, were in fact from aircraft cannons. In June 1943 Mr. Smeed of the ORC wrote that evidence had come to light that seemed to remove the possibility that Germans were using upward firing guns. In its May monthly report the ORC analysis showed that 36% of bombers were damaged from an unknown cause. Eventually, as the American army progressed into Germany, they found abandoned night fighters with upward firing guns.

We had an uneventful trip home. Once again it was a good feeling when our wheels landed on the runway. The raid on this railway target to the north of Paris was the first major test for the new 5 Group marking method, employing not only 617 Squadron's low level markers but the three Pathfinder Squadrons recently transferred from 8 Group. A few regular 8 Group Mosquitoes were also used to drop markers by Oboe to provide a first indication of the target's location for the main 5 Group marking force. Of the 247 Lancasters of 5 Group and twenty-two Mosquitoes from 5 Group and 8 group despatched, six Lancasters were lost. We lost two crews from our station that night, both from 57 Squadron, along with fifteen crews from other stations. Lancaster Mark 1 with the identification LL 893 DX-J, piloted by Squadron Leader S M Wigg, the Commander of 'A' Flight, took off at 2139 hours to attack the targets at La Chapelle but failed to return. The whole aircrew were found interred at Clichy New Communal Cemetery, which is thought to have been a second burial, as two photographs of one of the aircrew, Sergeant J Coulter, were found in the wrecked Lancaster in Avenue St-Milelet at St Omer. Piloted by Flying Officer H J Young of the Royal Canadian Air Force, ND 582 DX-S, a Lancaster Mark 1, managed to return to England though badly damaged. It attempted to land at Croydon airfield where it crashed into houses on the edge of the airfield at 0220 hours, destroying numbers 55, 57 and 59 Lavender Vale, Wallington. Three of the aircrew were killed in the crash and two were injured, one of these dying later of his injuries.

The bombing force had been split into two, with an hour's interval between them, each half aiming at its own half of the target. There were difficulties at the opening of the attack as the markers of the Oboe Mosquitoes were a fraction late and communications between the various controlling aircraft were faulty. The difficulties were overcome to the extent that both parts of the bombing force achieved extremely accurate and concentrated bombing.

The next day was dull and cold. Having slept until 1230 hours I had lunch and then spent quite a while in the Intelligence Library looking for information that I thought could be useful. I had thought that it was just a matter of luck whether or not one survived a tour of operations because statistics seemed to indicate that that was so. However, I had begun to feel that maybe there were things one could do to improve one's chances. It was obvious that the tame boar night fighters were the greatest menace on the way to and from the target. In the target area there was a lot of light which made it possible to see the wild boar single engined fighters but we could do nothing about the flak that was fired at us because in order to bomb accurately we had to make a long and steady run up to the target, during which time we ourselves were exposed as a good target.

Chapter 10

Nemesis Postponed

In the early part of the Second World War, bomber crews which were endeavouring to bomb targets in German cities in the dark were attempting the impossible. From the moment they were airborne they were suspended in a moving mass of air which was carrying them in some obscure direction of which they had little knowledge. They lacked the means to compensate for contrary weather difficulties and to correct for navigational errors to ensure that they had found the correct target city. In their forward planning, of course, navigators allowed for the movement of this air mass as it was perceived before departure but had no way of knowing the changes that had taken place en route. Consequently it was common for crews to miss their targets by many miles.

If they were fortunate enough to find the city where the particular target was located they were still unlikely to drop their bombs in the right place. Even if there were an absence of cloud, industrial haze would almost certainly make it impossible for them to have a view of the target of sufficient clarity and durability to ensure an effective attack. Crews had to look diagonally through such haze to see the target in good time if they were to be able to place their bombs accurately.

Later on, when some navigational aids became available, a Pathfinder force was able to lead the main bomber force to the right area and then mark the target, but only if there were no cloud. If the Pathfinders found the city was covered by cloud, after flying for four hours or more, all they could do was to drop sky markers above the clouds and tell the bomber force to bomb the sky markers. If the sky markers were actually over the correct target when they were released by the time the bombers began releasing their bombs the sky markers would probably have drifted in the air currents so that the total bomb load dropped by the attacking force of aircraft ended up being scattered over a wider area than was intended or necessary.

With such an outcome, it was possible for the precise target itself to escape unscathed, although plenty of collateral damage to industrial property, residential property and service and transportation installations could be caused, all of which would disadvantage the enemy to some degree. Yet the precise target, such as a ball-bearing factory – chosen for its vital contribution to the enemy's war effort - could remain intact. This in my view was the origin of what became known as area bombing. There were times when crews were simply obliged to bomb sky markers. I don't believe that any crew ever dropped bombs on a city just because it was a city. As Noble Frankland has put it, "Operationally, the idea of area bombing was to attack an aiming point which lay in the centre of a large area whose destruction would be useful. It was, in other words, a method of making bombs which missed the aiming point contribute to the destruction of the German war machine. Since nearly all bombs were missing the aiming point, there was a certain logic about the idea".

Our third trip was to Brunswick on Saturday night 22 April 1944. Being our first trip to Germany itself, we had reason to be a little more apprehensive. The precise target was an aircraft factory. In the morning we took 'O' for Oboe up for an air test and some practice flying. On landing, we practiced some ditching and dinghy drill. Briefing was in the afternoon, followed by our 'last supper' about 2000 hours. After supper I walked alone along the oak tree lined road from our Mess to the crew room where we donned our flying gear. As usual the place was full of chatter, concealing the anxiety that we all felt. WAAF transport girls were busy delivering crews to their respective aircraft, but since ours was parked nearby, we did not avail ourselves of the ride. Once at our aircraft, we followed the usual routine, including my run up to my seat up front.

At 2303 hours we were airborne and climbing for height above our airfield. Aircraft from 5 Group generally flew on their own sorties, independently of the other Groups of Bomber Command, owing to the particular target marking method which the Group had developed. This method was to dispatch the target marking aircraft, known as Pathfinders, a little earlier than the rest of us so that they could light up the general target area with flares by the time we arrived. We would then over fly the target while showering down bundles of tinfoil to confuse the German radar systems controlling the defending searchlights and anti-aircraft guns. Into this tinfoil screen other target marking Mosquito aircraft flew at very low altitudes, using visual identification to drop ground markers as precisely as possible.

Having distributed our tinfoil bundles, we would be advised by the master bomber on vhf radio where the marker was in relation to the target. We would then circle round with a clearly visible marker ahead and commence our bombing run. This system made it possible to bomb accurately and completely eliminated the problem of being unable to identify the target in time when having to look diagonally through industrial haze. Sometimes there were difficulties for the marker crews to get the target marked, in which case we orbited anticlockwise around the target area until we were told to bomb. Mostly the system worked well. Probably most crews didn't like having to spend so long in the target area with exploding anti-aircraft shells, groping searchlights and wild boar fighters around as a potentially immediate death warrant. It was certainly a stressful experience but it afforded a degree of satisfaction in providing a clear chance to see the enemy. It also gave one the macabre satisfaction in the teeth of battle to know that if one fell a victim at least it would be at the cost to the enemy of an effective attack. In fact, over my tour of operations I saw many more bombers shot down on the way to and from the target than I did in the target area itself.

Not long after we crossed into France I gave Dusty a call. As rear gunner, his lot as member of a bomber aircrew was definitely a lonely one. Unfortunately, from the moment I made contact with him his microphone developed a nasty crackle which impinged on the eardrums of every crew member. Such a noise can be very fatiguing and made the transmission of emergency messages ineffectual. It was crucial to be able to give and receive a message instantly and clearly for immediate action if a combat situation arose or if the condition of the aircraft merited an emergency rating. I told him therefore to switch his microphone off and to switch it on only at a time when he needed to speak urgently.

We reached the target area without incident but as we were distributing our bundles of tinfoil I suddenly heard our guns in action. We were being attacked by a night fighter but I had no idea from which direction the attack was coming. Dusty was later able to tell me that he had indeed informed me instantly but had forgotten that his microphone was switched off. I reflected on the absurd notion that if we had been destroyed in that attack I would never have known that little but important irony.

At the same time as I heard our guns I instinctively reacted by putting the nose down a little to gain speed for manoeuvring and increased power. I looked around frantically to see where the attack was coming from. While I was looking in the direction of the port rudder, Dusty, having realised that his microphone had been switched off, switched it on and said "he is still with us, just coming in for another attack". "Which way?" I yelled, feeling a desperate need to know exactly what was happening. "Starboard", he yelled back.

I knew that if the enemy fighter were attacking from the starboard side, I needed to make a quick turn to starboard to prevent him from being able to sight on to us. While looking in the direction of the port rudder I kicked on the starboard rudder and rolled the aircraft over to starboard. Ideally the manoeuvre should have been a severe but controlled defensive action but I think panic was breathing its hot breath down the back of my neck, because I overdid the manoeuvre and tipped the aircraft upside down.

Down we went, down in a terrible dive. My instruments were not designed to work upside down. Even if they had been working they would have been telling such a confused story that would have been impossible for me to translate into sense. My only hope I realised in those moments of terrifying chaos was to find out which way was up and which way was down by locating the whereabouts of the horizon - the difference between the earth and the sky that was difficult to discern at night time. I looked out through my side window, only to see that all windows were covered by a film of ice. I thought at that point that our last hope was gone. I was disappointed that we were about to join the majority who didn't survive more than five trips. I was also disappointed by the fact that I had let my crew down and because of that they were going to die with me.

The next point must have been when I passed through the panic barrier. I began to think clearly, realising that the lights I could see through the ice must be lights on the ground. With that realization I was able to get the aircraft the right way up, but still in that terrible dive. But at least there was hope. I had no idea how much height we had lost but I knew that we were not yet dead, if not far from it. In desperation I felt that if I could get the aircraft out of the dive before we hit the ground we would survive. I looked at the airspeed indicator which was the only instrument that told me something I could understand. It told me that we were approaching the ground at nearly 400 miles per hour – in other words time was running out fast and our lives with it.

I pulled on the control column only to find that it felt as though it were set in concrete. We had six tons of bombs on board. At the speed we were travelling and with all that added weight, the aircraft needed a lot of persuasion to get it to change direction. No doubt the adrenalin which would have been pumping through my system would have made me much stronger than normal but with all the energy that I could muster I was able to manage only a very small movement of the control column and to sustain that output of energy for only a few seconds at a time. I owe my life and the lives of my crew to the fact that I was born to grow tall. I used my long legs to wedge my knees between the control column and the instrument panel and thereby to lock in place each small movement of the control column that I could manage – one small movement at a time. I continued to do that until suddenly the airspeed indicator, from registering almost 400 mph, dropped down to 100 mph.

The sight of it gave me a fresh fright. It told me that we had come out of the dive and were now going almost straight up under the influence of our momentum. With our bomb load still on board we needed at least 120 miles per hour to avoid the stall and remain flying. It was imperative to attain that speed before our momentum ceased and we fell out of the sky. I knew that the spin following a stall in a heavily laden bomber would almost certainly be fatal. We had been trained to recover from a spin in the Tiger Moth but not in any subsequent aircraft types. Since then it has become customary to train pilots in the Royal Air Force to recover from spins after deliberately induced stalls. Pilots on the Empire Test Pilots' Course at Boscombe Down in Wiltshire have had to do it in as large an aircraft as the Andover. Pilots in training on the Tornado and other fast jets have to incorporate the skill of recovery from spins routinely in their courses.

As far as my knowledge and training went I knew that I had to get the nose down. Meanwhile the effect of this disastrous plunge on the other members of the crew must have been catastrophic both mentally and physically. Normally both gunners and myself wore harnesses to keep us in place but the bomb aimer, the engineer, the navigator and the wireless operator were free to move around as needs be. Consequently, those four members were subjected to the terrifying and unaccustomed forces of nature during that nightmarish plunge and recovery. When pulling out of that dive, the 'g' or gravitational pull on the body was extremely powerful and unpleasant, making it impossible to move. It felt as if the skin were being pulled off one's face. Although the jaw muscles are very strong, if one allows one's mouth to fall open in such circumstances, it is virtually impossible to close it again.

As a result, while we were coming out of that dive, everyone was firmly glued to the floor, completely unable to move. Now with the newly emergent need to regain speed, I was obliged to put the aircraft into another steep dive, having only just recovered from that uncontrolled plunge. This time however the dive was under my control from the outset and with real purpose. As I made the change from going straight up to going straight down the four unharnessed crew members changed from being stuck to the floor to being stuck to the ceiling. With the nose well down our speed quickly increased. Having just fought so hard to get out of the uncontrolled dive, I was apprehensive about allowing my chosen corrective dive to last any longer than was absolutely necessary to gain flying speed, as I imagined that the earth would come to meet us at any moment. As soon as I judged it possible I brought the aircraft out of the dive, bringing the unrestrained crew members back on to the floor. Unfortunately, however, I did it too soon. We lacked sufficient flying speed, making it necessary to put the nose down yet again and sending the roving crew members back up to the ceiling - but by the time I was able to allow them to regain their normal positions back on the floor, I had both the aircraft and myself finally under control.

My next thought was, "where is the enemy fighter now" and asked that question over the intercom. Had it stayed around to watch the debacle, probably thinking his first attack was responsible for it? Or had he concluded that we were a certain victim - or at least a 'probable'. He must have lost sight of us with satisfaction and passed on to pursue other business. Griff replied first saying "I can't see a damn thing. My windows are all iced over". Shortie spoke next saying, "I can't see a bloody thing, my turret is all iced over". Dusty, at the tail end, had an open panel to look through because his end of the aircraft was always going away from the wind. He said "I can see alright but I can see no sign of the fighter. Even if I could, I couldn't do anything about it because my guns no longer work". His guns no longer worked because the ammunition which supplied them was stored in containers located on either side of the fuselage. When we tipped upside down the stored ammunition fell out of the containers but did not fall back into them after we resumed our normal attitude. We all concluded that the fighter pilot had decided that he could not compete with the evasive capabilities of a Lancaster bomber, or perhaps he thought he had shot us down.

The fate of the rear-gunner's ammunition was shared by everything else in the aircraft that was loose or could be dislodged. Not least did this apply to the chemical toilet.

My next thought was "what height are we at now". We had been flying at 18,000 feet before all this happened, and I thought we must have lost a lot of height in that terrible dive. My altimeter had three hands, a long one which registered hundreds of feet, a shorter one which registered thousands of feet and a little one which registered tens of thousands of feet. Obviously, we normally never needed to monitor the little one very much. In the dark I was not able to see it anyway. I asked Jack what his altimeter was reading. Jack's altimeter had only one hand which gave him a general idea of height. He had a light in his office so he could see it clearly. Jack said we were flying at either ground level or 20,000 feet. In the event we were at 20,000 feet, in fact at 2,000 feet higher than we were meant to be. We had gained so much speed in the dive that we finished up higher than we started but until my instruments settled down I had no way of knowing anything except our speed.

Before all this happened we had been flying for more than four hours in a temperature of minus fifty-three degrees, but because the air was thin and could hold very little moisture, we had had no problems with ice, even though the whole aircraft and all the bombs on board were at well below freezing point. When we dived precipitately into warmer and damper air, the moisture in the surrounding air froze over everything it touched adding weight to the aircraft and increasing considerably to the difficulty of recovery.

Now that all our immediate problems had been dealt with, we had to get on with the job we came to do. Being a little higher than the other aircraft may have kept us out of further trouble because we had a good run up on the target marker although there was a great deal of enemy activity with searchlights, backpack guns and wild boar fighters. Eventually the night's mission was successfully concluded with an uneventful run home. We touched down at base at 0530 hours and I was in bed by 0730 hours.

The force attacking Brunswick included 238 Lancasters and seventeen Mosquitoes from 5 Group and ten Lancasters from 1 Group. Few night fighters were encountered, resulting in a minimal loss of four Lancasters. The raid was important in the history of Bomber Command's war effort in that it was the first time that 5 Group's low level marking method was used over a heavily defended German city. The raid was not a success. The initial marking by 617 Squadron Mosquitoes was accurate but many of the main force bombers did not bomb on it, partly owing to a thin layer of cloud which hampered visibility and partly owing to faulty communications between the various controllers. Some bombs were dropped on the centre of the city but many were dropped on the reserve H2S-aimed target indicators well to the south. The city records showing that forty-four people were killed suggested that little damage had been achieved.

After the manner in which I had treated my crew that night, I expected a lot of uncomplimentary comments about my ability as a pilot the next day but the episode was scarcely mentioned. That was a general characteristic amongst crews which I began to notice more and more as time went on. Unnerving experiences were part of the job. If you mentioned one of yours to someone else, the chances were that the person you were talking to had survived worse ones. There was also the 'Line Book' that was kept on the bar in the Mess. To get your name in it could cost you plenty. If a bystander happened to hear mention of a true experience which he thought was being a little embellished, he could shout "Line", which indicated that someone was 'shooting a line' or telling an exaggerated story. If someone else witnessed the telling of it (and it was never hard to find a witness) the hapless story teller was obliged to stand drinks for everyone in the Mess. For that reason, and others, the attitude prevailed that if one was still alive nothing else warranted a mention.

Of course the ground crew for our aircraft wanted to know how I had managed to pour good oil all over the engines. They managed to make me aware that they had better things to do with their precious time than cleaning up messes that I chose to make. Naturally, I promised very sincerely that I would try hard not to do it again. It was very good news to learn that our station had had no losses on that trip. It took us five and a half hours. We had completed three trips and we were still alive. I had learnt what I could do if I had to and that helped my confidence. I was learning much about the chances of survival.

In bed before going to sleep, I used to spend time thinking about all the possible emergency situations that could arise, determining what action I would need to take in each case. When things went wrong they did so fast, so I felt that if I had already given thought in anticipation of a negative situation I could take the appropriate action to deal with it more quickly. One subject that occupied much thought was the stark facts in each case of the bombers I had seen shot down. Notably I reflected, there had been no time for the pilot to take evasive action. In every case the sequence of events had been the same. Suddenly, five tracer shells could be seen going skywards at the same angle, then there was a pause of from eight to ten seconds before the bomber exploded.

During our training, we had been told that every third shell that the fighters fired was a tracer and was therefore visible. That meant that in each case fifteen shells of either twenty or thirty millimetre calibre had been fired into the petrol tanks of each bomber. Of all the bombers that I saw shot down, I never once saw any return fire. They were apparently all taken by surprise.

I reflected on the number of times I had looked up to the rear gunner of one of our bombers and had been convinced that he could not see our aircraft. While his pilot held a steady course it would have been easy for me to shoot him down. But why allow it to be so easy for a fighter to line up his sights in the first place? I thought. The night fighter pilots had to carry out a very precise and skilled exercise in flying to be able to put those shells into the right place into the bomber. That they were able to do it so consistently puzzled me. It seemed that the one factor on which the enemy pilot had to rely was that the bomber pilot would hold his aircraft on a steady course.

I visualised the effect of the corollary. The imaginary fighter pilot carefully positions himself beneath the bomber and adjusts his speed. When he had everything almost right the bomber changes its position. Patiently the fighter pilot begins the process all over again but once more, just when he was about ready to press the 'fire' button, the bomber again changes its position. The fighter pilot, however, is a tenacious, if growingly frustrated foe. He is not going to let that bomber get away, so once again he begins the tedious process of getting his aircraft exactly into the right position, only yet again to be deprived of a kill when the bomber shifts its position. This series of abortive attacks has cost a lot of time, so he finally accepts the inevitable. There are so many other bombers heading for the target. From experience he knows that there are plenty of bombers flying straight and level on a steady course, so he decides to break off the engagement with this bomber in favour of finding one that will give him no trouble by flying a steady course.

I resolved, from that time onwards, therefore, never to stay in the same place for more than a minute. Even if the sortie took ten hours or more, about once each minute I would roll the aircraft on its side to let Shortie, our mid upper gunner, look down below. In doing so I allowed the aircraft to drift thirty degrees off course. I would then roll the aircraft on to its other side for Shortie to look down again before bringing the course back sixty degrees, making the second leg a little longer or shorter than the first, depending on the wind direction, to stay overall on track.

Rolling the aircraft around as I did must have made Jack's job of navigating much more difficult. He needed to use his equipment but couldn't leave things loose on his desk, as the constant movement of the aircraft always tended to dislodge any unanchored objects, making it infuriatingly difficult for him to keep everything under control. However, he never complained and in fact expressed his complete support for the precautionary policy I was adopting. The other members of the crew must also have found the extra rolling motions of the aircraft physically uncomfortable, although as for learning to fly in the first place, the regular experience of it led to adaptation. As far as I remember none of them was ever airsick as a result of it.

About fifty years after the end of the Second World War and after I had retired from work I became a volunteer guide at The Royal New Zealand Air Force Museum in Christchurch, New Zealand, along with others with similar interests. Among the many interesting people from many countries whom I have met as a result was Frank Oftheimer from Bavaria in Germany. He and his wife had come to New Zealand to visit their daughter Maria and her husband Werner Denk, who had emigrated to New Zealand and settled in Christchurch. When I learnt that he had been the radar operator of the leading Luftwaffe night fighter team, I was most interested to talk to him. Maria kindly invited my wife and me to spend the evening with them, which we were very happy to do, and which enabled me to learn the true facts.

My attitude towards the enemy night fighter pilots who were out to shoot us down was that, like us, they were involved in a war of which they had no making. They were obliged to defend their country, and, like us, were doing an unpleasant job to the best of their ability. Frank told me that he and his pilot, Major Heinrich Prinz zu Sayn Wittgenstein, shot down eighty-three bombers. One night at Magdeburg, they shot down four in ten minutes, but a fifth one, flown by an Australian, Les Kelvingont, with Ted Muggeridge, a New Zealander, as bomb aimer, escaped with only damage. However, they did not intend to allow it to escape altogether and returned for a second attack. Tommy Tomson, a Scot, the bomber's rear gunner saw them creeping in below. He wisely held his fire until the critical moment before opening fire at an effective range.

Frank Oftheimer said he did not really know what happened. He only remembers that suddenly there seemed to be fire all around him. His pilot said "Get out", but before he could respond to that order he was thrown out. He parachuted to ground as the aircraft crashed in flames, killing the pilot. My guess is that the stream of bullets from the four guns in Tomson's turret, when hitting the fighter conveyed the effect and impression of fire. Probably the pilot was severely wounded but was able to order his crew member to bale out before he slumped forward over the controls, causing the aircraft to go into a steep dive - which then threw the radar operator out.

By the time I started my tour of operational flying with Bomber Command in 1944, Germany had assembled a formidable range of aircraft as night fighters. The need for night fighters was not appreciated in the early stages of the war by either side. Consequently both sides had to improvise, in the first instance by adapting existing aircraft to the new task. The mainstay night fighter employed by the Germans was the Messerschmitt Bf.110. It had originally been intended as a long-range day fighter but during the Battle of Britain in 1940 and subsequently had proved no match for the excellent stream of single engined fighters brought into service by the Allies. When it was fitted with radar in 1942 it proved to be an effective night fighter, being redeployed to combat the night bombing of German cities which built up to its crescendo from 1943 to 1945. With its longer range it was able to go out to meet the incoming aircraft of Bomber Command during their long flight to their targets. Other improvisations by Germany were attempted in support of the Bf 110, notably the Dornier Do. 217N-2, with a crew of four and armed with four cannons and four machine guns, the Heinkel He. 219A-2/R1 with a crew of two and armed with six cannons, both of which were introduced in 1943 and were equipped with radar.

The Junkers 88 G-7, an adapted version of one of the most successful aircraft of the entire Second World War, was then introduced in 1944 with its radar antennae prominently protruding from its nose. It had a crew of four and was armed with six cannons and one machine gun. It was also in 1944 that Germany threw into the night fighting its first twin-engined jet fighter, the Messerschmitt Me 262A-1A. Its two Junkers Jumo 004B-1 jet engines gave it a maximum speed of 540 mph at 19,685 feet, a ceiling of 37,565 feet, and a range of 652 miles. Armed with four 30mm. cannon, it had the makings of a decisive weapon against the heavy bomber.

All the German twin engined night fighters were able to waylay the bombers at a distance from their targets and even attack them over their own territory on their return from their bombing missions. They were dubbed 'tame boars' by bomber aircrews. More locally in the target areas themselves, single engined, short range fighters, notably the many variants of the Messerschmitt Bf.109 and Focke-Wulf Fw 190 were able to take speculative action against bombers caught up in searchlights, damaged by flak and confused in the mêlée of battle. They were dubbed 'wild boars'. They were not supplemented by radically additional types until 1945 - after the completion of my own tour of operations - when the revolutionary single jet-engined fighters were introduced but with the exception of the launch of the single seat Messerschmitt Me 163 B-1a with a Walter HWK 509A-2 engine in 1944. It had a maximum speed of 596 mph and a ceiling of 39,500 feet but fortunately for the bombers it had an effective operational time of only seven and a half minutes to use its limited armament of two cannon.

A substantial measure to counter the potentially formidable threat posed by the night fighter was Bomber Command's deployment of its Mosquito force. Once a night's target for the heavy bombers had been decided, as many as possible of the enemy airfields from which night fighters flew and which lay in the path or within range of the bomber stream's course to and from that particular target became subject to surveillance and suppression by Mosquitoes. One Mosquito arrived on station at an enemy airfield at an appropriate time ahead of the bombing force. It continually circulated the airfield as belligerently as needed to prevent night fighters from taking off. If they attempted to do so the practice was to drop its two 500 pound bombs on the runway at a suitable point to frustrate the take off. The overriding principle was to prevent the take off of the airfield's squadrons rather than to attempt to shoot down individual enemy aircraft on take off. The patrolling Mosquito would be relieved by another Mosquito at a precise time so that pressure on the airfield was maintained for the duration of the time that the bomber stream was exposed to attack from its night fighters. Another measure adopted was to fly Mosquitoes with the bomber force carrying electronic equipment for identifying the approach of night fighters so that the bombers could be better prepared to defend themselves.

Even from this brief and incomplete overview of the response made by Germany to the steady and relentless bombing campaign mounted by RAF Bomber Command, it can be seen that a substantial portion of its material resources and the war effort of its labour force had to be devoted to the purpose of defence against aerial attack. When the need to produce the aircraft required for defence is considered alongside the huge demand for anti-aircraft guns, searchlights, radar, armaments and other equipment, it may be further appreciated that Bomber Command's onslaught tied down a significant amount of military capacity on German soil and that of the occupied countries which otherwise could have been available for action on the front lines – on the Western Front but particularly the Russian Front.

German armour had always fought in close partnership with the Luftwaffe. The huge armoured battles of the Kursk salient involved 2,500 German and 2,650 Russian aircraft but a decisive result eluded the Germans. Colonel-General Hans Jeschonnek, the German Chief of Air Staff, committed suicide subsequently. His successor General Günter Korten determined that the Luftwaffe's first priority was the defence of the homeland against Bomber Command and the U.S. 8th Air Force. This policy decision led to a steady withdrawal of Luftwaffe units from the Russian Front, forcing the Panzerwaffe to operate with ever decreasing air support. In turn armoured and other vehicles had to be converted or built for anti-aircraft defence purposes, thus reducing the number of fighting vehicles.

It is now well documented how German war production in 1944 under the inspired leadership of Albert Speer rose to unprecedented peaks in spite of the fact that the tide on all fronts had turned against Germany – or, perhaps, because it had done so. Nowhere is such stimulus and response better illustrated than in the case of Bomber Command's campaign. Bomb delivery by Bomber Command remained at well under 10,000 tons per month throughout the war until April 1943, when it just exceeded that figure. It rose and fell on a monthly basis until March 1944 when it exceeded 20,000 tons for the first time, thereafter rising dramatically. With only three exceptions, the monthly delivery from then to the end of hostilities totalled between 40,000 and 72,000 tons. The difference between pre-March 1944 and post-March 1944 tonnage was of such an order that it would be fair to depict it as indicating two wars in one. The biggest monthly total in 1944 was that of August, a quantum increase to 70,000 tons, which was never exceeded again except by a small margin in the month of March, 1945.

It was therefore by chance that my own tour of operations took place across the time of maximum offensive effort by bomber command and maximum corresponding effort by the German defence to protect its assets under attack. In this effort they achieved considerable success as remarked by Webster and Frankland who have observed that "Outpaced, out manoeuvred and outgunned by German night fighters and in generally highly inflammable and explosive condition, these black monsters presented an ideal target to any fighter who could find them, and it was the night fighters which caused the overwhelming majority of the losses sustained by Bomber Command".

As the night fighter crews were able so consistently to put their shells into the petrol tanks of the bombers, I had concluded that they must be coming in fairly close beneath their victims to be able to see clearly where to aim – at probably about twenty metres. In fact, according to Frank they were creeping in at fifty metres or more below. With the aid of a laser beam they were able to manoeuvre their aircraft for the attack into exactly the right position. German technology and combat technique had reached a state of perfection which potentially spelled the apotheosis of the bomber as it was being operated at that date. Bomber losses in fact began to reach unsustainable levels but the course of the war itself was in favour of the bomber. The land invasion of Europe was drawing near. Soon the army would be capturing the airfields that the Germans were using throughout the occupied countries.

On reflection after our first three operations and from that limited experience, it seemed to me that although we needed a good share of luck to survive, there were probably also things we could do to help ourselves. The next night I thought that we might be able to learn some more because we were on the Battle Order again.

Chapter 11

Long Haul Targets

I slept until 1300 hours after our Brunswick trip. By the time I had had lunch there wasn't very much of the day left, so it was not strictly true to say that we had a day off. After chatting with the ground crew I spent my time writing letters in my hut. Usually I had peace and quietness there. It was fairly isolated so although six of us slept there most of us went there only to sleep. While we stayed alive we had comfortable conditions, including a dressing table with drawers to keep clothes and personal affects. On top of it was a photograph of Margie in her wedding dress. She stood there waiting for me to return from each operational sortie. We always cleared our pockets of all unnecessary items before flying into enemy territory so that, if captured, we would not be made subject to German interrogators who could conceivably use personal items to break one's resistance and gain important information. On all non-operational flying occasions, Margie's photograph went with me.

Next morning, 24 April, we found ourselves again on the Battle Order. We took our aircraft up for an air test which included some flying practice, after which we did some dry land sea ditching and dinghy drill. We pretended we were coming down into the sea and escaping into the dinghy which, if the circumstances were real, would automatically release itself from its stowage in the starboard wing. After that we practiced crash landing drill and abandoning aircraft in the air drill.

We were still very much in the learning stage, although we had been given a good training, we were all very conscious of the fact that nothing could substitute for the real thing.

Briefing was at 1700 hours in the large, cigarette smoke filled room packed with crews. We were beginning to get to know the form that the entertainment would take. At the far end was the curtain-covered map of Europe. Silence would suddenly descend when the senior officers entered and took up their positions on the dais. Having pulled back the curtain the Commanding Officer turned to us with a smile and said, "Good evening gentlemen. To-night's target is Munich in Southern Germany". He went on to impress upon us the fact that because we would first be flying almost to Milan in Italy, to force the night fighters to use extra petrol, we would be at about the maximum range of our Lancasters and would therefore need to conserve fuel as much as possible. He concluded by saying that "Squadron Leader Cheshire will, as usual, be marking the target and he expects, as usual, a high standard from us. Good luck".

Next the Meteorologist told us a daunting story about the fronts through which we would be passing and the high head winds which we could expect to encounter on our way home. On our way home? Those were the only words of encouragement he mentioned. He reminded us to ensure that we had ample height to clear the Swiss Alps. Navigators as usual had had an earlier briefing and had been provided with all the information they needed but the navigation leader for the squadron had a little more to say to us all, mainly about the planned route which should take us past the heavily defended areas.

Next the engineering officer told us that we would be topped up with fuel at the end of the runway just before take off and again stressed the need to conserve fuel. When everyone of importance had had their say, the CO closed the session by wishing us good luck again. When the senior officers had all gone, we made our way to the Mess for our 'Last Supper' of bacon and eggs.

After that, I walked alone with my thoughts along the oak tree lined road to our crew room where we dressed for flying. From then on the routine was the same as it had been for the previous three trips, again including the urge for me to run up to my seat. Once in my seat I felt alright as I had to be busy to get the four engines started and to carry out numerous checks. I then checked with each crew member individually in turn to make sure that we were all ready to start taxying. With permission to taxi, we moved into the line of dark moving monsters with whirling propellers, following the one in front of us. We stopped when it stopped and waited for the tankers to come alongside to top up our tanks at the very last moment.

To sit in my seat looking at the long line of bombers on each side of the runway was an impressive sight, especially when one reflected that a similar scene was being created at so many airfields around East Anglia. It was a sight that would bring apprehension to the enemy and hope to the people in the occupied countries of Europe.

Then, one by one, the propellers began to turn as anything between eighty and a hundred aircraft engines were started up again, according to the number of aircraft the station had been ordered to task for the particular night's operation. Soon, like a buzzing swarm of angry bees, the bombers began their take off runs. Immediately the first bomber had gained speed down the runway, another from the other side of the runway moved into position for take off. As the wheels of the first bomber left the runway, a powerful roar was emitted from the second aircraft as the pilot opened the throttles. While he was gaining speed, the bomber in front of us moved into position, awaiting the green light from the chequered caravan at the end of the runway. A flash of green light, a mighty roar from four Rolls Royce motors, and another heavily laden bomber was on its way, while the next one from the other side moved into position. As soon as that one began its take off run it was our turn to move into position. The whole process had been well rehearsed in training and practiced for real night after night. It worked like clockwork, usually without mishap.

Fig. 55. Control Tower at East Kirkby in the process of restoration in 1983. Author second from left, with Digger to the left and Dusty, Shortie and Jack to the right.

Fig. 56. Control Tower at East Kirkby as fully restored by 1997.

As it happened this night was to be one of the exceptions. From the bomber which had taken off first and was only at about five hundred feet high came a stream of black smoke from his starboard outer engine. That spelt serious trouble, immediately ruling out any likelihood that the aircraft could continue on its way to the distant target on three engines. The pilot must have doubtlessly decided to head for the open sea which was about fifteen miles away to jettison his bombs. He was already heading in that direction when black smoke also began pouring from his port inner engine. On three engines he had some discretion and flying options but with a full bomb load aboard on two he had none. With only two engines functioning he no longer had sufficient power to remain airborne and would have to crash. The pilot turned back towards our airfield, no doubt reasoning that if he had to crash, the best place would be where a fire engine and ambulance could quickly be on the scene.

The take off had been immediately suspended. The eyes of everyone were glued to the stricken aircraft whose fate seemed to be sealed. When he reached the airfield boundary the pilot realised that he was too high, obliging him to pass over the airfield and crash in open country. He put the nose of the bomber down and headed for the ground. As I watched I had thoughts of the disaster of a few weeks previously, when the pilot on failing to control the swing of his aircraft on take off crossed the road and exploded in the farmer's field, breaking windows fifteen miles away. With most of the bombers and aircrews from our airfield lined up nose to tail and a bomb laden bomber about to crash nearby everyone waited with bated breath in case a horrific disaster of incredible magnitude was about to happen. We could do nothing but watch and wait. The waiting seemed so long but could only have been a very short time.

A few seconds before the bomber was about to plough nose first into the ground, the pilot must have heaved back on the control column because the bomber suddenly flattened out and ploughed into the ground sending a shower of earth and white vapour skywards. After a few seconds we realised that a miracle had just happened. Earth particles had settled, the vapour had dispersed, bombs had not exploded, there was no fire, and the bomber lay apparently half buried in the ground. At that point the bomber sitting ready for take off was given the green light and started its take off run while we moved into position ready for our own take off, somewhat shaken but immensely gratified. It was not until our return that we learnt that the crew of the crashed bomber, piloted by Bill Bailey, had all survived with nothing worse than bruises, and had been given ten days survivors' leave.

It is remarkable in retrospect how we all reacted to events of that nature. A serious accident at home base costing the lives of aircrew members was the same for them as being shot down by the enemy. Those of us who survived had to see both kinds of events. We grew accustomed to seeing them. Reactions varied. The outward manifestations of them ranged from a quiet acceptance without comment to the seemingly stiff-upper-lip acceptance covered by the use of the famous nomenclature and vocabulary that became characteristic of RAF flyers as a breed. But inwardly there can scarcely have been a single individual who was indifferent to the risks and the awfulness of the possible manner of his end. We were all young and therefore possessed of the sanguine attitudes and competitiveness of youth. In common with all other forms of combat, the witness of the death of a colleague or fellow warrior was instantly registered psychologically by the realisation that the fatality happened to another person and not to oneself. It was an inevitable reflex, even if one felt a little guilty for it immediately afterwards but that was soon overshadowed by the counter realisation that there was still a job to be done and that any time it might be one's own turn to succumb.

When the green light pointed to me I opened the throttles to three quarters power, released the brakes and when I was sure I had the swing under control, applied full power. At 95 mph I had attained flying speed but I still had some runway left to me, so I stayed on the ground until the airspeed indicator showed 115 mph. If an engine failed at a speed of less than 130 mph it was not possible to maintain control even if we had flying speed. Had that happened to us, it was my intention to retract the wheels and skid along the ground, which I felt would give us a better chance of survival than being in the air and having to crash. It took only a few seconds for the speed to increase from 115 mph to 130 once we were airborne. Luckily I never had to deal with such a difficult problem as an engine failure on take off.

At 115 mph I retracted the wheels and continued to climb straight ahead until we reached a height of 500 feet, at which point I reduced power to normal climbing power, retracted the flaps and allowed the speed to build up to 175 mph. We were making for Selsey Bill, near Portsmouth, from where we would all set course at the same time on the first leg of our journey. As we flew I looked at each of those four roaring engines nonchalantly spinning its propeller. I somehow seemed to expect to see different emotions showing on their faces but no matter how anxious I might have felt, they never changed their placid expressions. They could work hard but felt nothing.

As we gained height with the air getting thinner, we reached a point where, if we needed to maintain power, we had to run our superchargers at high speed, in which case they required an extra 300 hp. to drive them. I thought that if I began climbing gently from an early stage maybe I could gain enough height to clear the mountains without having to run the superchargers at high speed, which would probably save some fuel. In fact, I did manage to clear the mountains in that way, probably saving some fuel, since after ten and a half hours' flying, we arrived home with enough fuel for another forty minutes' flying, while some of our aircraft were obliged to land elsewhere in England owing to insufficient fuel to reach home base.

It was a picturesque scene looking down on the glistening, white, snow covered mountains of France and Switzerland. Flying over Switzerland was technically illegal but it happened, I suspect, with the connivance of the Swiss. Although we had encountered a lot of cloud, the sky became clear. The starry sky and the snow capped mountains stood in sharp contrast to the dark and dangerous earth which normally lurked below. We felt a little more secure because we could see below. Soon the air raid sirens would be sounding in Milan followed by expressions of relief when we made an abrupt turn and headed for Munich. One of our squadron's bombers was attacked while we were over the mountains, but with the improved visibility the gunners were able to drive the fighter away.

It was an amazing and a very frightening sight as we approached Munich. Masses of searchlights seemed to encircle the city completely. If, as had been intended, our feint had persuaded many wild boar fighters to use up precious fuel in flying to Milan there were still plenty of them around Munich. It was my first encounter with searchlights in such abundance and knowing that I was going to have to fly into them terrified me.

To fight to escape from what appears to be almost certain death, as I had done at Brunswick, was one thing, but deliberately to fly straight into what seemed to invite certain death was quite a different matter. We had flown for nearly five hours to get ourselves into the target area, so now I had to do what was expected of me. My forehead was feverishly hot and sweaty and above me I sensed a black sheet waiting to envelop me and which, somehow, without any physical aid, I had to hold away. I knew that if it fell on me, it would be my end. Memories suddenly flooded back and I recognised that the black sheet above me was the same one which enveloped me before my operation for peritonitis at the age of five. I survived that occasion and hoped I would survive this one. My forehead became cool as though someone had placed a damp face cloth there. I took control of myself now and pointed the nose of the aircraft straight at the solid wall of searchlights.

Just as I was about to plunge into those searchlights they coned an aircraft on my left and one on my right, leaving a clear gap for me to fly straight ahead. We went through the gap and were able to see the target marker clearly ahead. Although there seemed to be fighters buzzing around everywhere, we had a good run up to the marker without any interference, capped by the welcome relief to hear Griff say "bombs away". However, the hardest part of the run still remained. Once the bombs had gone the aircraft felt so light that I felt I could dodge any enemy fighter but I was obligated to continue the steady bombing run until that little red light on my instrument panel told me that our bombs had landed and our photograph of their point of impact had been taken.

Had we been attacked during that phase I would have abandoned the photograph and concentrated on evading the fighter. Had we been attacked during the bombing run itself I would have had to concentrate on evading the fighter before commencing another run up to the target marker. Over the target where there was so much light from searchlights and fires, we encountered single engined fighters designed for the day but adapted to the night – the wilde Sauen or wild boars – which were able to attack the bombers without the aid of radar as the attackers were so visible in all the light – but by the same token we were able to see them too. They had been organized in the first instance by Major Hans-Joachim ' Hajo' Herrman and originally manned by ex-bomber pilots. While flying to and from the target the night fighters – the zahme Sauen or tame boars - were twin engined with a pilot and radar operator. They were always difficult to see. The first notice of their presence could be their armaments ripping into one's aircraft.

Having survived what at one stage had seemed impossible and set out on the compass course Jack had given me for home, I felt a little more relieved. I looked at each of the engines in turn but none of them looked the least bit perturbed. It was a long journey home into the head wind we had been told to expect. All the way on the return trip I continued my technique of not staying on one course for more than a minute, which I felt would keep us safe from attack by night fighters during a dangerous sector of the trip over part of Germany and occupied Europe.

We arrived back at base at 0730 hours having flown for ten and a half hours with no morning or afternoon tea or even a lunch break. As I parked 'O' for Oboe in its dispersal and shut down the motors one by one, I sat a moment or two in my seat just to savour the situation. We had just done a long and dangerous trip and we were home, unscathed and alive. It warranted a few moments of thanksgiving. Rising from my seat I picked up my parachute from its stowage position and sauntered slowly down the fuselage. There was no need to run.

Before we could have a meal and get to bed we had to attend the debriefing which simply consisted of reporting what we had seen and done, particularly if we had seen anything unusual. 630

Squadron lost two aircraft during the attack on Munich on that night of 24/25 April 1944. One of them was ME 717 LE-G, a Lancaster Mark 1 piloted by Pilot Officer L N Rackley. It took off at 2051 hours but was attacked by a night fighter, which wrecked its port inner engine. The aircraft was able to reach the island of Corsica in the Mediterranean where it crash landed at Borgo airfield at 0525 hours. The pilot brought the aircraft down safely but on the ground its tail assembly hit a parked aircraft, killing the rear gunner, Flight Sergeant N Dunbar of the Royal Australian Air Force. He was interred in the cemetery of the village of Bigulia, nine kilometres south of Bastia, which eventually contained the graves of sixty British and Commonwealth servicemen, including forty-one airmen. The aircraft had been delivered new to the squadron on 31 March and had only flown fifty-five hours.

The second aircraft lost by the squadron was JB 556 LE-, a Lancaster Mark 3. It was the one whose port inner engine burst into flame as it was taking off at 2054 hours. The aircrew, however, were dragged out of the blazing aircraft by the combined efforts of the Station Commander himself, Group Captain Taaffe, OBE, the Station Medical Officer, Squadron Leader S L Elliott, Flight Lieutenant Neison, and the crash rescue team. Sergeant H Allwright of all the members of the aircrew was the only one injured.

Nine Lancasters altogether – 3.5% of the total attacking force of 234 Lancasters and sixteen Mosquitoes of 5 Group, and ten Lancasters of 1 Group - were lost on this raid. The marking and controlling plans worked well, leading to the accurate bombing of the centre of the city. The intense flak and searchlight defences failed to prevent the low-flying Mosquitoes from carrying out their task properly. Subsequent German reports detailed extensive property damage, mostly of a public and domestic rather than industrial nature, although the railway system and railways installations received substantial damage. Some 1,104 buildings were destroyed and 1,367 were badly damaged, including eighteen military buildings, thirteen churches and seven hospitals. In view of the extent of the damage and destruction of property it was not known why among the casualty figures at eighty-eight killed, 2,945 injured and 30,000 bombed out, the figure for those killed should have been so low.

I awoke at 1630 hours having slept well. A strange phenomenon was occurring. I was at a loss to understand it. Once in bed and anxiously ready to drop off to sleep at the earliest possible moment, the roar of the engines was just as loud in my head as it had been during our trip, yet I knew the noise was not there. I was too tired to allow it to keep me awake but it puzzled me for many years until in later life, when my hearing began to deteriorate, an ear specialist provided the answer. He explained that the sounds we hear are transmitted to the brain by upright hair like structures which bend in different ways, according to the variations of sounds. When they are obliged to transmit the same sound for long periods of time, they become exhausted and are unable to resume their normal attitudes, so the same sound continues to be sent to the brain. Most bomber crew members developed hearing deficiencies in later life.

Having dressed, I made my way to the Mess for tea and read Daily Routine Orders on the notice board, noting that our crew was on the Battle Order for the following night's sortie. There was not enough of the day left to do anything particular so I confined myself to reading the paper and returned to my room to finish a letter to Margie as well as an aerograph to her. An aerograph was the nearest approach we had in those days to air mail. It consisted of one page written on a special form which was photographed and reduced in size to that of a postage stamp, making it possible to accommodate a large number in a mail bag. They would travel by sea to America, across America by air, then by sea to New Zealand, where they were enlarged to a readable size. An ordinary letter travelled all the way by sea and sometimes took as long as three months to be delivered. On that long voyage they were exposed to the attention of enemy submarines.

The next day, 26 April 1944, dawned sunny and bright. We followed the routine that was becoming so familiar. We checked our aircraft and equipment in the morning, went to the briefing in the afternoon and took 'Last Supper' in the evening. I then went on my lone walk with my thoughts along the oak tree lined road to our crew room, where we changed for flying. We went to our aircraft and climbed aboard, started the engines and checked all the equipment. When I had shut down the engines we all climbed out to sit on the grass for a last cigarette. When it was time to climb aboard again to be ready to start taxying I had to run quickly to my seat while the rest of the crew moved into their respective positions.

5 Group of Bomber Command, with 296 aircraft, was going to attack a ball bearing manufacturing establishment deep into Germany, at Schweinfurt, while the rest of Bomber Command was going to attack targets in Essen. By 1944 Bomber Command had grown into a powerful force capable of attacking several targets in different areas at the same time. This was to be our fifth trip, so according to statistics our quota of returns to base was due to run out any time now.

We got the green light from the caravan at the end of the runway at 2120 hours. Our friendly engines responded with gusto to what I asked of them. Once more the die had been cast. What would lie in store for us on this trip I wondered.

As soon as we crossed into Holland night fighters became very active - together with a surprise experience. Flying along in the dark and following my usual procedure of tacking and keeping a very sharp look out, I was suddenly exposed to a brilliant light suspended nearby in the sky. It made me feel like a wayward Romeo caught by an unexpectedly returning husband who turned on the bedroom light to find him in bed with his wife. Being accustomed to flying hour after hour in a dark world, it was decidedly shattering and scary to find us lit up when all we wanted to do desperately was to hide. For a few moments I was quite uncomfortable until I realised that not only did the light make it easier for the enemy to see us, it also made it easier for us to see the enemy. That was an opportunity we did not normally have. It happened that all the way to the target our route was lit by brilliant flares hanging on parachutes. The intention of the enemy clearly was to combat our distribution of 'window' and to give their wild boar night fighters the opportunity to see the silhouettes of the bombers flying at a flak free level of 15,000 feet by agreement between the Luftwaffe and the ground gunnery commands.

I think the enemy probably realised that lighting up the sky did not compensate for the surprise advantage the darkness gave them. It was the only occasion that I experienced such illumination. On the way home no such light was provided. The full significance of it may have lain in the fact that I did not see any bombers shot down on the way to the target but I saw a lot go down on the way home. From our force we lost twenty-nine, including three from our station - one from 630 Squadron and two from 57 Squadron. ND 789 LE-I, a Lancaster Mark 3 of 630 Squadron piloted by Pilot Officer J S Kilgour, took off at 2124 hours but was caught by a night fighter which brought it down near Méhlhausen. The whole aircrew were killed and at first buried at Méhlhausen but later at Dürnbach War Cemetery.

ME 679 DX-K, a Lancaster Mark 1 of 57 Squadron, piloted by Squadron Leader M I Boyle DFC and LL 920 KM-V, a Lancaster Mark 1 of 44 Squadron, collided near Oberkirchen. The entire aircrews of both aircraft were killed with the single exception of Warrant Officer D A Waddell of the Royal Canadian Air Force, who managed to bale out and was made a prisoner of war. The second loss to 57 Squadron was ND 786 DX-I, a Lancaster Mark 3, piloted by Pilot Officer G J Mee of the Royal New Zealand Air Force. It was attacked by a night fighter and shot down in flames near Miltenberg. Two members of the aircrew – the navigator and the bomb aimer - baled out and were made prisoners of war, the rest being killed. With 663 flying hours to his credit, the pilot was on his fifth operation. His brother, John Milward Mee had also been killed, just five weeks earlier, flying with 7 Squadron, Bomber Command. The losses at East Kirkby were mounting. On the same night 57 Squadron lost an aircraft on minelaying operations. Lancaster Mark 3, piloted by Flight Lieutenant A T Richards, with the identification ND 960 DX-I, took off at 2157 hours for the Baltic but encountered a night fighter which brought it down between Emtekaer and Naleke, seven kilometres south-west of Gelsted in Denmark. The whole aircrew were buried at Assens (Fyn) New Cemetery, used exclusively for Bomber Command burials.

The attack was not a success. Of the 206 Lancasters and eleven Mosquitoes of 5 Group and nine Lancasters of 1 Group which took part in it, twenty-one Lancasters, comprising 9.3% of the total force, were lost. The low-level marking provided for the first time by Mosquitoes of 627 Squadron was inaccurate. Unexpectedly strong head winds critically delayed the arrival of the Lancaster marker aircraft and the main force of Lancasters, whilst night fighters were out in force and pressed home their attacks throughout the raid. Most of the bombs fell outside Schweinfurt, if the figure of two people killed is taken as an index. This raid produced the heroic effort of Sergeant Norman Jackson, the flight engineer of a Lancaster of 106 Squadron, to save his aircraft which had been set on fire by a night fighter. He climbed out on the wing of the aircraft with an extinguisher, attached by the rigging of his opened parachute which another member of the crew held on to in an ineffectual effort to extinguish the flames. He and the rest of the crew survived in captivity. For that action he was awarded the Victoria Cross when he was repatriated after the war.

For me in particular it seemed to be a very successful trip. We had an uneventful run up to the target, secured a good photograph and, after nine hours flying, arrived home safely. We enjoyed the feeling of the wheels touching the runway. We knew then that we were almost safe but not absolutely so. Sometimes intruding fighters would join the stream of bombers heading for their home bases. If they did not catch any in the air by surprise, they would attack one coming in to land or actually on the runway.

Once clear of the runway our future was secured for at least another day. The slow drive round the perimeter track to our dispersal position where we parked our aircraft was always a pleasant one. Once there I followed my usual procedure of shutting down the engines one by one and watching each propeller stop before just sitting a while to savour the situation before picking up my parachute and sauntering slowly back down to the entrance door.

WAAF transport girls were busily gathering up crews and taking them to debriefing where we would be given a cup of coffee or tea while answering questions about things of importance. We were always asked about aircraft we had seen shot down but never how they were shot down. Since I was a relatively new participant, I concluded that most people would know much more about it all than I. One assumed the omnipotence of collective authority. I was therefore very surprised when, after the army had battled its way into France after 'D' Day and overrun some of the airfields used by the Germans, it was stated that the discovery that German night fighters captured on the airfields were fitted with upward firing guns was a revelation. Apparently the RAF was unaware of the fact. I naturally assumed that all operational crews were aware of it and therefore didn't mention it during debriefings.

With that particular debriefing over, I went along to the Mess for breakfast and got into bed by 0830 hours, falling asleep with engines still roaring. I slept until 1600 hours then got busy catching up with correspondence before going to the Mess for tea. During the meal the Commanding Officer told me that I had been promoted to Flight Lieutenant, which was a bolt from the blue since I had been a commissioned officer for only six weeks with the rank of Pilot officer, after holding the non-commissioned ranks of Sergeant and Flight Sergeant. The normal upward steps for commissioned officers were Pilot Officer, Flying Officer, Flight Lieutenant, Squadron Leader, Wing Commander, and Group Captain. Confusingly, Squadron Leaders led Flights. Wing Commanders led squadrons. Overall station commanders held the rank of Group Captain, or Air Commodore in the case of very important stations.

My promotion did not result from any special ability on my part. I jumped from Pilot Officer to Flight Lieutenant because I was the most senior Pilot Officer in 'B' Flight. Our Flying Officers and Flight Lieutenants had been eliminated in combat. As a Flight Lieutenant I was now one step below Roy Calvert, our Flight Commander, just because I was lucky enough to have stayed alive. Joe Lennon and I, apart from Roy, were now the two most senior pilots in our flight.

The subject of ranks and promotions was confused. When I went into the Air Force I don't think the state of Officer Cadet – which later became the norm for a commissioned officer in training - existed. I certainly never heard it mentioned. I joined with the rank of Leading Aircraftsman (LAC), bypassing the first two non-commissioned ranks of Aircraftman 1 and Aircraftman 2. When I qualified for my wings I was given the rank of Sergeant. Others became Pilot Officers. Before going overseas from New Zealand, Sergeants were promoted to Flight Sergeants, a rank that could be retained for the rest of a man's career in the Air Force at that time but subject to the fairly remote chance of promotion to the highest non-commissioned rank of Warrant Officer, or, on recommendation, being commissioned at a later date. Sergeants and Flight Sergeants could also apply of their own volition to be commissioned, those who were pilots being particularly successful in their applications.

On the squadron there were numerous Sergeants and Flight Sergeants as pilots, doing exactly the same job and sharing the same responsibilities and dangers as commissioned pilots but of course not sharing the same pay and living conditions. It was an unsatisfactory system - if it could be termed a system at all. My Flight Commander during my training to fly a four engined bomber suggested to me that I should apply for a commission. The six members of my crew were all either Sergeants or Flight Sergeants.

On surviving our trip to Munich as a crew we all went for a bicycle ride round some of the delightfully picturesque little villages nearby and had a few drinks along the way as a celebration. There were two hours of daylight saving time at that time of year so the evenings were long. The next morning we devoted to training drills, followed in the afternoon and evening by bombing practice and air to sea firing practice. It was an extended work out. I didn't get to bed until 0200 hours.

When I reported at our Flight office on the morning of Saturday April 29 I was told that we could have ten days' leave, news which was greeted with great enthusiasm by all members of the crew. The English members invariably went home. Those of us from overseas always needed to make prior arrangements so a little warning was always helpful. I had previously been in contact with relatives of Margie's who had invited me to visit them when I had leave. As it happened, they lived in Norfolk not far from Shortie's home. Like most people in those days they didn't have a telephone so there was no way I could tell them I was coming. Shortie and I set off together in the afternoon to walk about three miles to catch a bus to take us to Boston, where we could catch a train. We arrived in Boston just after our train had left but we were able to get another one two hours later. That one broke down en route, but we did eventually arrive in Norwich just before midnight. We walked to Shortie's sister's home where we woke the family up and asked for a bed for the night.

Next morning he and I looked around some of the sights of Norwich before catching a train for Worstead, which from the map looked as though it would be fairly close to where Margie's relatives lived. We found the right place and were made most welcome after walking a further four miles. Shortie's home was only about two miles from there - which of course minimized the difficulties I would otherwise have had. He owned a motorbike at home and often called over to see me during our leave. He showed me a lot of the local area, with me riding pillion. When we returned to the squadron he took it back with him.

Margie's relatives were farming people. Being a farming boy myself, I felt very much at home there and enjoyed a very relaxing leave. It was a family environment - a daughter of twelve at school, a son of seventeen working on the farm, a daughter of nineteen in Scotland, and another daughter of twenty-one nursing in Norwich. I was able to catch up on a lot of sleep and correspondence. All too soon my leave came to an end. I had to make my way back to the squadron. Near the end of my journey I dozed off to sleep and overshot the station where I should have left the train and had to hitch hike back to East Kirkby.

Fig. 57. House of Margie's relatives in Norfolk, a place for leave and two roof top visits.

Chapter 12

Working for D-Day

Back from my leave, I awoke next day to a mostly clear sky with a few white, fluffy clouds and an atmosphere that seemed to breathe peace and contentment. I allowed my mind to wander to the other side of the world, reflecting on the many peaceful mornings I had experienced there in my pre-service farming days. Before breakfast I read the DROs on the Mess notice board and noted that our crew was listed on the Battle Order for that night. Looking around the mess I saw only faces I did not know, such was the turnover rate and the passage of time taken up by our ten days' leave. It had been a relatively quiet period for the station between the raid on Schweinfurt on the night of 26/27 April 1944 and the attack on Annecy on the night of 9/10 May. In that time the station lost one aircraft from 57 Squadron on the night of 3/4 May during an attack on Mailly-le-Camp. Taking off at 2143 hours to attack the military camp there, Lancaster Mark 3, ND 468 DX-M piloted by Flying Officer R.A.F. Scrivenor, who came from the then Northern Rhodesia, was shot down by a night fighter south-west of Le Vaudoue (Seine-et-Marne), twenty-three kilometres south-west of Melun. All the crew were buried in Le Vaudoue Communal Cemetery. They were unusually young , with an average age of twenty-one.

We did an air test and some bombing practice in the morning. After a late lunch, we went to the briefing for the night's sortie to find that we were on target to a small ball bearing manufacturing plant at Annecy, on the boundary between Switzerland and France We were also told that we would be part of an experiment. We would have a bomb load of six bombs, one of which would have a pyrotechnic device attached to it that would enable it to be seen from the time it left the aircraft until it reached the ground. No other details were mentioned. The Meteorologist told us that as there would be a cold front over the English Channel, we had better cross the Channel at a height of only 500 feet and climb to 18,000 feet after passing under the cold front and reaching the coast of France.

We got the green light for take off at 2124 hours and cruised down to our rendezvous point at 500 feet. We were always allocated an operational height at which to fly, to minimise the possibilities of collision. To-night we were allocated the lowest height, which was 16,000 feet. Of course there would be other aircraft at that height but this practice distributed the bomber stream as judiciously as possible to avoid collisions. However, I didn't fancy the idea of going through the target area at 16,000 feet when all the other bombers were up above us, showering their bombs down. Consequently, I said to Jack that we needed to be exactly on time at all turning points so that, with a little luck, we might be first to the target.

Having crossed the English Channel at 500 feet, I opened the throttles to climb to our allocated height and was horrified to see the flames that came from our exhausts. They were so conspicuous in the night sky. They lit up the underside of the aircraft to the extent that I felt we would be easily seen by enemy night fighters. Making us even more vulnerable was the fact that in our climbing attitude we had a reduced speed. With our nose up, we were in an impossible position to make quick manoeuvres. I felt that great care should have been taken by the planners and commanders to avoid placing us in such a dangerous position, unless it was completely unavoidable and justifiable. With aircraft flying between England and the Continent by night and by day, it seemed to me that it should not be difficult to ascertain the weather conditions in different places. We were told to radio a cloud report every hour while on operations. I'm sure we wouldn't be the only ones doing so. On this occasion there was in fact no cold front over the English Channel. There had been no reason for us to run the unnecessarily extra risk.

Fortunately we had no opposition. Over all, it was a very quiet trip in a clear sky with a bright moon. I saw no aircraft shot down. I think it was the quietest and easiest trip of all, the only anxiety arising on reaching the target. Along the way Jack kept us precisely on time at each turning point. On reaching the target right on time we saw that the target marker was already glowing for us to aim at. Everything was exactly as I wanted it to be, so of course we went straight into our run up to drop our bombs.

As Griff was directing me on the run up, the target marking aircraft and his deputy in another aircraft suddenly began conversing with each other by radio. Their voices were so loud that I was unable to hear what Griff was saying. Our radio was not within my reach so I yelled to Les, our engineer, to switch it off. Les could not hear me for the same reason that I could not hear Griff. I reached across and punched Les on the shoulder and pointed in a condemnatory way at the radio. He guessed what I wanted and switched it off, by which time we had overshot the target. I quickly did a turn around for another run up but it was too quick. I had not allowed sufficient time to line up with the marker, so I had to make a third attempt. By the time we finally commenced our correct run up, all the other aircraft had arrived. As I listened to Griff's instructions I was looking up to a stream of pyrotechnics cascading down from above, many of which seemed to be heading straight for us. I knew that for every bomb with a pyrotechnic marker that I could see, there were five others that I could not see. Good management had ensured the chance to avoid the danger in the first place. Bad luck had neutralised the advantage but good luck had come to our aid.

Our homeward journey was just as uneventful as the outward one. I still continued my practice of shifting our position every minute. In those times we didn't have power assisted controls so to maintain my procedure I needed to expend a good deal of energy over many hours. There were times when I asked myself if it was really necessary and the answer I gave myself was "risk your own life if you want to but you are not justified in risking the lives of the rest of the crew unnecessarily".

We felt our wheels touch the runway after just under nine hours of flying and by 0800 hours I was back in bed, still listening to the roar of the engines as I dozed off to sleep. Later reconnaissance photographs showed that our operation had been a very successful one. No aircraft had been lost from the force of thirty-nine Lancasters and four Mosquitoes of 5 Group. The bad weather en route had assured that only two of the Mosquitoes for marking the target actually reached it. Nevertheless the factory was accurately bombed.

I slept until 1600 hours the next day and on going to the Mess, found that Margie had sent me a fruit cake, a packet of cheese, a tin of home made assorted biscuits, and some assorted goods that she knew I would like. The fruit cake and biscuits were sealed into separate tins then sewn into a jute bag which once contained sugar. The address was written with a felt pen on the jute covering of the parcel. Clearly, much loving care had gone into accumulating the ingredients which in wartime were in such short supply and in doing all the cooking and packing for their long journey by ship. Needless to say, every crumb was relished by our crew. It disappeared all too quickly. Along with the parcel were many letters from New Zealand and 100 cigarettes from the Anzac club in New York. I looked at the notice board in the Mess and saw that our crew was on the list for the following night. There was not much of the day left so I used it on catching up with correspondence and sent letter No 58 and a couple of aerographs away to Margie.

The date was now 11 May 1944. No doubt the Germans, like us, must have been aware that if there were going to be an invasion of the continent, it had to come fairly soon. It transpired that we were going to be involved in many operations of a preparatory nature for this inevitable onslaught against the Germans in the West. At the briefing we were told that our target was a large military camp at Bourg-Léopold in Belgium. Since we would not have far to fly we would be able to carry a bomb load of 12,000 pounds, which would include a 'Cookie' of 4,000 pounds.

Unfortunately the wind turned out to be very different from the 'met' forecast on which our navigators had based their flight plans, resulting in our late arrival at the target. Our target markers, in Mosquitoes, being able to fly much faster than us, had marked the target on schedule but by the time we had arrived, the marker flares had burnt out. We were flying en route at 4,000 feet to get below the cloud base. Enemy fighters were very active. Each time a bomber went down in flames the cloud base reflected the light from it, making it very easy for the fighters to see the bombers. Bomber pilots became nervous and dropped their bombs, despite being told to cease bombing so that the target could be marked afresh.

Since we were carrying 'Cookies', which were thin-walled blast bombs and generated very big explosions, it was not safe for the target markers to come anywhere near the target area until they could be sure that no bombs were going to be dropped. All Pathfinder and mainstream aircraft had to ensure that they were not less than at 5,000 feet in altitude over any target area when 'Cookies' were being dropped, since their blast effects were calculated to reach 4,000 feet. That moment never came. Eventually the bombing controller said with a very disgusted tone of voice, "O K, abandon sortie and take your bombs home. On the way home we dropped our 'Cookie' in the North Sea since there was no way we could defuse it. Landing with a sensitive 'Cookie' still in the bomb bays was a risky thing to do but it was reasonably safe to land with the rest of the bombs.

Two aircraft of 630 Squadron were lost on this attack on Bourg-Léopold. Taking off at 2228 hours, ME 737 LE–S, a Lancaster Mark 1, piloted by Pilot Officer W A Watt of the Royal New Zealand Air Force, is believed to have been attacked by a night fighter. It crashed at Blauwbroek, three kilometres south-east of Herenthout (Antwerpen) and seven kilometres south-west of Herentals. Two aircrew members, the engineer, Sergeant R V C Witham and the bomb aimer, Flight Sergeant K A M Stuart of the Royal New Zealand Air Force, survived its destruction and were made prisoners of war. The other five members were all killed and buried at Schoonselhof Cemetery, Antwerpen. It was Pilot Officer Watt's seventh operational flight. He was twenty-five years old and had completed 525 flying hours.

The second aircraft to be lost that night was ND 580 LE–G, piloted by Pilot Officer A T Jackson. It took off at 2220 hours but was lost without trace. The names of all its aircrew members are inscribed on the Runnymede Memorial. Situated at Runnymede, near the River Thames, west of London, this Memorial commemorates the aircrew of the Royal Air Force and Commonwealth Air Forces of Bomber Command who died on operations but have no known grave.

57 Squadron also lost an aircraft on the same night tasked for minelaying. Lancaster Mark 3, piloted by Flight Lieutenant A T Richards, with the identification ND 960 DX-I, took off at 2157 hours for the Baltic but encountered a night fighter which brought it down between Emtekaer and Naleke, seven kilometres south-west of Gelsted in Denmark. The whole aircrew were buried at Assens (Fyn) New Cemetery, used exclusively for Bomber Command burials.

The trip turned out to be a very frightening and disappointing exercise. Haze over the target hampered the marking of it by the eight Mosquitoes of 5 Group. In all six Lancasters were lost.

As the trip to the night's target had taken only three hours and forty minutes, it was possible to get to bed at a reasonable hour, permitting an early rise the next day. We did some emergency drill practices after lunch and after tea a little socialising as a crew. There were no operations laid on for that night so we went into Sleaford for a few drinks, some darts and some fish and chips. Dusty's car and Shortie's motorbike were on station so we were able to please ourselves. I was always surprised by the fact that in a time of rigid food rationing in Britain we could always buy fish and chips.

We were supposed to do some bombing practice and fighter affiliation exercises the next day but our aircraft was unserviceable, so we were free for the rest of the day. We were briefed for 'ops' the next day but the trip was abandoned before we took off for it because of bad weather over the target. The unfavourable weather on the Continent persisted the next day. A few crews were gathered together for firing practice during the day and at night some bombing practice. Two stormy days followed during which our main preoccupation was trying to keep warm in May!

After dinghy and parachute drills in the morning and an air test in the afternoon, it was 1830 hours on Friday 19 May 1944 when we sat down to our 'Last Supper' of bacon and eggs before being briefed for 'ops' for that night. The target was a railway marshalling yard at Amiens in France, clearly of great importance to the Germans with regard to their defence of the French coast when the impending invasion finally landed. But it was also in the centre of the night fighter area. Night fighter bases were at a short distance giving the German aircraft maximum time for attacking the invading bombers.

We had been issued with .38 Smith & Weston revolvers. The wags ran the gamut of jokes about their possible purposes, especially how they might be useful against the night fighters. They were seriously issued to be of use if we had successfully baled out and could use the weapon to threaten someone to help us to escape, or were able to shoot someone to escape. We had not been properly trained to use them and lacked experience in using them so the chances of their effective use in practice seemed remote. I felt it would probably get me into more trouble than it was likely to get me out of, so I always left it at home. What might have been more useful would have been a wad of local money or – as Tornado pilots carried in the First Gulf War – a string of gold coins for bribing people to effect an escape.

We took off at 2211 hours and flew unopposed to the target area which nine Mosquitoes from 5 Group and 8 Group had attempted to mark but where we found complete cloud cover. We reduced height to 6,500 feet but were still in cloud so were told to take our bombs home. The Master Bomber ordered the attack to cease after only thirty-seven of the 112 Lancasters involved had dropped their bombs. Again we had an unopposed homeward journey, which was just as well because our rear turret had become unserviceable just as we arrived in the target area. We arrived home at 0315 hours and for once were early to bed. One aircraft had been lost.

The next day was cold and cloudy with no flying, so we practiced a few escape drills. In the evening, Griff and Les were nowhere to be found so Dusty took the rest of us for a drive around some of the nearby villages. We had a few drinks here and there as well as two lots of fish and chips along the way, all of which made for a very pleasant and relaxing counterpoint to the tensions of repeated sorties.

Next day was still cold and cloudy but 'ops' were on and we were on the Battle Order for the night of 21/22 May. At briefing we were told that most of our aircraft would be attacking other targets but Bill Bailey, Joe Lennon and Doug Hawker would be placing mines in Kiel Harbour. It was impressed upon us that we must make very sure that our mines went down in the right place, since if one fell on land, the surprise element would be lost. The night's operation for minelaying was substantial. Altogether Bomber Command despatched seventy Lancasters and thirty-seven Halifaxes to the Frisians, Heligoland, the Kattegat and Kiel Bay for the loss of three Lancasters.

Mines were normally dropped from a height of around 500 feet in strategic places but because our mines were to go into Kiel Harbour, where it would be dangerous for a bomber to fly at 500 feet, we would be dropping special mines that would descend on a small, speed-retarding device, from 15,000 feet. We were the most experienced crews in our flight so were chosen for this precision exercise. Joe and I had done eight trips and Bill had done seven. Of course the briefing followed all the usual procedures, during which, owing to the presence of a cold front in the North Sea, we were instructed to fly at 500 feet until reaching the coast of Denmark, then climb to 15,000 feet. Take off was to be at 2249 hours. I wasn't enthusiastic about having to climb over enemy territory but didn't feel experienced enough to express my thoughts.

When the first aircraft began to take off we didn't have the mines on board and there was no sign of their arriving. The Commanding Officer drove into our dispersal, and I guess he noticed the concerned look on my face because he patted me on my shoulder and said, "Don't you worry, we will get you away on time". I knew that the others would all be gone before it would be possible to get the mines loaded onto our aircraft. I was visualizing how the voracious night fighters which had been brought into action by the earlier bombers would relish the chance to attack a lone bomber, competing to shoot it down. I never knew why the mines had not been delivered to our aircraft on time.

On the basis of simple logic, clearly it was not possible for us to do what was being asked of us. To place the mines carefully where they needed to be, a long, careful bombing run was required while holding the aircraft steady on a precise course. It was always the most dangerous part of any trip because while the aircraft was being held as steady as possible, it was a good target for anti-aircraft guns and night fighters. It was bad enough when there were many of us doing it at the same time. That was the reason we flew strictly to time so that we would be all together and the defences would be unable to concentrate on any one aircraft in particular. For a lone bomber to survive in the situation into which we were likely to go was expecting the impossible. It was not uncommon for a bomber to fail to return but to send a trained crew on an impossible errand seemed to me to be an unjustifiable expense. Dead crews contributed nothing towards winning the war. Our squadron was always short of aircraft and crews. Furthermore, if we were shot down on dry land our special mines would be discovered and the surprise element lost.

Fifty minutes after the last aircraft had gone from our station, we took off on our mission impossible. My only hope was that by climbing as quickly as possible we might arrive at the target area before the last of the bombers attacking Kiel itself had turned for home. As soon as I had retracted the undercarriage I set maximum permissible continuous power to the motors and began to climb. At 15,000 feet, we were able to travel much faster than the rest of our aircraft which were flying at 500 feet. Of course, there was a cold front barring our way but to fly through that would be a lot less dangerous than being alone over the target. Cold fronts could be very dangerous. They were one of the hazards of flying I had thought a lot about while in bed at night. I was aware that we would get a rough ride but had confidence in the Lancaster's ability to survive the severe buffeting. Our greatest danger would be from ice but I had a plan for that eventuality.

We were nearly half way across the North Sea when Jack called up to tell me that we had gained thirty five minutes. That was great news. If we were in fact nearly half way across the North Sea it seemed to indicate that we could conceivably reach the target on time. Even if we didn't, we would certainly arrive before the others had all left. On we flew in the dark expecting any time to feel the aircraft begin to buck as we neared the cold front. I looked at the motors on the left, then the motors on the right, half expecting to see smiles of relief on their faces but they just seemed to be concentrating on their job of keeping those propellers spinning, even though I had asked them to work so hard without a relief spell of any sort. I felt I would like to reach out and pat each of them on the head by way of thanks. Fifteen minutes passed and still the air was smooth. At that stage Jack came on the intercom again with the seemingly incredible news that we were going to reach the target on time. We were going to do the impossible all because the 'Met' man had got it wrong. There was no cold front over the North Sea.

In fact we reached the target area two minutes ahead of time. We did not have to wait for a target marker to be put down as the aircraft visiting Kiel city did because we knew exactly where our cargo had to be delivered. With good visibility we immediately commenced a long, steady run up to the dropping point. Anti-aircraft shells were exploding freely. Shortie became very nervous. From where he sat on top of the aircraft, he had a good view of all the frightening sights. Griff called "Bombs gone" and I turned immediately for home, feeling that we had done a good job. With normal cruising power set to the motors, I dropped the aircraft's nose a little and flew slightly downhill all the way home.

At briefing we had been instructed to fly under the cold front as far as the Danish coast on the outward journey but on the way back to drop down to 500 feet at the Danish coast, to fly under the cold front on the way home. We were the only ones who knew that there was no cold front, so we were able slowly to lose height all the way home. Although we were flying at normal cruising speed, as the others were, we were flying faster because we were higher and were flying slightly downhill. When we reached base we were surprised to see that no lights were on, so I called Control. The lights came on and we were told to land. We were first back home.

As we taxied slowly round the perimeter track, Control called and asked, "Didn't you go to the target?" I replied, "Yes, we have been to the target" but felt the time was not appropriate for any further explanation. As we neared our dispersal I think there may have been a tiny smirk on my face as I visualized the looks of surprise, doubt, incredulity, and disbelief on the faces of those present in the watch tower. They were asking each other, "How could he take off fifty minutes late, get to the target and be first back? It's impossible. There has to be something wrong somewhere". Next day Jack was summoned to the navigation section with his records after which no further questions were asked.

I don't know the total number of bombers involved that night, but the loss rate seemed high. I couldn't help wondering how many losses were due to having to climb over enemy territory. Two were lost from 630 Squadron. Despatched on the same mine-laying operation, LL 950 LE-Y, Lancaster Mark 1, piloted by Pilot Officer R W Bailey, took off at 2218 hours but was attacked by a night fighter and crashed in Denmark. The whole aircrew were buried at the Esbjerg (Fourfelt) Cemetery. One member of the aircrew, Flight Sergeant J M Henderson was, at thirty-five years of age, well above the average age of bomber aircrew members. The second lost had been tasked to Duisburg. Taking off at 2251 hours, JB 672 LE-F, a Lancaster Mark 3, piloted by Flying Officer H W Smith of the Royal Canadian Air Force, was attacked by a night fighter and crashed near Kilder (Gelderland), twenty-seven kilometres east-south-east of Arnhem in Holland, killing the entire aircrew. Six are buried in the Roman Catholic churchyard at Bergh (Kilder). The name of the seventh, Sergeant R V Lawrence, is on Panel 233 of the Runnymede Memorial.

Monday 22 May 1944 dawned fine and warmer than usual. We were listed on the Battle Order again so followed the usual routine. This was to be our tenth operation. We were by then old hands. The butterflies in my gut were noticeably less active than formerly. Familiarity bred accommodation but never contempt. I was fairly confident that the policy I was following while flying to and from targets was keeping us safe from the greatest danger of all - the twin engined night fighters. When reaching a target area itself on the run up to bomb we had to depend on luck. Our target for that night was Brunswick again, the previous scene of near catastrophe.

On arriving without incident, we found a patch of cloud completely obscuring the target. On our airborne radar Jack could see where the target would be but the marker boys had as yet been unable to mark it. Following normal practice we proceeded to orbit the target in an anticlockwise direction. We were about halfway round when a Pathfinder aircraft ahead was hit by a fighter and jettisoned its flares which lit up whilst hanging in the sky. We continued on our orbit of the target when suddenly ahead I saw a bomber coming almost straight at us but a fraction lower. Shortie had seen it too and was yelling "Pull up Doug, Pull up Doug" which is precisely what I was trying to do with great despatch. While I was dragging back on the control column I saw a second bomber also coming straight at us, but fractionally above. Griff in his compartment saw it too and yelled "Dive Doug, Dive Doug". From dragging back on the control column I suddenly had to ram it forward with all my might. As that second aircraft passed overhead our whole aircraft vibrated. Even in the instant of emerging from it I saw a third bomber in the gloom coming head on, a fraction lower than us but not low enough. Again I frantically dragged back on the control column while Shortie was yelling "Pull up Doug, Pull up Doug". I think the whole sequence of those three events took place in less than twenty seconds – quite a short time in which to die three times. Brunswick was not our favourite target.

All our aircraft were not fitted with airborne radar. Consequently, unpredictable events had to be met with improvisation. I realised that other pilots had mistaken the flares in the sky for flares marking the target so they were proceeding to orbit anticlockwise round it, putting them on a collision course with us. It was a contingency that scarcely could have been predicted. Needless to say I found somewhere else to fill in time. This turned out to be a classic case of area bombing. For twenty-five minutes the marker aircraft attempted to put a marker beside the target, while we filled in time. Searchlights, anti-aircraft shells and fighters all did their best to make life unpleasant while we waited but it proved impossible to mark the target. We did not take our bombs home. We dropped them somewhere near the target.

We arrived home at 0400 hours only to find that an aircraft had crashed on our runway, preventing us from landing. We landed at Strubby - another airfield in our Group, where we had breakfast and then dosed off to sleep in chairs in the Mess. We had insufficient fuel to take off but were unable to be re-fuelled until late afternoon, finally arriving home at 1800 hours. I looked at the notice board in the Mess and saw that we were on the Battle Order for the following night. The Brunswick raid had cost the squadron two aircraft and their crews. Aircraft JB 546 LE-A, a Lancaster Mark 3, had taken off at 2240 hours but crashed at Quakenbruck, having been attacked by a night fighter. Four members of the aircrew were killed and buried at the Rheinberg War Cemetery. The pilot was Pilot officer E F Champness of the Royal Australian Air Force. Three members of the aircrew survived to become prisoners of war - Flight Sergeant V S J Zusker, of the Royal Australian Air Force, Sergeant E Adair and Sergeant L Jones. The second aircraft was ND 655 LE-J, another Lancaster Mark 3, piloted by Pilot Officer V W Brown of the Royal Australian Air Force. It was lost without trace. The names of all its aircrew members are on the Runnymede Memorial.

In addition three aircraft from 57 Squadron were lost. Under the command of Pilot Officer L H Winneke of the Royal Australian Air Force, ND 878 DX-B, a Lancaster Mark 3, had taken off at 2216 hours but was caught by a night fighter over Ottersberg, sixteen kilometres east-south-east of Bremen. The aircraft exploded, killing the entire aircrew, who were buried at Beckingen War Cemetery. The second loss was that of Lancaster Mark 3, ND 879 DX-H, piloted by Pilot Officer J C Marland which took off at 2212 hours but crashed in Germany, all its aircrew members being buried at the Reichswald Forest War Cemetery. The third was NE 127 DX-J, also a Lancaster Mark 3. Taking off at 2223 hours, it crashed at 2345 hours at Dorkwerd (Groningen), only five kilometres from the centre of the city, after being attacked by a night fighter. Sergeant N G Wharf and Sergeant P I Dalseg, both of the Royal Canadian Air Force survived to be made prisoners of war. The pilot, Flight Sergeant F N Henley and the other members of the aircrew were interred in Hoogkerk (Kerkstraat) General Cemetery. It had been a black night for the station at East Kirkby.

Altogether thirteen Lancasters had been lost on the raid to Brunswick — 5.5% of the total force of 225 Lancasters and ten Mosquitoes from 1 Group and 5 Group. Again I wondered how many of that night's losses were due to having to climb over enemy territory. The failure of this raid owed most to the complete covering of cloud in contradiction to the forecast of clear weather over the target. In addition the Master Bomber's radio communications were faulty. Most of the bombs fell in the country areas around Brunswick. Few fell in the city itself. There were no casualties. Ironically, a reconnaissance aircraft only one hour after the raid had ended found the skies over the city completely clear.

Next morning we went down to 'O' for Oboe with the intention of taking it up for an air test but the ground crew were busy patching holes from the flak that we had suffered while filling in time over Brunswick. Since we couldn't do the things we needed to do, we fiddled around doing a few jobs on Dusty's car. We finally got our aircraft at 1800 hours and took it up for an air test before going to the briefing. By now the routine had almost become second nature. After our 'Last Supper' I still liked to walk alone down to our crew room, but no longer felt compelled to run up to my seat in the aircraft. I guess I wasn't alone in still wondering each time if it would be the last one but we didn't mention such matters to each other.

At briefing we were told that our target would be the Ford and General Motors plants at Antwerp, which had been taken over by the Germans for making tanks for the German army. It was good news for us because it would be a short trip with the minimum time over enemy territory. It turned out to be a relatively short trip, taking only three hours and five minutes. There was much opposition from fighters and flak. No losses were suffered by the total attacking force of forty-four Lancasters and seven Mosquitoes from 5 Group and 8 Group. We were home just after 0100 hours and in bed by 0230 hours. The factories escaped but nearby dockside buildings were hit.

The next day was cloudy and rather cold. Operations were on again that night so we spent the day following all the usual procedures. As we arrived at our aircraft and were about to climb aboard we received news that the night's operations were cancelled. Nobody seemed disappointed. It was somewhat of an anticlimax because for most of the day we had lived with the knowledge that we would be going into enemy territory again and that was almost as bad as actually doing it.

As no 'ops' were scheduled for the following night, I arranged with 'Chiefie', our ground crew boss, to have a little get together with the ground crew during the evening but it did not eventuate because they were working until late on our aircraft. I received three parcels from Margie, one containing a beautiful fruit cake, another containing home made biscuits, and the third containing a scarf, gloves, chocolate and a few other sundries. It was like having another birthday. The crew were just as pleased as I was to see a fruit cake arrive.

Saturday 27 May 1944 was sunny and brought us a listing on the battle order for the night. We took our plane up for the usual equipment check, in the process of which we flew across to Shortie's home area, near where I had spent my last leave. We descended to tree top height. It was strictly illegal. From inside his turret Shortie was able to wave to his family. Then we flew to Margie's relatives, still at tree top height. As we passed over their house, they waved to us from the garden. As they waved, Digger, who was lying in Griff's compartment passed the remark that, "The old boy is getting a bit thin on top". We all enjoyed the experience, although we were breaking the rules of course. Afterwards, I decided that since we risked our lives night after night and endured only anxiety, we ought to enjoy a little fun while we were still alive. From then on, I purposely did low flying from time to time.

At briefing we were told that the target consisted of five coastal battery positions on the French coast, including that of our own particular target, St.Valery-en-Caux, where six heavy guns were facing the sea. That was the area from where the 51st Highland Division had had to retreat in 1940. The American 8th Airforce had unsuccessfully attacked them and other Bomber Command Groups had also tried to neutralise them unsuccessfully. The night's work was to be on a big scale, involving 208 Lancasters, forty-nine Halifaxes, and fifteen Mosquitoes, from which one Lancaster and one Mosquito were lost. With a grin on his face, the Station Commander pointed out that a 1,000 pound bomb should fit nicely down the barrel of each of them. We took off at 2250 hours, carrying eleven 1,000 pound and four 500 lb bombs on the short flight to the French coast. We were not allowed to bomb until the marker aircrews were completely satisfied that their marker was in the right place, which meant that we had to orbit for twenty minutes, during which time one bomber was shot down. Even after we had bombed we did not feel sure about our success. Reconnaissance photographs, however, showed that all targets had been satisfactorily bombed. In the case of our site we had destroyed five of the guns and all the control gear - so we were pleased with our night's work.

Chapter 13

Longest Day at Last

By 1 June 1944 we had survived twelve trips, and had been briefed for our thirteenth. The superstitious found going on their thirteenth trip a traumatic experience. The facts researched in 1942 showed that crews were the most vulnerable during their first five missions – inexperience being the plausible explanation. However, a secondary rise in vulnerability arose in the middle of a tour from about the fifteenth to the twentieth missions, suggesting that vulnerability followed on from having reached a peak of efficiency plateau which induced complacency. I was aware of that survey. My own personal experience tallied exactly with its findings. Because of my inexperience our third trip had been nearly our last but surviving it provided a valuable learning shock.

As my experience grew, my confidence grew, and accordingly, my competence. Being aware of the survey I realised that an "It can't happen to me" attitude was creeping up on me, so I made a conscious effort to guard against it. Also I became aware that I was beginning to develop a very callous attitude of mind. Watching yet another bomber going down in flames induced the tendency to think only that someone else had been unlucky, rather than feel concern for the human beings, that maybe my personal friends were being burnt to death while struggling to escape. In fact, as time went on I did become emotionally dead. I ceased to feel anything. Maybe it was nature's way of preserving my sanity but it was a condition that I had to live with for a long time after the war.

Our thirteenth target on the night of 1/2 June was to be the railway junction, marshalling yard and bridge at Saumur in France. It was a small scale raid by fifty-eight Lancasters of 5 Group. The selection of that type of target suggested that the object was to disrupt the movement of enemy materials and troops as much as possible. We took off in bright moonlight, having an uninterrupted trip to the target and back. Photographic reconnaissance showed severe damage to the junction. The main lines had been torn up. There were no losses. We could hardly believe it. It really had been our thirteenth trip. So much for superstition.

Bad weather kept us on the ground for a couple of nights, until Sunday 4 June when we took off in the early hours of the morning to destroy a gun emplacement at Maisy on the French coast. 52 Lancasters of 5 Group from the total force sent out were directed to Maisy as the fourth of the four gun emplacements attacked that night. The other three were deception targets in the Pas de Calais. Our target was the genuine target in the interests of the imminent 'D' Day landings. It was situated between what were to become known as the Omaha and Utah beaches, where American troops were due to land within thirty-six hours. We flew in cloud all the way and on reaching the target area, found it so covered in cloud that the Pathfinder marking crews were unable to see the target which could only be marked by Oboe sky markers. We then dropped our bombs on top of the glow from the marker. They were far from ideal conditions for accurate bombing. Two of the other targets in the Pas de Calais that night were also obscured by cloud but the third was well bombed. We had to fly all the way home in cloud. This was a major raid involving 259 aircraft – 125 Lancasters, 118 Halifaxes, and sixteen Mosquitoes drawn from 1 Group, 4 Group, 5 Group, 6 Group and 8 Group. All the aircraft returned safely.

Unknown to us the long-awaited Allied landings across the English Channel were about to take place. In support of that historic event Bomber Command was asked to play a major tactical part. On the night of 5/6 June 1944 an incredible force of 1,012 aircraft, consisting of 551 Lancasters, 412 Halifaxes and forty-nine Mosquitoes was despatched to bomb coastal batteries at Fontenay, Houlgate, Longues, Maisy, Merville, Mont Fleury, Pointe-du-Hoc, Ouisterham, St Martin de Varreville and the site to which we were specifically directed at La Pernelle. Cloud proved to be a serious handicap for this great effort. In the event 946 aircraft carried out their assigned bombing tasks. Three aircraft were lost – two Halifaxes from 4 Group on the Mont Fleury raid and a Lancaster from 6 Group tasked to Longues. Only two of the targets were free from cloud – Ouisterham and our own target, La Pernelle. All other bombing had to make use of Oboe marking. At least 5,000 tons of bombs were dropped, the greatest tonnage in one night to date in the entire war. For us it meant an early morning take off at 0120 hours to demolish the gun emplacement at La Pernelle on the Cherbourg peninsular. At briefing it was impressed upon us that we must stick precisely to the planned route there and back and to ignore anything which may seem unusual to us. We did precisely as we were told and had yet another easy and uneventful trip but unbeknown to us, it was anything but an uneventful occasion.

Our route had been planned to keep us clear of the paratroop transports and glider towing aircraft. Could we have seen through the clouds, we would have seen the largest fleet of ships ever assembled, crossing the English Channel. Most of the big guns along the French coast had been destroyed by Bomber Command by the time that the armada arrived. At 0700 hours German radio reported that a small landing had taken place but was being repulsed. At last the long promised day had arrived when the western Allies finally launched their ground assault against the shores of the Continent of Europe. It was a memorable and gigantic operation with its mixed fortunes, starting at the turn of midnight and persisting in full flood until the end of that day into the next. It had indeed been the 'Longest Day' as subsequently depicted in the acclaimed film by that name.

Bomber Command had made a significant contribution to the preparations for the landings which eventually proved successful. During the particular night of the landings, a record 1,211 aircraft were sent out, the majority to destroy the defences and batteries of the Normandy coast that were designed and prepared to resist the expected invasion. Support operations were also mounted. 101 Squadron was detailed to patrol German night fighter bases governing the beaches. Two Stirlings of 149 Squadron with others dropped dummy parachutists away from the landing areas to distract German attention. Altogether 1,590 aircraft of Bomber Command during the months of 1944 up to 'D' Day were missing, had crashed during domestic flights, or had been destroyed in ground accidents, representing a large loss of aircrew.

Next day I slept until nearly 1500 hours. After rising and going to the Mess, I learnt that the invasion of Europe had begun. That night the squadron lost an aircraft piloted by Pilot Officer A W Wilson of the Royal Australian Air Force. It was ND 685 LE-Q, a Lancaster Mark 3, which took off at 0029 hours to attack Caen in support of the Allied landings in Normandy but was brought down. The pilot and three other members of the aircrew were buried at the Bayeux War Cemetery. The other three became prisoners of war. We ourselves were not needed so I took the opportunity to catch up on some correspondence, including writing letter No 89 to Margie.

On the night of 7 June we flew to Forêt de Cerisy, near Belleroy in France where the German 7th and 21st Panzer Divisions were reported to have parked their tanks and established fuel dumps in the forest, en route to the front for a counter attack against the Allied landings. We took off at 2230 hours, each carrying eighteen five hundred pound bombs, which we deposited in the area, returning having encountered no opposition. We were in a total force of 112 Lancasters and ten Mosquitoes drawn from 1 Group, 5 Group and 8 Group. An accurate attack was also carried out on a six-way road junction half way between Bayeux and St-Lô. Two Lancasters were lost, neither from our station.

After having had the following night off duty, during which Digger, Jack, Griff and I went into Skegness, we were readied for our next mission which was a railway junction and marshalling yard at Étampes, south of Paris. It was a miserable night, cold and wet. We took off at 1930 hours and flew to the target area, all the way in rain with some icing. Arriving at the target, we had to come down to 4,000 feet to see the target. It was not marked on our arrival, so as usual we orbited in an anticlockwise direction. Enemy fighters were quickly on the scene. Bombers began to go down in flames. Each time this happened the flames from the burning bomber reflected on the cloud base, lighting up the whole area and making it very easy for the fighters to see the bombers. It was a very unpleasant environment. As had happened before, each time the master bomber told us to hold our bombs, some nervous person released his bombs, making it impossible to mark the target. We were too busy trying to avoid the night fighters to take much notice of the confusion taking place.

The whole exercise became completely disorganised to the point that in a disgusted tone of voice the master bomber said "OK, complete your bombing and go home". By this time it was possible for the light flak to concentrate on each bomber as it went through the target area. Of course in order to put the bombs in the right place we had to do a steady run up, which made us very vulnerable to flak as well as night fighters. As we went through the target we got a shell through our port main spar. Digger's radio was dismantled by it.

We learned later that the cause of all the problems was that when the master bomber who was to control the event arrived at the target, he discovered that his radio was not working, but of course was unable to tell anyone. Eventually his deputy realised that something was wrong and took over, by which time the night fighters were having a ball and putting the attack at risk. The attack, confused as it was from my point of view at the time of our contribution to it, was eventually facilitated by accurate but late marking. The damage to the town had evidently taken place in the interim. However, the upshot of it all was that the bombing spread from the railway area into the town, which suffered 25% destruction or damage, over 400 houses being destroyed, 133 people killed and fifty-one injured. Six Lancasters were lost, including one from 630 Squadron. Aircraft PB 121 LE-F, a Lancaster Mark 3, having taken off at 2148 hours, was attacked by a night fighter which, on its second pass, brought the aircraft down in flames at Omerville (Val d'Oise), seven kilometres west-south-west of Magny-en-Vexin. The pilot, Flight Sergeant C M Houghton AFM and five other members of the aircrew are buried in Omerville Communal Cemetery. There was one survivor, Flying Officer D C Percy, who was made a prisoner of war.

Following the attack on Étampes there were two reasons why we did not fly on any operations for thirteen nights. One was that Jack had developed a high temperature and was sent to hospital, and the other was that our aircraft was also in hospital being repaired. There were nevertheless still jobs that had to be done in the squadron and with some time on my hands, they tended to fall into my lap. The tension of operational flying was relieved to some degree but the awareness that it was only a brief respite did little for overall anxiety levels.

We were back on operations on the night of 22 June. Our target was a synthetic oil refinery at Wesseling on the banks of the Rhine, about fifteen miles south of Cologne. During briefing we were told that our bomb load would be one 4,000 pound high capacity 'Cookie' and sixteen 500 pound general purpose bombs. Black night fighters had been seen attacking the American bombers during the day, which might mean diminished opposition to our attack. There was a cold front over the English Channel and we had to fly at 500 feet until clear of the front and then climb to 15,000 feet. That meant climbing over enemy territory which I was particularly averse to. All the usual routines followed. On resuming operations after such a relatively long break I boarded the aircraft but found myself with the thought again "Will this be the last one?" and ran quickly up to my seat.

There was always a bit of anxiety in getting the engines started from cold. Instead of a choke, which cars of that era needed, we had a small pump with which we fed extra fuel to the engine while operating the starter motor. If the engine did not start reasonably quickly we felt uncertain whether it was because we had pumped too much fuel or not enough. Sometimes the fuel we had pumped would start coming out the exhaust stubs and would catch fire. We would then be looking at flames licking up the side of the engine – a disconcerting sight for any aviator. Usually the engine started and blew the fire out and I never had cause to call on the ground staff man who used to stand by with a fire extinguisher. With all engines running smoothly we joined the line of bombers snaking round the perimeter track making for the take off point. We took off at 2230 hours, passing over the hole in the boundary hedge which Flying Officer Murray's aircraft had made a few weeks before when he had lost control of the swing on take off and crashed, causing his bombs to explode. As we flew down across England I looked ahead but could see no signs of cold front clouds so I said to Jack that I was going to climb to 15,000 feet as we flew towards the South Coast. Jack said that if I did that I would disrupt his flight plan. I replied that I thought it might be better for all of us if he modified his flight plan.

We arrived over the coast of France at 15,000 feet. There was no cold front. Immediately fighter flares began to light up the sky and bombers began to go down in flames. We were supposed to record the positions of aircraft we saw shot down. Normally I would tell Jack where a stricken aircraft could be seen relative to our position and he would note the position on his chart. At that precise time I was reporting the positions of aircraft going down in flames faster than Jack could plot the positions on his chart. I soon ceased to mention them because I felt such a devastating spectacle would be so demoralising for the rest of our crew. All the way to the target and all the way back, aircraft were going down in flames. In the target area itself the flak was very heavy as well. Clearly the Germans were desperate to protect their oil on which their continuation of the war depended.

The weather forecast for the target area had been for clear conditions but in the event complete low cloud was encountered. When it was found that the customary 5 Group marking method could not be used because of the cloud cover, the reserve H2S method was employed. Later reconnaissance revealed that the plant had sustained only slight damage. Much of the bombing went astray as was borne out by the fact that fifteen Germans, five foreign workers, and one prisoner of war were killed in the nearby town of Wesseling itself. A secret German official report subsequently published in the British Official History quoted a forty percent loss of production as a result of the raid, although the duration of the loss remained unknown. .

The losses that night were truly horrendous. There was no doubt in my mind that climbing over enemy territory contributed to a major proportion of our losses. I felt even more convinced after this attack that the heavy losses on the previous Kiel sortie had been for the same reason. Enemy fighters had been given an excellent opportunity to get amongst the bomber stream and stay there. Altogether thirty-seven Lancasters were lost from a total attacking force of 128 Lancasters and six Mosquitoes from 5 Group, supplemented with five Lancasters from 1 Group. The overall average loss rate for the night was 27.5% of the Lancaster force. From East Kirkby we sent out thirty aircraft from the two squadrons but only nineteen returned. It was a night of unmitigated disaster for the station, 57 Squadron losing six aircraft and 630 Squadron losing five, in both cases an unprecedented and catastrophic loss rate.

From 57 Squadron and taking off at 2300 hours under the command of Flight Lieutenant R A W Beaumont DFC, NN 696 DX-H, a Lancaster Mark 1, was attacked by a night fighter and crashed west of Gelsenkirchen, killing all members of the aircrew. Five are buried at the Rheinberg War Cemetery. Flying Officer M A Clark and Warrant Officer C H T Hurley are commemorated on two panels in the same cemetery.

JB 526 DX-D, a Lancaster Mark 1, took off at 2300 hours, piloted by Pilot Officer S Weightman, but was attacked on the outbound flight by a night fighter which brought it down one kilometre north-west of Goslar and three kilometres west of Julich in the Harz Mountains. The aircraft is known to have caught fire. In the explosion which followed, it is probable that the pilot was thrown clear by it, as he was the sole survivor and became a prisoner of war. The six other members of the aircrew were buried in the Rheinberg War Cemetery. Pilot Officer N R Carr of the Royal Australian Air Force, the pilot of LM 573 DX-U, a Lancaster Mark 3, was also the sole survivor, probably as a result of also being thrown clear, when it exploded after catching fire. He became a prisoner of war. The aircraft had taken off at 2310, but crashed between Vlijmen (Noord-Brabant) and Nieuwkyk, six kilometres west of s'Hertogenbosch. The six members of the aircrew who died were finally buried in Bergen op Zoom War Cemetery. Both the air gunners were nineteen years old.

Flying Officer J R Mounsell and Flight Sergeant Q D Naysmith successfully evaded, but two other members of the aircrew were made prisoners of war, when LMII5 DX-M, a Lancaster Mark 1, which had taken off at 2306 hours, crashed at Oud Turnhout (Antwerpen), three kilometres east of Turnhout in Belgium. The pilot, Flying Officer A F Bayley and two other members of the aircrew were killed and finally buried in Schoonselhof Cemetery. A stern attack from a night fighter brought Lancaster Mark 3, LM 580 DX-L, down at As-en-Campine (Limburg), six kilometres north-east of Genk in Belgium. It had taken off at 2307 hours, piloted by Pilot Officer G P Guy, who was the sole member of the aircrew to be killed, being buried at As-en-Campine Communal Cemetery, alongside the aircrew of a Wellington from 214 Squadron which had crashed in July 1941. All six other members managed to bale out, three becoming prisoners-of-war and three evading capture.

Pilot Officer A E Nicklin of the Royal New Zealand Air Force was the pilot of Lancaster Mark 3, ND 471 DX-A, which took off at 2302 hours. It suffered sufficient damage to require ditching off the East Anglia coast. All the aircrew were rescued by ASR Launch RML 514 from Great Yarmouth. We had heard that German fighters were now using rockets against the American daylight bombers. During the debriefing of our own station squadrons several crews said that they had seen rockets being fired. It was the first time we had heard of rocket attacks by night. Nick Nicklin and his crew in Lancaster 'A' Able seemed to confirm the fact a few days later. Leaving the target they had just set course for home when the yellow glow of a rocket streaked past them at a distance of a few feet above them, followed by another which seemed to explode underneath. While crossing the Belgian border another explosion occurred underneath them, and with the coast beneath them, yet another. Within minutes three engines had cut out, the petrol tanks showing empty. Two hundred gallons of fuel had been lost. Quickly the engineer switched to the main tanks which contained 600 gallons. The engines were revived, but only for a few moments, since the fuel lines must have been shattered. With one engine still running but only delivering half power the crew took up their ditching positions. When, after completing their air test on that selfsame morning, Nick had suggested a ditching practice, his suggestion was not well received by the crew, but they were pleased to have had second thoughts. Although Nick was firmly strapped into his seat, the impact of the aircraft hitting the water sent him through the windscreen. The rest of the crew followed normal procedures, quickly settling themselves with Nick into the dinghy, which automatically released itself from the starboard wing. All felt the utmost relief when they were finally picked up by the Air Sea Rescue Launch.

From 630 Squadron and taking off at 2327 hours, piloted by Pilot Officer R C Hooper DFC, Lancaster Mark 1, ME 843 LE-U, crashed in flames between Hamont (Limburg) on the Belgian-Dutch border and Bocholt, three kilometers north-north-west of Bree, having been attacked, it is believed, by a night fighter. All members of the aircrew were buried in the Heverlee War Cemetery. Squadron Leader A E Foster DFC was the pilot of Lancaster Mark 3, ND 531 LE-K, which took off at 2330 hours and disappeared without trace. Its distinguished aircrew included two holders of the DFC and two holders of the DFM. All the names of the aircrew are inscribed on the Runnymede Memorial.

LM 118 LE-V, a Lancaster Mark 1, took off at 2317 hours, piloted by Pilot Officer J H G Smith, but was caught by a night fighter and crashed four kilometres south of Boxtel (Noord-Brabant), eight kilometres east-north-east of Oisterwijk. All members of the aircrew were buried in the Eindhoven (Woensel) General Cemetery. Piloted by Pilot Officer T G Hart of the Royal Canadian Air Force, ME 782 LE-N, another Lancaster Mark 1, took off at 2308 hours but crashed four kilometers north-east of Turnhout (Antwerpen), having been attacked by a night fighter. All the members of the aircrew were buried in the Schoonselhof Cemetery.

Lancaster Mark 1, ME 795 LE-G, took off at 2324 hours but had to be abandoned on its return at 0338 near Henlow, Bedfordshire. Piloted by Flying Officer L N Rackley of the Royal Australian Air Force, known as Blue, from Queensland, 'G' George struck trouble for the second time, having previously faced disaster when an engine of his Lancaster caught fire over Munich on 24 April, forcing him to land at Borgo on the east coast of Corsica. Barely had he crossed the coast into Belgium when he was attacked by a night fighter. The mid upper gunner replied, scoring hits which caused the fighter to disappear into clouds on fire. However, Rackley's aircraft had sustained serious damage and was almost uncontrollable. With the greatest of difficulty and much help from the crew, Blue was able to turn the aircraft round and head for home, jettisoning his bombs in the sea on the way.

They crossed the English coast near Ipswich. Since it would be impossible to land the aircraft, Blue told the crew to prepare to bail out. There was a huge hole in the fuselage making it necessary to help the rear gunner to get past it. He was used to living dangerously as he had been the rear gunner and sole survivor in the aircraft which had crashed on our station earlier in the year when the pilot, Flying Officer Murray, lost control on take off. Safely back over England the crew began to bail out. It was then discovered that the rear gunner's parachute was damaged and unusable. The bomb aimer had no hesitation in telling him to attach his harness to two metal D-shaped rings hanging from the bomb aimer's harness at his back over his bottom - to which a small dinghy could be attached when baling out over the sea - so that they could both go out together. They successfully left the stricken aircraft but sadly, when the bomb aimer opened his parachute the shock of the sudden slowdown in descent pulled out the attachments to the two Ds and the rear gunner went down without a parachute. His luck had finally run out in a dramatic way. Apart from Blue, all the rest of the crew landed safely. Blue did his best to set his aircraft on a course which would take it safely out to sea but because of its uncontrollable condition he was unable to do so. No sooner had he baled out than the aircraft began making ever decreasing circles in his direction. As he landed his parachute caught on a London bound train and he was badly bruised before he was able to release himself from his harness – but he survived.

In the immediate aftermath of the overwhelming event of that night it was not known how many of the aircrew members had been killed. Potentially the figure was seventy-seven from the Messes of East Kirkby, many personally known to us. But as the news came in of the North Sea rescue, hopes for many more survivors were entertained but it could not be known that twenty-five altogether had been rescued, had baled out over England successfully, had evaded, or had been made prisoners of war and that fifty-two had been killed. Armageddon had finally struck the station.

It was always heartening to hear that an aircrew member had managed to evade in occupied territory, although news of such evasions filtered through only after long delays. During my tour a rear gunner in 57 Squadron, Len Manning, successfully evaded during July 1944. Having been burnt in the aircraft before baling out and severely winded by his landing, he staggered eight miles to collapse at the door of a farmhouse. The farmer put him to bed. A man from the Resistance soon appeared to check his identity and gave him a sten sub-machine gun to defend himself. A doctor treated his injuries. German patrols visited the farm but the farmer was able to deter their enquiries with persuasive disclaimers. He was then moved several times and supplied with cigarettes, money and forged documents, ending up in a room above a café which was frequented by German military personnel. He was warned off the postman who was suspected of being a collaborator. Germans visiting the café on one occasion when there was no time to hide saw him having a meal in the back room with other wanted illegals on the run but to their amazement took no notice of it. The courtyard became full of German tanks but they moved on. Several weeks later in a complacent mood he walked into the café to find Germans sitting there but the owner chased him out pretending he was a servant. Eventually Resistance workers arrived to take him to the advancing Americans. He went to Paris to the reception centre set up by the RAF for evaders and returned to England after a three months' ordeal.

We were all introduced to the practice of formation flying. The inference was drawn by many people that senior officers were thinking that we might operate in daylight as the Americans did. Operations were laid on for that night but were cancelled in late afternoon so in the evening I took the crew into Horncastle for a little celebration.

Next day, 24 June, we again practiced formation flying in the morning and were briefed in the afternoon for the night bombing of a launching site for unmanned flying bombs, which twelve days previously had begun landing in London, causing much concern. We took off in the late evening and flew to Pommerval just inside the French coast. It was a short trip but the opposition was much greater than we had expected. We ourselves saw four bombers go down but the losses that night totalled twenty-two Lancasters from a large force of 739 aircraft, including 535 Lancasters, 165 Halifaxes and thirty-nine Mosquitoes, drawn from all Groups. They were directed against seven flying-bomb sites, including our own particular target at Pommerval. It was a clear moonlit night for these attacks. It is not known why all the losses were confined to Lancasters. They were caused by night fighters aided by searchlights. It was difficult to ascertain the results of these attacks as the ground around the sites had been so disturbed and pitted from previous attacks but evidently the Germans had been able to sustain operations from at least some of the sites.

Germany's secret weapon launching sites became our next target as well. On the night of 27/28 June a total force of 721 aircraft – 477 Lancasters, 207 Halifaxes and thirty-seven Mosquitoes – attacked six sites. Our own particular target of these was at Marquise Mimoyecques but it was only later that we learnt that we had bombed an additional German secret weapon, known as the V3, the V1 being the unmanned motorised flying bomb, and the V2 being the rocket propelled armament which descended on London without warning. It was apparently a gun, reputed to have twenty-five barrels, which had been built inside a hill, making it virtually impregnable to bombing. It was designed to land one shell per minute on London, the shells being rocket assisted to give them the required range. It never actually fired any shells to London. The theory was that although bombs might not penetrate to the gun itself, they could damage the surrounding area to an extent that made it impossible to supply ammunition to the gun. The Americans bombed it too, reputedly with the effect that one of their smaller bombs went down one of the gun's barrels, demolishing everything from inside. All the attacks that night were believed to have been effective at the cost of three Lancasters, none of which came from our station.

As it dawned I remembered that Saturday 1 July was Margie's twenty-first birthday. We were on the battle order again so we took our aircraft up for an air test, incorporating some low flying for good measure. As usual Joe Lennon and his crew, who were also on the battle order, were testing their aircraft too. They saw us low flying and joined us. We flew up the beach at Skegness in formation. Some teenagers had the temerity to pick up stones from the beach and threw them at us. As we approached the pier we had to gain height in order not to collide with it. Two big bombers in close formation flying so low must have presented a rather spectacular and formidable sight. When we landed back at East Kirkby we learnt that operations had been cancelled - to our great pleasure. I wished that the reason for the cancellation was Margie's birthday but found it was on account of the bad weather.

I sent Margie a cable for her special occasion and Jack had also sent one on behalf of the crew. Back in the Mess Joe and I decided that with the cancellation of operations and Margie's twenty-first birthday, there was plenty justification for letting our hair down with a little celebration—-which we did. Next morning we were told that we could go on leave. All the good things were happening at once.

It was a wonderful feeling going on leave, even though we weren't able to make any prior arrangements. For those of us from overseas who did not have anywhere in particular to go, there was an organisation in London which provided a list of people who would happily welcome us. However, I didn't need to use the service as I was going to Margie's relatives in Norfolk where I had spent my previous leave, although they did not know that I was on my way.

Dusty, Digger, Griff, Jack and I boarded a train to Grantham, from where Jack and I went to London. We arrived there about 2200 hours by which time it was too late to go further, so we spent the night at the Strand Palace Hotel. There we were introduced to the unpleasant habits of German flying bombs and rockets, respectively known as V1s and V2s. I did not mind the latter, which arrived at such a high speed that it was possible neither to see nor hear them. If you heard the explosion you knew that it had missed you so there was no need to feel concern. If it hadn't missed you, well, you still would be unable to have any concern.

Flying bombs, however, were quite unpleasant and a positive cause of insomnia. Their arrival was preceded by the distant sound similar to that of a small aircraft. We knew that when the engine stopped the bomb would fall to the ground and explode, which tended to make one concentrate on listening to the sound. Hearing the explosion allowed a brief period of relaxation before beginning the listening process all over again. I remember at one stage during the war concluding that there was little that one could not get used to. I think that that conclusion included flying bombs apart from their affront to one's privacy.

Before going our respective ways the following day, Jack and I visited a Daily Express exhibition of photographs of the invasion of Europe, followed by a visit to a News Theatre. Then Jack boarded a train for Essex and I boarded one for Norfolk. Since Shortie had his motorbike on the station he had been able to make his own way home but this time without having to bother to help me to find my destination as he did on our previous leave. It was wonderful being on leave. I caught up on a lot of lost sleep and felt very much at home with the Graham family who made me most welcome. Every day with them was precious. There were six of them in the family during my leave. With their parents were Jean, Gladys and Sandy, but also Isla, their daughter from Scotland was home. Sandy and I went boating on the Norfolk Broads with Isla. We also took numerous walks together around the countryside. The experience was a tonic for me. Isla was a very sweet person and reminded me very much of Margie. Their being related seemed to bring Margie much closer. Shortie called a couple of times, once when Gladys was home from Norwich. In turn he gave Gladys, Sandy and Mrs Graham a ride on the pillion seat of his motorbike.

All too soon the seven days slipped by. I found myself on the train heading back to work, arriving in Boston at 1900 hours after which I was able to hitch a ride most of the way back to East Kirkby. On reporting for duty next morning, I learnt that during my absence our Wing Commander and crew had been lost - a major loss for the squadron.

On the night of 7/8 July, Wing Commander W I Deas DSO DFC and Bar was the pilot of Lancaster Mark 3, NE 688 LE-R, which took off at 2244 hours but crashed at 0130 hours at a location eleven kilometres south-south-west of Magny-en-Vexin, south-east of Villers-en-Arthies (Val d'Oise). One member of the aircrew survived to become a prisoner of war. The pilot and the other five crew members, who included Flight Lieutenant G G H Farara DFC DFM , previously of 97 Squadron, were buried in Omerville Communal Cemetery, alongside six aircrew members of 630 Squadron who died on 10 June 1944.

The usual arrangement of command was to have a Group Captain as the overall commander of a base such as East Kikby, responsible for every aspect of the multifarious activities by hundreds of personnel in every describable trade and level of expertise which were necessary to maintain the offensive operations of its bomber squadrons. To keep one man in the air required the work of many men and women on the ground. Each of the two squadrons based at East Kirkby, 630 Squadron and 57 Squadron, was headed by an officer of Wing Commander rank. Each squadron was divided into two flights, 'A' Flight and 'B' Flight, each flight having a Flight Commander, usually of Squadron Leader rank.

Flight Commanders flew fairly frequently, but not invariably since there was a certain amount of administrative work to be done. Wing Commanders had even more administrative work to do so they flew even less but did need to fly often enough to keep up with changing operational conditions. Since they flew infrequently, they did not have a regular set crew. Consequently when they did fly they needed to gather a crew together from wherever possible. On the night that Wing Commander Deas flew, he took with him the Flight Commander of 'A' Flight, who was a navigator and as his engineer he took the Engineering Leader of the squadron. As his bomb aimer he took the squadron's Bombing Leader and as his rear gunner he took the squadron's Gunnery Leader. Finally, as his wireless operator he took the squadron's Signals Leader. They were a distinguished aircrew. Suddenly nearly all the leaders in the squadron were missing.

It was a catastrophic loss as a result of which Roy Calvert, who was Flight Commander of our Flight, 'B' Flight, took the Wing Commander's position as overall squadron commander and I took our Flight Commander's position, while another Flight Lieutenant in 'A' Flight took over that Flight Commander's position. In each case there was nobody to explain the requirements of the new jobs to the new officials. They assumed their jobs in a vacuum as a result of a hazard of war and immediately settled down to discharge the stream of orders coming to our station for operations to continue the war.

Chapter 14

Touch of Disillusion

Within a short time I also learnt that the loss of the 630 Squadron commander together with our squadron's other leading and experienced crew members was not the only reversal suffered by the station during the week of my leave. 57 Squadron took another heavy blow during two attacks mounted on the nights of 4/5 July and 7/8 July against a target at St Leu, losing six aircraft. On the first of these two attacks, Lancaster Mark 3, JB 486 DX-F, piloted by Flight Lieutenant A E Grubb took off at 2324 hours but was shot down at 0200 hours by a night fighter at Cormeilles (Oise), eight kilometres west-north-west of Breteuil. All members of the aircrew were buried in the Poix-de-la-Somme Churchyard. Piloted by Pilot Officer R R Smith of the Royal Australian Air Force, another Lancaster Mark 3, JB 723 DX-P, took off at 2322 hours but crashed at the village of Aubermesnil-aux-Erables (Seine-Maritime), two kilometres south of Foucarmont, all members of the aircrew being buried in the village churchyard. Pilot Officer R N Taft was the pilot of Lancaster Mark 1, ME 867 LE-N, which took off at 2313 hours but crashed at Lannoy-Cuillere (Oise), four kilometres north-west of Abancourt. One member of the Aircrew was buried in the Lannoy-Cuillere Communal Cemetery, the rest in the Poix-de-la-Somme Churchyard.

On the occasion of the second attack, Lancaster Mark 1, ME 868 DX-K, took off at 2219 hours, piloted by Pilot Officer M Rose of the Royal Australian Air Force but crashed in open country between Fresnay-le-Long (Seine-Maritime) and St Maclou-de-Folleville. Three crew members were killed, including the pilot. One was made a prisoner of war and two successfully evaded. The seventh member died from his injuries and was buried in the local churchyard at St Maclou-de-Folleville. Having taken off at 2221 hours, Lancaster Mark 3, JB 370 DX-O, crashed in open country nine kilometres south-east of Montdodier (Somme). All the aircrew survived. Three were made prisoners of war. The pilot, Pilot Officer N T Owen and three others evaded, one of whom, Flight Lieutenant K J Stevens DFM of the Royal Australian Air Force, was on his second tour of operations with 57 Squadron. Finally, Lancaster Mark 3, LM 522 DX-G, took off at 2218 hours also to attack the flying boat storage site but crashed between Envermeu

(Seine-Maritime) and St Nicolas d'Abermont, both villages being eleven kilometres south-east of Dieppe, killing the entire aircrew. The pilot, Pilot Officer S Findley was buried in the Envermeu Communal Cemetery, with his colleagues in a French military cemetery.

For our first sortie on returning from leave we were briefed to attack Culmont Chalindrey in France. We carried a bomb load of 13,000 pounds to railway targets there as part of a total force of 378 Lancasters and seven Mosquitoes drawn from 1 Group, 5 Group and 8 Group, despatched variously to include attacks also on railway targets at Revigny and Tours. Only half of the force designated for Revigny managed to bomb their target owing to the cloud cover encountered but Culmont and Tours were accurately bombed. Ten Lancasters were lost from those tasked to Revigny and two from those to Culmont.

Flying Officer Dennett flew with us as a 'second dickie' on the trip to Culmont but because it was such a relatively quiet trip I had little opportunity to teach him anything. I did demonstrate my method of keeping clear of night fighters and with a layer of white cloud beneath us was able to demonstrate the fact that if it were possible to find such a layer and to fly 100 feet above it, any night fighters attempting to creep up from behind became clearly visible as soon as they broke through the cloud.

On arriving back at base we found cloud down to 400 feet. On our normal circuit for landing we had to take account of a hill 300 feet high with trees on top. We were the first aircraft back so were given permission to land, followed by Joe Lennon. After that a lot of aircraft arrived at about the same time, causing congestion in difficult conditions and necessitating their diversion to other airfields. Being diverted was always an unpleasant experience since if the weather was bad, it was impossible to return for several days, leaving one deprived of all the bits and pieces such as shaving gear, tooth brush, and clothing which are taken for granted but without which life can become tedious.

There were no 'ops' next day so I spent the time getting unanswered letters dealt with and sent letter No 96 to Margie. In the mail there was a parcel from Margie. The contents of her parcels were always much appreciated and enjoyed. In the evening I indulged a bicycle ride with Griff by way of relaxation.

Our twenty-second operation as a crew followed quickly on the night of the 15/16 July 1944 when we were briefed to attack the railway system of France yet again – this time at Nevers and Châlons-sur-Marne. We ourselves took a bomb load of 13,000 pounds to Nevers. The attacking force that night consisted of 222 Lancasters and seven Mosquitoes to mount the two raids. Two Lancasters were lost at Nevers and one at Châlons-sur-Marne, none of them being from East Kirkby. That mission was followed immediately by our participation in a major effort in support of the British Army in France.

On the morning of 17 July we did some practice high level bombing. In the late afternoon we were told that there would be an 'ops' meal at 2230 hours, with the briefing at 0030 hours. At briefing we were told that the British 2nd Army was being held up in France at Caen. The target was to be some enemy strong points to enable them to break out. We took off at 0330 hours and were soon in the target area for the dawn attack. By the time we had deposited our bombs on the markers daylight was lightening the eastern sky and broke as we flew home. I could hardly believe the sight that met our eyes. The sky was full of aircraft of all shapes and sizes, presenting a daunting sight for enemy forces on the ground. Bombers of varying sizes were coming and going, while fighters keeping a watchful eye for enemy fighters were circling comfortably above. Below, in the English Channel, masses of ships were like birds searching for grain on an empty wheat field, all busy about the business of maintaining the invasion forces which struggled to break the German forces opposing them.

942 aircraft took part in the attacks to the east of Caen, including 667 Lancasters, 260 Halifaxes and fifteen Mosquitoes. The object was to destroy five fortified villages that lay in the path of the projected armoured attack code-named Operation Goodwood. Clear weather conditions for the attacks prevailed. Four of the five villages were satisfactorily marked by Oboe. At the fifth, Squadron Leader E K Cresswell, the master bomber and other Pathfinder crews were able to use visual methods successfully. More than 5,000 tons of bombs were dropped by the Bomber Command aircraft. American bombers also supplemented them with a tonnage in excess of 1,500 tons. Elements of the 16th Luftwaffe Field Division and the 21st Panzer Division were caught in the attacks and were badly affected by them. Operation Goodwood was able to get under way. The attacks were probably

the most useful and effective direct support which Bomber Command was ever able to give the army.

Interestingly, although we bombed from only medium heights between 5,000 and 9,000 feet, losses were limited to only six aircraft – five Halifaxes and one Lancaster. Both naval gunfire from coastal areas and army artillery units subdued German defensive anti-aircraft capability in the area of the attacks before the event. Allied air superiority over the battlefield area being complete, no German fighters appeared to molest the attacks.

None of the aircraft lost at Caen came from our squadrons but the satisfaction from that fact was very short lived. Later the same day as the attacks at Caen, both 57 Squadron and 630 Squadron supplied aircraft for a night attack on Revigny. 57 Squadron suffered one loss. When coned by searchlights on crossing the French coast, Lancaster Mark 3, JB 318 DX-L, which took off at 2256 hours, strayed off course and was shot down by a night fighter, crashing at Basseville (Seine-et-Marne), twelve kilometres east-south-east of La Ferte-sous-Jouarre. The pilot, Flight Lieutenant J A Bulcraig DFM and three other members of the aircrew were killed. They were buried in Basseville Communal Cemetery. One crew member was made a prisoner of war and the remaining two members successfully evaded. The pilot had completed a full tour of operations as a navigator in 50 Squadron for which he was awarded the DFM, as was another member of the aircrew, Sergeant N L E Gale DFM, who received his award as a member of 106 Squadron.

However, 630 Squadron was mortified to learn piecemeal of the losses of four aircraft on this same mission, a blow that was exacerbated by the loss on the same night of an aircraft sent up on a night flying training sortie. At the time we had no way of knowing that thirteen members of the combat crews had survived to be made prisoners of war or to evade capture, whilst one of the four man crew on the training flight survived.

LM117 LE-J, a Lancaster Mark 1 piloted by Flying Officer B W Brittain of the Royal Australian Air Force, having taken off at 2245 hours was homeward bound at 0200 hours when it was hit by ack-ack and crashed near Togny-aux-Boeufs (Marne), thirteen kilometres south-south-east of Châlons-sur-Marne. All the members of the aircrew successfully baled out with the exception of the wireless operator, Flight Sergeant Beckhouse of the Royal

Australian Air Force, who was found near the village with wounds or injuries which proved fatal. He was buried in the local cemetery. The pilot and two others of the aircrew evaded capture. The other three were made prisoners of war.

Taking off at 2250 hours, ME796 LE-S, a Lancaster Mark 1, piloted by Flying Officer G E Maxwell of the Royal Australian Air Force was orbiting the target awaiting orders to bomb, when first a night fighter attack, followed by hits from ack-ack , caused it to crash at 0130 hours at Villers-le-Sec (Marne), 40 kilometres south-east of Châlons-sur-Marne. The pilot and three of the aircrew were buried in the local churchyard. The other three successfully evaded.

Lancaster Mark 3, LM 537 LE-X, took off at 2250 hours but was hit by ack-ack at 0200 hours and brought down at Chassericourt (Aube), sixteen kilometres north-north-east of Brienne-le-Chateau. The pilot, Flying Officer P B Dennett of the Royal Australian Air Force and two other members of the crew were buried in the local churchyard. Of the four other members of the crew, one was made a prisoner of war and three successfully evaded.

When outward bound after take off at 2247 hours, Lancaster Mark 3, PB 236 LE-F, crashed at 0121 hours, at Neuvy (Marne), fifteen kilometres west-north-west of Sezanne, having been attacked by a night fighter. The pilot, Pilot Officer A J Sargent, and all the other members of the aircrew were buried in the local communal cemetery. One of the crew members, Sergeant N Barker at thirty-five was well above the average age for aircrew members.

On a navigational exercise with Flying Officer W A Sparkes as pilot, Lancaster Mark 1, ME 729 LE - took off at 2204 hours but trouble with two engines forced the crew to abandon the aircraft at 0059 hours at Mossdale Farm, Dunure, six kilometres south-west of Ayr. Three of its crew of four were killed.

On my return from Caen I reflected that it was a far cry from those desperate days in 1940-41 when German submarines were causing havoc by sinking ships far faster than they could be replaced, German bombers were bombing British cities with impunity at night, the British Army had been defeated in Europe and had suffered serious reverses in the Mediterranean theatre. Bomber Command had been Britain's only means of retaliation and, despite its limited resources, the only light on an otherwise unrelieved picture of gloom and doom. We knew now, that even if we ourselves did not survive to see it, the goal for which the war had been fought would be achieved.

We did an air test on the morning of Wednesday 19 July having been told that we would be preparing for our first daylight operation. During the morning Wing Commander Guy Gibson VC DSO DFC, who was famous for the dramatic bursting of the dams in the Ruhr Valley and had recently been posted to East Kirkby as its Base Operations Planner, came to me as Flight 'B' Commander and announced that we were going to undertake a daylight operation on which he would like to fly with us. He requested that I find and allocate a crew with whom he could fly. He was not officially available for operational duties but he told me that he had arranged it officially. Of course, knowing who he was, his rank and his famous reputation, I did as I was asked and arranged for him to fly with Flight Sergeant E Bowers in aircraft PB 244 LE-N, an aircraft that was lost a month later. What I did not know then was that he had not arranged it officially. Roy Calvert, who was currently our Squadron Commander, knew nothing about it. Obviously realizing that we had recently lost most of our senior personnel it seemed in retrospect that he was taking advantage of the fact.

Everything was prepared to include him on the mission. The target consisted of two V1 launching sites and a supply dump at Creil Thervigny, north of Paris. The attacking force consisted of 132 Lancasters and twelve Mosquitoes drawn from 5 Group and 8 Group.

Briefing was at 1730 hours and we took off at 1900 hours. Those times might not seem appropriate for a daylight operation, especially as we had only just passed the longest day of the year but the take off times were calculated to take into account the two hours of daylight saving time which were in place in England. Visibility was excellent as we flew across Southern England, enabling a wonderful view of the picturesque scene below. We were not officially trained for formation flying, so to stay together we followed our night time procedure by keeping strictly to allotted times.

Before we crossed the English Channel Jack told me that we were already running ahead of time, so I said I would hang back a bit. As we crossed into France, again Jack told me that we were still ahead of time. I said "I can't hang back any more Jack. We are already at the very back of the force and if I hang back any more we will become the obvious attraction for a fighter attack". With ninety-nine other aircraft flying ahead of us I knew there would be plenty of warning that the target was imminent because I would see the bomb doors being opened up on aircraft ahead of us but I was puzzled as to why we were running so far ahead of time when, night after night, we normally stayed resolutely on time.

Next came a call from Jack saying that according to his calculations we must have reached the target, quickly followed by Griff's voice saying "Yes, there it is below." I found it difficult to grasp the significance of what I was hearing. I looked ahead and could hardly believe what I could see. All the aircraft ahead of us had their bomb doors open and were showering bombs down on the open countryside away from the target.

My policy had always been that if we were lucky enough to reach the target at all, then the maximum use must be made of the bombs we had carried to it. Bombs just had to be delivered in the right place irrespective of all dangers. I always consoled myself with the thought that when we had effectively bombed a target if we were unable to make it back home we could die or become prisoners of war knowing that our job had been successfully accomplished. The thought of dying or ending up in captivity on a basis of failure seemed to be anathema to me.

I therefore turned back and commenced a second run up on the target. As we did so I saw another aircraft on our port side doing the same. I thought to myself, "That will be Guy Gibson. A man of his calibre and reputation would not want to be associated in any way with such an incredible fiasco". All the work and organising that had gone into the planning of the operation as well as the petrol and bombs had been entirely wasted. I knew the letters on the aircraft he was in would be LE-N but when the aircraft was close enough to read the letters, I read LE-X. That was the aircraft piloted by my friend Joe Lennon, who was a very conscientious person who invariably brought back a photograph of his bombs landing on the appointed target.

Since we were then alone over the target, the anti-aircraft guns took full advantage of their opportunity and directed all their fire at the two aircraft, one after another. Joe's aircraft suffered numerous shrapnel holes and our aircraft required a new aileron and a new aiming head for the bomb sight. Griff had been looking through the aiming head when it disintegrated in front of his eyes, together with the perspex window through which he had been looking. Suddenly I heard Griff shout, "They've got me", but as his voice sounded strong I guessed that although the blast had been dangerous he probably wasn't injured as badly as he at first thought. I told him to poke his head up so that I could see him and was able to assure him that he was alright – in the sense that he was not fatally injured. When the perspex window had been smashed the finely powdered remains had peppered the small portion of his face that was showing between his oxygen mask and his leather helmet. Undoubtedly it must have been very painful for a brief moment, understandably causing him to think that his face had been blown off.

Back in the Mess that night I approached Guy Gibson, thinking that he would be most disappointed to have witnessed such an amazing demonstration of incompetence. Much to my surprise, however, he was ready and willing to make excuses, saying that the crews must have been frightened on undertaking a daylight raid to which they were not used. It was far from being an explanation for a fiasco and of course was not a valid excuse at all. Fortunately no aircraft were lost.

He went on to tell me that he had stayed in the area afterwards, taking photographs of the countryside. But I knew that when Joe Lennon and I had extracted ourselves from the flak and headed for home, all the other aircraft in the operation were almost out of sight in the distance. We knew that we were last to leave the target area. The only camera with which Guy Gibson could have taken photographs was the one which automatically took a series of photographs when the bomb doors were opened. It seemed obvious to me that he was providing an excuse for having scenes of the countryside on the camera in Lancaster LE-N. Surprisingly, he entered that sortie in his log book, falsifying some of the details in doing so. No mention of Flight Sergeant Bowers was made. He pasted into his log book one of the photographs that the camera in the aircraft had taken, claiming that it included the aiming point. Jack sent me a copy of that photograph but although I had perforce been able to look down on the target area twice, I could not see it in the photograph.

The facts about this particular attack in which Wing Commander Guy Gibson took part are in conflict with published data about the same event. He has been quoted as flying in Lancaster LM 216-N, the correct designation for which was LM 216 LE-K, but he did not fly in that aircraft. As his participation was unofficial, the pilot, Flight Sergeant E Bowers of Lancaster PB 244 LE-N, the aircraft he actually flew in, had to fly as a supernumerary. His claim over the photographic record of the attack was different from the data in my possession as Flight 'B' Commander and derived from my own observation.

The next night we were tasked to attack railway marshalling yards and a triangular-shaped rail junction at Courtrai in Belgium. At this juncture of the land invasion by the Allies in Northern France, there was no respite in the efforts made by Bomber Command to support it by attacking transportation networks used by the Germans for carrying reinforcements and supplies to the battle areas, as well as some direct tactical attacks in the vicinity of those areas. A total of 302 Lancasters and fifteen Mosquitoes drawn from 1 Group, 5 Group and 8 Group was despatched on the night of 20/21 July. A report by Bomber Command reported that both targets had been devastated. Nine Lancasters were lost but none from our station. We saw two of those aircraft go down during this short flight of only three hours. A night fighter made a provisional attack on our aircraft but hung back and then broke the engagement off when both Dusty and Shortie opened fire on him. We had to have a new rudder fitted as a result of it.

After two days we took part in a disparate range of activities by Bomber Command on the night of 23/24 July. While a force of 180 aircraft drawn from training units was sent on a diversionary sweep over the North Sea, twenty-seven Mosquitoes were sent to bomb Berlin and to maintain the relentless pressure on the German capital to deny its population any sleep, with a further five to Déren. Among the other operations that night, two Stirlings were tasked on a mission to Brest and twelve aircraft were engaged in operations in support of Resistance groups in the occupied territories. We ourselves were one of six Lancasters sent to Kiel. Four of them had to attack a target in Kiel itself while Joe Lennon's aircraft and ours were laying mines in the harbour. By this time we were veterans. All the stages of preparation to the point of take off were so familiar to us but after our 'Last Supper' I still walked alone with my thoughts from the Mess, along the oak tree lined road to the crew room. Being our twenty-sixth operation as a crew – and my twenty-seventh – I had not become complacent about the potential of each trip for being our last but at least I no longer felt compelled to run up the fuselage to my seat in the front of the aircraft after climbing aboard.

Our take off was at 2200 hours. Joe Lennon's aircraft and ours each carried four mines. Unlike my previous trip to Kiel on a similar mission, there was no delay in loading up our mines. We left as scheduled and flew above cloud all the way. On arrival we found the target area completely obscured by cloud, compelling us to put our mines down by using our airborne radar and which required a long and careful run up to the dropping point. Jack had his eyes glued to the H2S screen so that he could tell Griff the exact moment to release the mines. He had also set up a camera to photograph the H2S screen at the moment of his instruction to Griff. All went according to plan. We felt we had done a good job in spite of the heavy flak in the target area. The other four Lancasters were obliged to drop their bombs on a sky marker owing to the cloud. Air markers were never a satisfactory method of bombing.

The cost of all Bomber Command's operations that night was one Lancaster which came from 630 Squadron. Setting off for Kiel Bay at 2244 hours, PB 211 LE-H, a Lancaster Mark 3, piloted by Flying Officer R T Hayes had to be ditched in the sea thirty-six miles north-east of Cromer while outward bound. The pilot and four other members of its aircrew died and are commemorated on the Runnymede Memorial. The two remaining crew members were seven hours in the water before being rescued by the coastal minesweeper HMS Coursor.

Later on during the morning of 24 July after our return from Kiel we carried out a ground check on our aircraft. A night attack on an oil storage depot at Donges near St Nazaire in France was planned for the night. Take off was at 2230 hours. The force of 104 Lancasters and nine Mosquitoes was from 5 Group and 8 Group. The attack on Donges cost the loss of three Lancasters, one of which was from 57 Squadron. Piloted by Flying Officer R H Simpson, Lancaster Mark 3, ND 560 DX-N, took off at 2154 hours but crashed. All seven members of the aircrew were buried in Orleans Main Cemetery.

There was no night fighter opposition en route or during our return. The expanding capture of occupied territory by the invasion forces was constantly recovering Luftwaffe airfields and eroding the German defensive capacity. Flak however was heavy in the target area and searchlights were in abundance. Alf always reckoned to sit on his tin hat in the best interests of his manhood whenever the flak was as heavy as it was that night.

Searchlights had ceased to worry me as they once did. It was possible to learn techniques for coping with them. There was always a master beam which could be identified by its colour and which was radar controlled. It used to come groping for us in a series of systematic movements. At the point that the beam would reach us on its next movement I learned to turn suddenly and fly through the beam, which would then reverse to follow me upon which I repeated the manoeuvre. By successively repeating this method it was possible to pass gradually out of the searchlight's range. Of course, it was imperative to deny an opportunity for the master beam to lock on to the aircraft as that would be the signal for all the supporting searchlights to form a terrifying cone on it. Ack-ack could then have a clear apex of illumination of the target for their armaments. It was practically impossible to escape once an aircraft was coned in that way. I have seen aircraft surrounded by the red hot fragments of dozens of shells which sooner or later would deal them lethal blows.

Without respite on the night of our return from Donges we had to prepare to take part in a resumption of the attacks on the traditional longer distance missions to German industrial cities, this time involving an eight and a half hours trip deep into Germany to the city of Stuttgart where the particular target was an aircraft factory. The force consisted of 412 Lancasters and 138 Halifaxes, of which eight Lancasters and four Halifaxes were lost, making a 2.2% loss rate. One of the Lancasters lost was from 630 Squadron.

It was still daylight as we flew southwards over England and saw that we were flying close to Bill Adams and his crew. Radio silence of course was strictly incumbent on us so Digger flashed them a good luck message by using the Aldis lamp. We struck extensive opposition on reaching the Kammhuber Line – the radar controlled belt stretching from the North Sea at Denmark across the Continent to South-West France in a defensive arc around Germany, through which invading bombers had to pass at one point or another. Five aircraft went down in quick succession but once through it the flight became less troublesome as we passed across Germany itself.

On arriving at Stuttgart we were pleasantly surprised to find less opposition than we had expected for such an important target. The run up to the drop point was unrestricted, leaving us to be confident that we would take home a picture of our bombs landing squarely where they were intended to land. Soon after turning for the return journey, however, Digger's voice came over the intercom to say that he was watching a suspicious blip on his 'Fishpond' screen. He declared that it seemed to be following us. I replied that I would change course thirty degrees and hold steady as a trial manoeuvre to validate his suspicion. After about one minute into the new course Digger came back on the intercom to announce "Yes, he is following us". Upon that confirmation I told Digger to let me know when the range had closed to 400 yards. When he did so I undertook a standard manoeuvre that we called a corkscrew, for which we dived first right, then left, followed by a climb to the left and a climb to the right. This set of manoeuvres was then repeated for as long as it took to shake off an enemy night fighter. It was a difficult manoeuvre for an enemy fighter to follow. Usually only one complete sequence was needed to discourage an enemy fighter. Most enemy pilots were only too glad to find an unsuspecting bomber that continued to fly on a steady course.

Digger's 'Fishpond' screen was part of our airborne radar equipment known as H2S. It was very helpful to the navigator to be able to check our location by referring to points on the ground. However, some enemy fighters had the equipment to pick up the signals emitted by H2S so it was crucial to keep a close watch on the 'Fishpond' screen, particularly when H2S had been used.

I was glad to arrive back yet again, but I had pause to consider the vicissitudes of fortune. In spite of our signal on our outward journey while still over England, Bill Adams didn't come back. His Lancaster Mark 3, PA 992 LE-Y, had taken off at 2139 hours but crashed at 0130 hours between Tramont-Emy (Meurthe-et-Moselle) and Tramont-Lassus, respectively fifteen and sixteen kilometres from Colombey-les-Belles. Two members of the aircrew died but Flying Officer W Adams of the United States Air Force and three other crew members successfully evaded.

We were dog tired, having had three successive nights of operations. It was doubly good to feel the wheels strike the tarmac on touchdown. After taking a few minutes to park the aircraft and shut down the engines, I took a moment to savour the moment of our return before picking up my parachute and sauntering along the aircraft to the exit door. It had been our twenty-eighth operation as a crew in the aircraft I was about to step out of, Lancaster Mark 3, ND 527 LE-O, but how was I to know that we would not be able to fly in it again. We thankfully were able to get into bed by 0600 hours.

The next day produced yet another call on 'B' Flight. I thought that the intended operation would not be too demanding so I chose the less experienced crews, exonerating ourselves, believing that four nights in a row was really too big a demand on us. The operation was to Givors. A force of 178 Lancasters and nine Mosquitoes of 5 Group carried out an effective attack on the railway yards there. However four Lancasters and two Mosquitoes were lost. Two of the Lancaster losses resulted from a collision which brought to a final end the veteran aircraft ND 527 LE-O which had served our crew so well and others before us. The whole aircrew of Lancaster Mark 3, ND 527 LE-O, were buried in the Clermont-Ferrand Communal Cemetery. Having taken off at 2117 hours, it crashed at 0245 hours at St. Ignat (Puy de Dôme), fourteen kilometres east-north-east of Riom. The pilot, Flying Officer Wilson and three other members of the crew were from the Royal Canadian Air Force.

The loss of Mosquitoes was unusual in that although they were vulnerable when flying low for target marking purposes, their high speed guaranteed them virtual immunity from night fighter attack. It has been estimated that 60% of all losses of Mosquitoes during the later months of the war at night which fell to night fighters were accounted for by the Luftwaffe's newly introduced Heinkel He 219.

It turned out to be only a short break for us as we were briefed the day after for a continuation of the attack on Stuttgart. However, the aircraft we were going to fly developed a faulty fuel pump which could not be fixed in time for the appointed take off. Joe Lennon went on it to log up his thirtieth operation, which normally would have been his end of tour and release from operations but the CO told him that as we were short staffed with so much work to be done he would have to stay on operational duty a while longer, which is exactly what happened in my case. George Joblin also went on this operation for his thirtieth operation but he failed to return. It always seemed a cruel irony to be shot down on one's final operation. It was as if experience were no guarantee of immunity. It was as if random factors played a decisive part in

Fig. 58. Lancaster LE-O lost 26/27 July 1944 on its mission to Givers

one's survival or otherwise, a consideration which most people referred to as luck.

Of the 494 Lancasters and two Mosquitoes despatched for this attack forty were lost.

As it happened we lost three aircraft from the station - two from 57 Squadron and one from 630 Squadron. From 57 Squadron, Flying Officer A V H Wardle DFC was the pilot of Lancaster Mark 1, ME 864 DX-E, which took off at 2144 hours but crashed at 0120 hours. Of the seven aircrew members, four were made prisoners of war and three were buried at Dürnbach War Cemetery. The pilot, Flying Officer W A Nicholls, and three other members of the aircrew were successfully able to evade when their Lancaster Mark 1, PD 212 DX-F, having taken off at 2150 hours, crashed at 0030 hours, possibly near the River Aube, north-east of Romilly. The other three crew members were made prisoners of war.

ND 497 LE- W, a Lancaster Mark 3 from 630 Squadron, was piloted by Flight Lieutenant G R Joblin DFC of the Royal New Zealand Air Force. He was twenty-four years of age, with 647 hours' flying on his record. The aircraft took off at 2153 hours but was attacked by a night fighter and crashed near Magstadt, thirteen kilometres west-south-west of Stuttgart at 0230 hours. At low level, three members of the aircrew managed to bale out but only the bomb aimer's parachute opened in time. Flying Officer W C J Beeson, the sole survivor, was made a prisoner of war. The other six members of the aircrew were buried first at Magstadt then permanently at Dürnbach War Cemetery.

On 29 July we took our aircraft for an air test after its fuel pump repair. By comparison with an operational flight an air test was less than dangerous, yet hundreds of aircraft were lost in the course of flying over home territory for one purpose or another. Fatalities on such flights for Bomber Command alone amounted to over 8,000 men. As it happened 57 Squadron lost an aircraft the day after we took our own air test. Lancaster Mark 1, LM 284 DX-, piloted by Flying Officer D L Davies DFC, and a test aircrew from 55 Base, mainly from 207 Squadron, was lost on a test flight. It was presumed to have come down in The Wash. The body of Flight Sergeant C Gidman DFM was washed up on the beach at Brancaster in Norfolk and buried there. The other five members of the limited aircrew included three holders of the DFM and Pilot Officer F W Logan DFC of the Royal Canadian Air Force. They are commemorated on the Runnymede Memorial.

Rising at 0200 hours on 30 July we were duly briefed and took off at 0530 hours for a daylight attack at Cahagnes in Normandy. This was one of six German positions in front of a mainly American ground offensive in the Villers Bocage-Caumont area to be assaulted variously by a giant total force of 692 aircraft – 462 Lancasters, 200 Halifaxes and thirty Mosquitoes. Owing to heavy cloud only 377 were able to bomb their intended targets, using Oboe markers. Two of the six targets were effectively hit. In our own case we were unable to see our target and brought our 10,000 bomb load back to base. Four Lancasters were lost, none of them from East Kirkby. As it was my personal thirtieth operational flight, on my return I half hoped that the CO would absolve me from flying on any further operations but he didn't mention the fact and I decided it would be imprudent for me to raise it.

The very next day we were tasked to carry a 12,700 pound bomb load on another daylight attack on the French railway system. A force of 127 Lancasters and four Mosquitoes from 1 Group and 5 Group carried out an effective raid on the railway yards at Joigny-La-Roche near Paris in clear conditions. It was an amazingly easy trip facilitated by the German retreat from many airfields in France which used to be home to both day and night fighters of the Luftwaffe. On return we found that cloud had descended to ground level. The dulcet voice which usually welcomed us back from operations told us to divert to Syerston. Only one aircraft was lost on the mission but it came from 57 Squadron. Having taken off at 1741 hours, Lancaster Mark 3, ND

954 DX-Q, crashed at 2145 hours, being unable to maintain formation. The pilot, Flight Lieutenant J B P Spencer, and four other members of the aircrew were buried in Banneville La Campagne War Cemetery. Two were made prisoners of war – Flight Lieutenant R T Clarke DFM, the Squadron's Engineer Leader, and Pilot Officer N E Hughes-Games. The latter died at Sagan on 28 September 1944 and was buried in Poznan Old Garrison Cemetery.

Chapter 15

Closing the Account

By early afternoon 2 August 1944 the cloud had lifted and we were able to return to base. I spent most of the remainder of the day in the office, except for the time spent responding to a summons for Lennon and me to report to the Station Commanding Officer. It seemed clear that our low flying antics had caught up with us - we could think of no other reason. Joe and I discussed what our fate might be, deciding that whatever it turned out to be it would be a lot safer than flying on operations.

We knocked on the CO's door. A firm voice commanded us to enter. We did so, feeling like lambs being taken into the slaughterhouse. On entering, we found him standing beside a table with a big grin on his face. We were surprised at what we were seeing - it was like arriving at the target and finding no opposition. On his table was a series of reconnaissance photographs. They showed Kiel harbour as a scene of devastation, with ships that had been beached, ships with only their masts protruding from the water and a general appearance of chaos all around. Clearly our mines had landed in the right places and the enemy had been taken completely by surprise. Our CO was pleased - but no more so than we were. We had two good reasons to be pleased. We had obviously succeeded in doing a good job at Kiel in the face of heavy flak. We were also not in line to be carpeted. The success of the sortie to Kiel was really due to the skills of our respective navigators, who, with only a small screen to look at had timed the release of the mines to perfection. As the subject of low flying was never mentioned our escape from reprimand was icing on the cake.

Next day, 3 August, we found that during our absence, a brand new aircraft had arrived to replace the one that had been lost in the hands of another crew over Nevers. After having used the same aircraft for all of the first twenty-eight of our total of thirty-four operations together as a crew, we used several different aircraft including this brand new one for the remaining six operations. After breakfast, we were briefed to attack a flying bomb supply site at Troissy St.Maximin, north east of Paris. Our new aircraft took off much more easily than the old one, which in becoming a veteran had begun to show a measure of wear and tear as a result of the hard work to which it had been exposed. Our attacks on flying bomb sites were becoming crucial. Enough flying bombs were reaching London to be more than just a nuisance. Some were being shot down by fighters or anti-aircraft guns, but many were getting through, particularly at night time. Of course they could not be aimed at a specific target so the damage was random and people were being killed in the capital.

We took off at 1000 hours carrying eleven 1,000 pound and four 500 pound bombs. Flying in daylight seemed much easier than flying at night. The weather was clear at all the targets attacked – altogether one flying bomb launching site and three supply sites. As it was possible to see all around us we always felt that we had a chance to escape if things went wrong. We had a fighter escort too, which made us feel much safer. On our way to and from the target there was no opposition but in the target area there was very heavy flak. Most aircraft including ourselves came back peppered with holes but only two Lancasters - both from 5 Group and both engaged in the attack on the Bois de Cassan site - were lost from a total mixed force sent out consisting of 394 aircraft, including 234 Lancasters, ninety-nine Halifaxes, forty Mosquitoes, twenty Stirlings and one Lightning. Good results were claimed.

An attack on another flying bomb launching site was planned for the following day, 3 August but the repairs to our aircraft as a result of the previous day's assault on the site at Troissy St Maximin had not been completed, so we were grounded, enabling me to spend the day in the office and take a bicycle ride with Griff in the evening.

On Saturday 5 August in daylight we bombed yet another flying bomb site, this time at "St.Leu d'Esserent, once more near Paris. On this occasion we flew in formation with a fighter escort as the Americans did but the outcome was not satisfactory, largely as a result of the fact that broken cloud made identification of the target difficult. Since we all released our bombs when the lead plane did, the inevitable result was that bombs were spread over a large area. Had each aircraft gone into the attack individually as we normally did on targets for night bombing, I feel that a much better result would have been achieved. It was a pity that the results were disappointing. Weather conditions were good. A large force had been despatched, no less that 742 aircraft, including 469 Halifaxes and 257 Lancasters with sixteen Mosquitoes, all drawn variously from 4 Group, 5 Group, 6 Group and 8 Group. The Forêt de Nieppe site was also attacked by this force. Thirty-one

Lancasters and eight Mosquitoes attempted attacks on four other sites by using the Oboe leader techniques but only nine aircraft succeeded in bombing. One Halifax was lost from the attack on St Leu d'Esserent.

Fig. 59. Flying home, mission completed.

I was desperately striving to catch up with the office work so I didn't fly again for four days. During that time – on the night of 7/8 August - 630 Squadron lost an aircraft. This was the first loss suffered by the squadron since the night of 28/29 July. Flight Sergeant G V B Patterson of the Royal New Zealand Air Force, who hailed from Levuka in Fiji, was the pilot of Lancaster Mark 1, LM 262 LE-G, which took off at 2105 hours as part of a huge fleet of 1019 aircraft - of which seventeen were lost – to attack five strong points in the Normandy battle area. It was tasked to bomb an enemy concentration in front of Allied troops at Secqueville but crashed en route in France, being brought down twelve kilometres west-north-west of Lisieux, exploding on impact at the farm of Monsieur Cholet at Montreuil-en-Auge. Three members of its crew survived, two being made prisoners of war and one evading. Three of those killed were buried in the St Valery-en-Caux Cemetery and the other in St Desir War Cemetery. The pilot and three other members of the aircrew were killed. He was twenty-three and on his first operation, with 464 flying hours to his credit. His brother had already been killed on 15 November 1941 as a pilot flying with 99 Squadron. The other three members of the aircrew survived, including Flying Officer A A Thomas, the navigator, also of the

Royal New Zealand Air Force and the engineer, both of whom were made prisoners of war. The wireless operator evaded capture.

On 9 August we were tasked to attack an oil storage complex at Forêt de Châttellerault in Southern France. It was our penultimate mission as a crew. We were in a total force of 176 Lancasters and fourteen Mosquitoes drawn from 1 Group and 5 Group from which two Lancasters were lost. We were obliged to orbit for twenty minutes as there was some difficulty in marking the target. I became concerned about the delay because having been named as second deputy controller, I didn't want to be suddenly responsible for something I knew virtually nothing about. Eventually the markers appeared and we were told to commence our attack. There was no opposition, although we did see the two bombers that were lost go down. They were probably hit by bombs from other aircraft flying above them. Afterwards, Joe Lennon told me that the CO had told him that he could finish then. It was his thirty-fifth operation. Joe had got one ahead of me so I was pretty sure that if I managed to survive the next one, I too would be paid off.

My thirty-fifth and last operation turned out to be on 10/11 August 1944, in a force of 215 aircraft including 109 Lancasters, 101 Halifaxes and five Mosquitoes drawn variously from 5 Group, 6 Group and 8 Group. We bombed submarine bases at Bordeaux and La Pallice using armour piecing bombs. Our own target was the former. We were airborne at 1730 hours on a bright sunny day. The view as we flew down across Southern England was delightful. After crossing the channel, Brittany with all its hedges and varied landscape was most picturesque. Darkness descended as we crossed the Bay of Biscay. Reaching the target we found the defences to be minimal, giving us no trouble apart from the searchlights. We had a perfect run up to the target which seemed to be a fitting feature for our last trip.

On returning to base and feeling those wheels touching terra firma was an experience of unbelievable relief. Having parked the aircraft at its dispersal site as usual, I shut down the motors one by one. I watched the propellers stop and then just sat for a while. I looked at each motor in turn, gave each one a smile and a nod, picked up my parachute and sauntered slowly down the fuselage. It would have been a cruel anticlimax if the CO had asked me to do some more but he was waiting to say "Congratulations, well done, you've done enough". As a crew we had completed thirty-four operations. I had completed thirty-five, taking into account my trip to Aachen as 'second dickie'.

Next day we were told we could have ten days survivor's leave. For a change we had a chance to make some prior arrangements. Shortie was going to his home in Norfolk. Jack was going to his home in Essex. Les was going to his home in Yorkshire and Digger was going to his home in Carlisle. Griff was going to stay a while in Carlisle with Digger and family. I had made arrangements to stay with other relatives of Margie in the Scottish Highlands.

As Flight Commander, I arranged for a new crew to do a practice cross-country flight, taking Carlisle as a turning point. Digger, Griff, Joe Lennon (who was going to Newcastle) and I all dropped off at Carlisle. Travelling in those times was always a very tedious experience owing to the crowded conditions created by woefully inadequate public transport services. It was a big time saver for us to be able to reach Carlisle by using our own transport.

We all spent the night as non-paying guests in the hotel managed by Digger's father. Next day we explored Carlisle in the morning. In the afternoon Joe left by train for Newcastle. At 0245 hours the following morning I caught a train for Inverness, where I changed trains for Invershin, my final destination where I was given a warm welcome by Margie's relatives who ran a guest house in the Highlands. It couldn't have been a more ideal place for someone like me to be. I had a profound need for peace and quietness. As on my previous leave in the Highlands, I awoke each morning to the sounds of singing birds and a mountain stream splashing its way down across the rocks. There was not a single sound of an aircraft. I had nothing to do but relax and catch up with correspondence. Of course I wrote to Margie - letter No 99 - as well as to numerous others.

I could only stay there one week. I had used a day's leave to get there and needed two days to return to East Kirkby. I set out again for Carlisle. Next day Digger and I headed back to East Kirkby We had good seats until we reached Newcastle where many ladies were amongst those who boarded the train so we felt obliged to stand for the 270 miles to Peterborough. We had seats from Peterborough to Boston, however, and arrived back at our airfield at 2200 hours.

In the Mess I found lots of mail waiting for me including four parcels from Margie, one from my mother, and a second one from Mrs Fox on behalf of the community of Scargill in North

Canterbury where I grew up. We had the resources for one last feast together before we split up.

Every item of the wide range of equipment we needed and used for flying operationally belonged to the Ministry of Defence. Before being permitted to leave an airfield on a new posting we had to produce documents to indicate that all appropriate equipment had been returned. We spent all day gathering the necessary documentation. Roy Griffin and I along with Joe Lennon and his navigator, all New Zealanders, were posted to Westcott, a New Zealand Operational Training Unit in Oxfordshire. Jack Warwick, Alf Dawson, Les Meace, Ron Adams, and John Miller were posted to different airfields to be instructors.

I was posted to the No11 Operational Training Unit at Oakley. My first flight there was in a Wellington on 2 October 1944. I then flew almost every day until my last flight – also in a Wellington on 13 September 1945. In between those dates I flew a few times in Wellingtons and a very few times in Master aircraft but overwhelmingly I flew Hawker Hurricanes engaged on cine work.

Fig. 60. Author and Hawker Hurricane in 1944.

Fig. 61. Author flying a Hawker Hurricane over Oxfordshire in 1944.

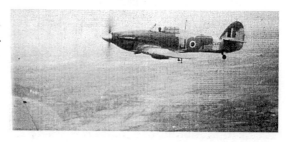

During this period I was informed that I had been awarded the Distinguished Flying Cross. I was of course proud to be the recipient of it. However, I could not help reflecting that many who deserved to receive the award never became recipients of it. Many brave deeds went unrewarded because they remained unknown and unreported. Citations for such awards generally picked out one particular event to substantiate the justification for them. In my case our determination to press home our attack on Munich was quoted. Such awards were normally presented by King George VI at Buckingham Palace but I had arrived back in New Zealand by the time that my turn was scheduled. Consequently, the DFC was pinned on my tunic by the King's representative, the Governor General of New Zealand. By a nice coincidence, the Governor's Aide-de-Camp who was holding the cushion on which the medal rested before being affixed to my tunic was Squadron Leader David Roberts, the pilot of the Lancaster in which I had taken my first operational flight as 'second dickie' to Aachen.

On the completion of our full tour of operations I was eligible to recommend any of my crew members for a commission. I asked each in turn if he would like me to do so. Jack, Griff and Dusty agreed and were duly commissioned. Jack and Dusty went on to become Flight Lieutenants. Griff, who had falsified his age to be eligible to join Air Crew, was sent home and discharged.

As far as possible after the war we kept in touch with each other. Les joined the RAF Fire Service but was tragically killed in an accident. Nearly sixty years later I had the pleasure of meeting his wife and son in 2002 while attending a squadron reunion. With the passage of time, Griff, Dusty and Shortie have also joined those lads we knew who gave their lives as young men so long ago. In 2003, Digger, Jack and I were together at our squadron reunion - a pleasant and rewarding if nostalgic experience to be with them again after so many years.

The relief we all felt at the time of our completion of operational flying was palpable. Life had seemed so unreal. Night after night we had watched others being burnt to death or blown into infinity or just disappearing and not being around any more, the while knowing full well that within seconds, minutes or hours, our own fate could be sealed. We savoured our chances of survival - chances that were at best about one in five. Having arrived safely back from one sortie the mind was plagued with the thought that the next might well be our last, as we might not return from it. The horror of it all had to be sublimated by various means which were manifest in the culture developed by the flyers of the Royal Air Force over the years – the nonchalance, the jokes, the diversionary nature of the specialist vocabulary, the veto on talking about experiences in open court. The reality was too indescribably horrific to contemplate if sanity had to be preserved. So many who experienced or witnessed what could happen were themselves victims. Few lived to be able to tell the tale. Many crews were overtly given to carrying mascots and following set routines as imagined assets to ward off the unimaginable.

Superstition was a well known temptation to which so many bomber crews succumbed. If, for any reason, the normal sequence of events were different, many crews felt it was an ominous sign. One night when Dusty was settled in his turret and we were about to move off, he realised that he was not wearing his scarf. As it was the first time he had forgotten it, he was concerned, not simply because he needed it for warmth but because it was the first time he had gone without it and that could mean ill-luck in the annals of the superstitious.

I was not at all superstitious and took every opportunity to do the things that, according to superstition, I should not do. I had of course taken the bed in the corner of my hut whose former occupants had gone missing, in spite of the dire warning of the other inhabitants, on my first arrival at East Kirkby. In addition in those days I smoked and liked to have the third light for a cigarette, or if there were a conveniently placed ladder I would purposely walk under it. One evening when we were sitting on the grass beside our aircraft, having completed our pre take off checks. I went to get the third light for my cigarette whereupon Griff rushed forward and blew out the match before I was able to do so. I said "All right then, I will walk under this ladder." and went to walk under the ladder which provided us with an entrance to our aircraft. All the rest of the crew made such a fuss that I felt it prudent to desist from walking under the ladder completely. Had I completed my action and incurred disaster on the next trip, none of us might have been alive to attribute our fate to it but the others were unwilling to run the risk. I would have liked to do it to scotch the superstition on return from the next mission but how was I to know that we would return from it? That was the night a shell came through the main spar on our port side, dismantled Diggers radio, and put our aircraft out of action for nearly a month. Of course they all blamed me. I had evidently only half exposed them to disaster.

The stress of combat flying amid high loss rates induced such strange but understandable psychological defence mechanisms. They were fuelled by apparently inexplicable happenings. For example, at one stage during the war, there was a reputedly authentic report of a Hawker Hurricane fighter which, during the Battle of Britain, landed back at its home airfield but stopped at the end of the runway and failed to taxi in. On investigation it was found that the pilot was dead with a bullet through his head. Another pilot who took over the undamaged aircraft one day had a strange experience. The aircraft of its own volition seemed to have deliberately avoided an enemy fighter which came up from behind. Realising that such a story would be met with abject derision in the Mess, he made no mention of it. Later, the aircraft was being flown by a different pilot who had a similar experience but he too did not mention it for the same reason. When a third pilot also had a similar experience but did venture to mention it, all three imagined there was a strange factor at work. It was thought that there must be a malfunction of some sort, perhaps in the control mechanism which needed to be rectified. However, ground staff were unable to find any possible mechanical explanation so the aircraft was returned to the makers who almost dismantled it, finding nothing unusual. The maker's name and aircraft manufacturing number were given, seemingly adding authenticity to the story.

Occasionally an aircraft was lost as a result of other causes but the vast majority of lost aircraft were brought down by either night fighters or ack-ack. All too often whole crews were killed in the ensuing explosion of their aircraft in the air or its disintegration on hitting the ground. Infrequently, all the members of the aircrew of a stricken bomber baled out but then not without mishap. The most common outcome was a mixture of fates. Some members were killed in the aircraft or so injured in the aircraft that they were unable to jump. Among those who jumped there were casualties when parachutes failed to open or when a parachutist's landing caused death or injury. Occasionally there were freak accidents, as when a Lancaster pilot jumped but had failed to disconnect his intercom which strangled him. Those who reached the ground safely were either made prisoners of war or successfully evaded capture by their own efforts or those of the Resistance organizations, returning to Britain or reaching a neutral country or hiding out until the cessation of hostilities.

The bare description of the fate of an aircrew member, however, indicates nothing of the terror, trauma and suffering that may have preceded it. For those who died their personal experience up to their deaths could not be known, unless witnessed by a colleague who survived to tell of it. One crew member who was fortunate to escape from a fatally crippled aircraft has recorded his experience. With special operational responsibilities, James Arthur Davies was an additional member to the normal complement of seven aircrew members of Lancaster Mark 3, DV 267 SR-K of 101 Squadron which took off from Ludford Magna at 2338 hours on 19 February 1944 for an attack on Leipzig but crashed near Tolbert, Groningen in Holland after being attacked by a night fighter. Of the eight men on board, three were killed and five were made prisoners of war. Part of his description of the final moments of the aircraft is as follows.

"At that moment the port wing fell off, the starboard wing went down, then the nose. In a loud, clear, almost detached voice, our skipper gave the final command. Abandon aircraft, Abandon aircraft, Abandon aircraft. And no more".

"I glanced over my shoulder to see our Wireless Operator, Cass Waight, enveloped in flames without his parachute harness. He had been told many times to wear his harness at all times, but he always refused, saying that it was far too uncomfortable and he could not work in it. It was a terrifying sight".

"I was probably the last crew member to leave the burning bomber which was about to be blown to pieces. The rear-gunner, Royston, had already jumped and I had to wait for mid-upper gunner Bolt to go. We were about to jump when both of us, crouched before the now wide-open door, were hit again and we were knocked sprawling against the fuselage. I had the curious sensation of drowning and then lost consciousness. It could only have been for a second or two. When I awoke, Bolt had gone. It was now my turn".

He was a Special Duties Operator. It was only his second operational trip. He landed with slight injuries and one boot less in the vicinity of the crashed aircraft about fifty miles from the border with Germany. He met up with the Resistance who told him that the pilot went down with the plane. Bolt's parachute failed to open.

Resistance people reached the plane before the Germans and found the pilot's mutilated body and also the bodies of Bolt and Waight, without a parachute, in the same area.

Another fortunate airman was an aircrew member, Len Manning, a rear gunner in 57 Squadron at East Kirkby. On 18 July 1944 he was in a Lancaster tasked to Revigny on northern France. He has recalled that it was coned by searchlights soon after crossing the coast of France. In taking evasive action their aircraft fell out of the bomber stream. Shortly after that there was an enormous explosion in the port wing, the aircraft being hit by cannon fire from a night fighter. Immediately flames were streaming past his turret which had jammed as a result of the destruction of one of the port engines that maintained the hydraulic pumps. He centralised his turret by hand, opened the door and climbed into the fuselage. He saw the mid-upper gunner clipping on his parachute, opening the rear door of the aircraft and leaping out.

The fuselage was already a mass of flames and molten metal. His own parachute that was stowed in it nearby was smouldering. As the aircraft went into a steep dive he pulled it from its stowaged position and struggled to clip it onto his harness, a task made difficult by the gravitational pull of the plunging aircraft. He managed to fix it with one clip but failed to affix the other. With everything on fire he determined that he had to jump immediately and leapt into the night. As he fell he pulled the rip-cord which to his unimagined relief opened the parachute. He found himself hanging to one side. Something brushed his face. It was his intercom cord attached to his helmet. It had been whipped off as the parachute opened and was entangled in the silk shrouds. He grabbed it and hung on to it – an act which probably saved his life as it helped to take his weight – the while realising that his parachute was on fire. On his way down he heard a terrific explosion as their Lancaster hit the ground near Basseville. He landed flat on his back and lay winded, while his parachute burned. He tried to smother the flames and hid the burnt remains in a hedge. He had survived.

Then there were always the perils of the sea over which we had to fly so much. On the night of 21/22 October 1943 their aircraft, a Lancaster Mark 3, EE 184 KM B, of 44 (Rhodesia) Squadron, which had taken off from Dunholme Lodge at 1726 hours, was hit by flak and lost its fuel over Leipzig. The crew reviewed their chances and decided to try to return to base as opposed to baling out to certain captivity or death. The aircraft had been delivered direct from the factory on 11 June 1943, since when it had been in continuous use, accumulating 322.45 flying hours.

After a while, however, it became clear that insufficient fuel remained to get them back to England. There was a strong headwind to make matters worse. The aircraft was put down in the North Sea in what turned out to be a Force 9 gale. In accordance with dinghy drill the upper escape hatch located near the mid-upper gunner's turret was jettisoned. The crew calculated that they were about ten miles from the coast of England but did not know they were quite close to the Spurn lightship. The aircraft came down some sixty miles south-east of Grimsby in Lincolnshire.

Crew members took up their ditching positions. The navigator, Sergeant Connor, decided to stay with the pilot, Pilot Officer R H Watts of the Royal Australian Air Force. The bomb-aimer pulled the toggle to release the dinghy housed in the starboard wing and grabbed the Very pistol and cartridges, stuffing the pistol in his boot. Two of the five crew members were able to get into the dinghy. The other three jumped into the sea and hung on to the side of the dinghy subsequently with great difficulty as it had already shipped a lot of water. But they managed to get into it. By then there was no sign of the pilot and navigator. It took a while for them to realise that the front of the aircraft had already disappeared.

Conditions were atrocious, danger being their constant companion in the stormy waves which threatened to swamp their frail little craft. The bomb aimer had lost the pistol in the sea but they found the emergency rations in the dinghy together with another small pistol, which he fired off. Unfortunately he aimed it vertically so that it fell back and narrowly missed them. The terrible shock of losing their two comrades finally hit them. They fired off more cartridges and eventually saw a light which turned out to be a vessel coming towards them. It was the minesweeper HMS Loch Moidart which had picked up signals from their aircraft and had plotted their position. It was a close run thing. A boathook punctured the dinghy during the rescue in the darkness of the night, endangering the five airmen yet again as huge waves threatened to tip them back into the sea. But their rescue was achieved. Pilot Officer Watts was buried in Bergen op Zoom

Canadian War Cemetery. Sergeant Connor is commemorated on Panel 145 of the Runnymede Memorial.

Fig. 62. East Kirkby Perimeter track in 1983.

Fig. 63. East Kirkby main runway area in 1983,
with Shortie on the left, then Jack, Alf and the
author

When seven men lived such an existence in bomber aircraft for hours on end, apparently alone in the darkness and in the confined space of an aircraft which might suddenly explode but always be surrounded by danger, a very strong bond developed between them because every experience was shared. I remember once thinking to myself, that there was nothing that one cannot get used to. When it was all over and the strain and tension no longer existed, the time came when we realised just how great the tension actually had been. Equally, all seven of us enjoyed the relief that came with knowing that it was finally over. The basis for that bond was then forever broken but not the friendship that it generated.

Thoughts and feelings can better be portrayed in poetic form. Audrey Grealy had the insight to express my thoughts and feelings better than I.

Life was a fleeting moment, when we lived from day to day.
A morning dawned, the sun broke through, we savoured every day.
For well we knew that, with the dusk, there was a price to pay
When we were young.

We lived our lives up to the hilt, we laughed and loved, and prayed.
We learnt to crack a flippant joke, if we should feel afraid.
These things were all accepted for, by us the rules were made
When we were young.

The dangers which we faced became a common bond to share.
The friendships forged upon such fire were rich beyond compare.
So many of them all too short, their loss so hard to bear.
When we were young.

So many years have passed since then, the flames of war have died.
The individual paths we chose are scattered far and wide.
But we remember proudly, those whose lives to us were tied.
When we were young.

Chapter 16

Perspectives

In retrospect there are clearly three main considerations regarding the events in which I took part, events which themselves were part of the war-long contribution that Bomber Command made to the British war effort overall, which required first a defence against the German invasion of the British Isles and then to win back the conquered territories and ultimately to overthrow the German hegemony in Europe. That it remains a topic of critical interest and concern is testified by the fact that Der Spiegel devoted twelve pages of its issue 2/6.1.2003 to the subject. The three considerations are (1) the experience of people on the ground, (2) the cost to the personnel and aircraft involved, and (3) the material effects of the bombing as a significant factor contributing to the prosecution of the war.

In the managerial climate of thought and practice of the present day it is fundamental to conceive an objective clearly, to marshal and use the necessary resources for reaching it and to use them both effectively and efficiently. But in war it is the lives of people which enter into this equation in a manner and to an extent that never applies to the economic and social processes of a peacetime population.

Presumably people on the ground could afford little but negative thought for those who were bombing them. As has been remarked regarding the bombing of Britain by an author who lived through the German bombing attacks on East Anglia "...half a century has passed since the sounds of Dorniers, Heinkels, Ju 88s and many more heralded frightening moments. It was hard to realise that aboard them were people, and many like ourselves caught in terrifying situations not of their choice or making".

In this context it is worth remembering that the Luftwaffe itself maintained both purposeful and seemingly indiscriminate attacks on British towns and cities throughout the four years of the war from May 1940 to May 1944, often including the daylight machine-gunning of civilians in the streets by low-level attacks. In 1942, even as Bomber Command was beginning to build up its own offensive capability against German targets, the Luftwaffe flew a total of 3,532 sorties on night-bombing operations to Britain between April and August alone. Operation 'Steinbock', launched in January 1944, involved the use of as many bombers as Germany could muster to attack London and other places. Over 600 sorties were despatched during that one month. The campaign was organised by Pelz, newly promoted to Generalmajor, the Luftwaffe commander who had been responsible for the 'Jabo' raids on south-coast towns earlier in the war. The subsequent vicious attacks on Plymouth in April 1944 and Bristol in May 1944 were supplemented by intruder raids right up to the end of March 1945. During the last few months of the war, hundreds of V1s, from June 1944, and V2s, from September 1944, fell indiscriminately on South-East England. They were meant to terrorize the population and if possible to regenerate the fortunes of war for Germany. The will and the intent to destroy British assets and people were ever-present and given expression as far as resources permitted. It was just fortunate that enemy resources and bombing capacity were so miniscule by the end of the war compared with those of Bomber Command.

I often thought about the state of mind of the people on the ground as we flew over them. In the occupied territories I used to think that the sound of our aircraft offered them hope. Over German territory I used to think of the dread and even the terror of people which were generated by the sound of our engines over their heads. It must be remembered, however, that so many of the population in the occupied territories in or near the legitimate targets which we attacked eventually also had every reason to fear the sound of approaching Allied aircraft. The loss of life and damage to friendly people on the ground proved in the end to be of substantial proportions. I have been able to talk with people who have emigrated to New Zealand and who as children or young people were subject to the effects of British bombing during the Second World War in different parts of Europe. Those in the occupied territories were widely prepared to suffer with great stoicism in the belief that it was part of the price that had to be paid for ultimate freedom from oppression.

With the passage of the years, all aspects of the aerial bombing by Allied Air Forces have come to be represented and betokened by reference to the attacks on two particular cities – that on Dresden for the European theatre of the war in respect of the British Bomber Command's war and Tokyo for the Pacific theatre of the war with respect to the bombing carried out by the American Air Force - which inflicted 84,000 casualties in one day in the city.

The cost of the bombing in terms of the loss of life of the airmen engaged in delivering it and the civilian population on the ground may be a matter of logistics and collateral calculation for those in politics and military command who were directing the course of the war but for each individual lost and his or her family and friends the perspective is very different. The story is told of the old man who daily walked a beach in California picking up starfish stranded by the movements of the tide and returning them to the ocean. A modern young woman living nearby one day accosted him with a starfish in his hand and queried the necessity of his task. "There are so many of them, surely it doesn't matter if a few of them get stranded?" she challenged. "But it matters to this one", he replied.

I have invited testimony from survivors of the attacks on both these cities to record their experiences and impressions in this narrative. Both have been obtained directly from their authors and are translated from the original text as validly as possible.

The account regarding Dresden is supplied by Heidrun Krämer who has continued to live in Dresden. She married Rainer Krämer and had two children. It is the text of a letter from her father written to her on her tenth birthday.

The historic city of Dresden, located some 125 miles south of Berlin and close to the frontiers with Poland and Czechoslovakia, lay in the path of the advancing Russian armies into Germany. The Russian troops, often out of control, inflicted widespread and unmitigated brutality on German people as they overran them, notably in Silesia, some 150 miles due east of Dresden. Those who could escape fled westwards. For example, a woman from Neisse in Silesia reported "We others fled via Glatz and Bautzen, without any luggage, mainly walking all the way, eventually reaching Dresden on February 12, 1945". Thus, Dresden itself was home to an additional population of refugees, probably several hundred thousand in size at the time of the British bombing attack on the city on the night of 13 February 1945.

Until that date Dresden had escaped major bombing but became a target so late in the Second World War ostensibly by being perceived as a military centre that could play an important part in the continuing German resistance to the Russian advance.

It was a relatively undefended target. Bomber Command of the Royal Air Force lost only eight aircraft on the mission – a low loss rate for such a distant target. The death toll was consequently high. German estimates put the death toll of the native population at over 40,000 – placing it at a stroke among the highest totals suffered by any German city — but record that the actual toll could have been as high as 200,000, taking into account the facts that refugees often had no identification and that so many bodies were incinerated and buried under the mountains of rubble from the collapse of the city's multi-storey dwelling houses.

The destruction of so much of the delectable historic heart of the city emerged as regrettable. British Bomber Command in general and its Commander at the time, Marshall of the Royal Air Force Sir Arthur Harris, in particular, attracted the obloquy of people of disparate political and philosophical views but who were united in condemning an allegedly unnecessary and wanton action. It must be remembered however that there was no respite for the survivors of Bomber Command's attack, since next morning, 14 February 1945 the American 8th Air Force attacked Dresden with 316 bombers. It did so again on the following day with 211 bombers, and yet again on 2 March with 406 bombers. A further attack by the American 8th Air Force was carried out on 7 April with 572 bombers. Not only American writers but also some British writers appeared to have a strange desire to accuse only Arthur Harris and Bomber Command for wantonly bombing Dresden.

However, it has been pointed out by way of reply to this censure that a state of total war existed, in which nothing could be justified yet everything could be justified. The evidence cited to justify the attack on Dresden may or may not be convincing but the sudden and apocalyptic nature of it, at a point in the war when all the signs were of the imminent triumph of the Allies over Germany, has left a permanent scar in the collective memory.

Dresden, 13 February 1955

My Dear Heidrun

It is now ten years since we celebrated your first birthday. It was at the end of the carnival (Fastnacht). The streets were full of people who were enjoying the celebrations. The normal residents of the city had been joined by many thousands of refugees, fleeing from other parts of Germany to the East that were already being overrun by the Russians. But for the moment the war was forgotten and the Carnival was in full swing

The children in particular were making the most of the happy atmosphere throughout the city. They had been less affected than the adults by the war that had been going on for well over five years at that point. Many of them had been born during the war and had never known peaceful conditions. In contrast, the adults had become war weary. The reversals of the war for Germany had induced great anxieties and fears – and grief for loved ones lost. There had already been enormous losses of German lives on the Eastern Front and in the cities and towns of Germany as a result of bombing. Yet up to the day of your first birthday our lovely city of Dresden had not suffered any serious attack from the air. Perhaps we had deluded ourselves that we were going to escape the ravages of war completely. Hope, at least, was always there.

Unexpectedly at 9.30 pm that evening the air-raid sirens went off. It was not long before we could hear the approaching drone of heavy bombers. We had little time to pick up our belongings and some warm clothing - since it was a cold night in February – and make for the air-raid shelters.

Within a few minutes the first bombs began to fall in what would turn out to be one of the most devastating aerial attacks on a city – some say it was definitively the worst – of all time. The bombs rained down on beautiful Dresden. From our shelter it gave us all the feeling of being in a massive earthquake. Our thoughts were that no one and nothing would survive it

Throughout it we were expecting the end to come for us too and prayed that if it came it would be swift, in preference to being so injured or burnt that death would only be delayed until a long, lingering agony had been endured. It needed strong nerves not to panic. It was probably worse for your mother than giving birth to you. Your mother tried everything she knew to comfort you and your sister Maritta. She read fairy tales which Maritta appreciated, although you were too young to understand what she was reading.

The pounding went on incessantly without any change in its intensity until about 11 pm. When we emerged from the shelter we were confronted by an indescribable scene. To start with, it was almost impossible to breathe as the air was full of acrid dust, which soon clogged our nostrils. And then there was the heat. You could feel it all around you. From going down into the shelters in the February cold we had been violently transported into an inferno. The sight of it all was unbelievable. We could see beyond any doubt that out beautiful city was in ruins. Fires were raging everywhere, sending showers of sparks high into the night sky. The smoke from the inferno must have been filling the whole sky but little of it could be seen in the darkness beyond the huge canopy of light from the cauldron below it.

The city burned for five days. It was beyond the power of man to save it. It has since become known that 35 – 40,000 of the city's own identifiable people died - but it has been estimated that anything up to 200,000 people might have perished. The city had been the temporary Mecca for refugees on a very large scale. Although the total number who had arrived was never known, subjective estimates put it in the hundreds of thousands. Many thousands of those people were simply incinerated in whole families, leaving no one to mourn their loss or to know of their fate. Thousands were buried under the rubble and mutilated beyond recognition.

I helped the Rossgers family, your Grandpa and Grandma and your Uncle Hans to their homes. We were fearful of what we would discover but apart from superficial damage we were relieved to find that their homes were still habitable. Grandma Lina should have stayed with us all but she insisted on going off by herself. She was so anxious to rescue her things that she wouldn't wait for me to go with her. She arrived at her house to find it burning. She felt compelled to save what she could reach and apparently nearly died in the flames and smoke that eventually destroyed her house. She managed to save herself but disappeared to our great consternation. It was some days later that we discovered she had been found in a distressed state in a caravan in Cossebaude, though we never knew how she got there.

In the event we had little time in which to recover from the attack. At 1.30 am we were stunned to hear the air-raid *warning sirens going again in Radebeul. We thought that it was a mistake. It was not a mistake, however, simply a tactical move by the enemy to catch all those engaged in fire-fighting and rescue work in the open, made worse by the fact that many night workers had by then returned to the city from factories dispersed in the suburbs and environs to protect their families and homes.*

The second attack seemed worse than the first - if that were possible to conceive. Those who could not get to underground shelters, including many of those engaged in rescue and firefighting from the first attack, made for the parks, or fled to the banks and fields on the side of the Elbe. There they were at risk of stray bombs falling on them but at least they were away from the firestorm and falling debris. However, it is believed that they were exposed to machine gun fire from the raiding aircraft. When able to look around, those people must have had a spectacular, if terrifying, sight.

We were all very lucky again to survive. Not far away from us on the railway, a wagon of a goods train carrying ammunition went up in a mighty explosion.

We decided without a second thought to move away from the burning city. Your mother carried you wrapped up in a blanket on her bicycle. I carried Maritta on my bicycle. We actually saved your birthday cake. Your mother tied it on to her bicycle. We decided to go to the Lutzens family in Boxdorf. I wanted to go the shortest way but your mother suggested that we should go via Wahnsdorf. It turned out to be a good idea.

At 11 o'clock on the morning of that very next day following the night attacks on the city, there was a daylight attack. Refugees were bombed and strafed. They walked as petrified, semi-dead people. And so occurred the death of our city. It had become a monument to the capacity of men to inflict terrible things on each other.

I hope it doesn't happen to you or other people ever again. That is my birthday wish to you.

Your Daddy

Supplementary Testimony from Inka Pöhland, Heidrun's Daughter 2003

My grandfather who wrote that letter was born on 8 May 1909 in Dresden. Until he was thirty year old, he worked at a well-known tailor's shop in the city, never being called into military service or war work. I do not know the reason for that. It might have been on grounds of poor health or it may have been that the facility was used to produce clothing for military use. His first daughter was eighteen months old when war was declared. He was a good man in the sense that he gave no offence to others, he cared for his family - augmented by the arrival of my mother on 13 February 1944 - he worked hard and wished only to see his family in a prosperous state and enjoying a happy life. He was interested in natural history, the theatre and astronomy. He cherished the desire to travel the world with his family.

He realized his ambition during or just before 1939 to start his own business. It was to provide the lifestyle for his beautiful wife and children that he passionately wanted for them. He personally never dabbled in politics but loved the Fatherland that he saw as the essential historic traditions of German culture, not the revised version of it produced by the Third Reich. His relatives variously were involved as party members or fellow travellers. The pressures to conform for most people then were compelling. Options were limited.

The early years of the war were quiet. He made a good living – good enough to keep his family fed well, even when food became scarce during the later years of the war. A thriving black market developed in the city. Women went out to work to obtain extra food coupons. Hunger became a reality. My grandmother told me of women who came to the shop crying in despair for their children.

Grandfather used to ride his bicycle out to the countryside to visit farms. Farms had to meet quotas imposed on them by the government. The quotas became more and more demanding as the war went on, so it was not easy for farmers to find food for others. But, of course, he was a tailor. Farmers needed clothes and were willing to trade food for clothes. Grandfather's experience then was the perfect instance of the example used to illustrate the quintessential nature of the subject with beginners in the study of economics. The hungry tailor and the trouserless farmer needed each other.

As the war turned against Germany with calamitous effects, the family began to take their own precautions. In Dresden many people lived in houses with multiple storeys. The fear spread that the collapse of such high-rise properties would bury their occupants in the rubble. Nevertheless, the cellars were the safest places to be. My family prepared small cases with documents and other vital and precious possessions in them for flight to the countryside if needs be. Many babies were born in those Dresden cellars. The treatment of sick people was carried out in them and even surgical operations were conducted in them.

By good fortune, on the night of 13 February 1945, all the family members had assembled in the cellar of my grandparents. All the properties of my relatives were destroyed except that of my grandparents. On their flight from the city early the following morning, my grandfather's decision to travel a circuitous route through a forested area may have saved their lives, as the long columns of people fleeing the city were machine-gunned by low flying aircraft.

Those who survived of course were traumatized. The children had had no childhood. The experience of war for Dresden people left an ineradicable stamp on their lives. It shaped the psyche of a whole generation. My grandfather died in 1983.

Inka Pöhland

Testimony from Tokyo is provided by Hisa Nomura, born in Tokyo in 1929, as follows.

When war broke out the first thing I remember was the air raid siren reverberating through the air. It was 18 April 1942. I had never heard an air raid siren before so I didn't know what to do but a senior student led me to the air raid shelter. Then I realized that Japan was at war. Towards the end of 1940 the education of children had become very militaristic. My younger brother at eleven was given military training at school.

There was great piety for the Japanese god and the royal family was blindly worshipped. At school each morning we *worshipped before portraits of His Majesty and Her Majesty. It felt strange but was evidently educational policy.*

As time passed the air raid warnings became more frequent. We were not able to sleep as we had to get up and go down to the shelters every night. Life was made worse because provisions began to run short in 1943. We always felt hungry. Many children were evacuated from central Tokyo to the outlying parts of the city, including four of us children. It felt as if the family had been torn asunder.

In 1944 we began to feel that the war had turned against us. Almost every night American bombers called B29s bombed Tokyo and nearby towns. We saw many parts of Tokyo on fire. The night sky was full of conflagration. In July 1944 I was mobilized for work in a factory making munitions. We made parts of aircraft.

In 1945 Japan was fighting on knowing it was a losing battle. But the military authorities tried to persuade us it was a winning battle. On 10 March and 25 March the city was subjected to an unimaginable firestorm. All around my school everything was devastated and burned. As many of us as were left went to the fire-ravaged school to see what could be rescued. I was still fifteen when the end of the war came via the speech by the Emperor on the radio. I saw many grown up people weeping.

The second testimony from Tokyo is provided by Keinosuke Obi who was also born in 1929. He relates his experience as follows.

As wartime continued, food supplies decreased. We had little chance to eat rice which had always been the staple food of Japanese people. Instead, people made wheat dumplings and dipped them in salty soup, swallowing them whole. They didn't taste good. Those who lived in urban areas and wanted to have rice secretly took their valuable kimonos to nearby farm villages and bartered them for rice. When all their kimonos had gone, and their rice ran out, they began cooking a little rice mixed with lots of potatoes. They had little chance to eat meat or fish. Those who managed to get some pickled plums felt themselves very fortunate.

When I was thirteen years old, as a second grader in secondary school, one class period was assigned for daily military training. An officer sent from a nearby regiment taught us how to use a gun and how to stab a man. During this training, we were given mock-guns made of wood. But we carried heavy real ones when we marched a long distance around the foot of Mt. Fuji. Still very young, we were completely exhausted by this hard trek. Many of us fell unconscious by the roadside. But with no real idea about war or battlefields, we felt nothing negative during our military training. Rather, we had some heroic sentiments. Not a few of my classmates yearned to be enrolled in the Military Training Schools.

After 1943, squadrons of American bombers began round-the-clock air raids over Tokyo. Every household was required to cover its electric bulbs, and the inside of the houses got very dark. I used to see American airplanes flying high above, their silver wings glittering. In the clear blue sky, those strange objects seemed exquisitely beautiful to my eyes. And so it was that I looked forward to seeing the terrible beauty of those shoals of aircraft.

To protect themselves from the bombing, people were ordered to make shelters in their backyards. My mother and I dug bit by bit every day and finally completed our own shelter. My father was out of the house almost every day because of his office work and scarcely helped us. Digging a mass of earth was very hard work for a woman and a little boy. We had a comparatively large backyard, which we worked hard to cultivate, growing potatoes and vegetables for food.

Several air-raid shelters were built in the school yard, too. The moment we heard the warning siren, we ran out of the classroom and dived into the shelter. Once while we were in the shelters, we heard the thundering sounds of bombing close by. After the bombers had left we went out and found a massive hill had appeared next to our shelter. It had been thrown up by the near misses. We felt extremely relieved that none of us had been injured.

My family lived in the suburbs about forty minutes by electric train from the central part of Tokyo. Thanks to this remoteness we scarcely experienced an air-raid at the beginning of the war. Gradually, however, as the war went on, we sometimes saw fighters flying overhead. Once I was pursued by one of them. I was extremely scared when I saw fighter bullets embedding themselves in the pillars of the nearby railway station.

We got information about the war only through radio broadcasts and the newspapers. Both of them repeatedly announced that Japan was continuing its great victories on every battlefield. We used to hear slogans like "Holy War!", "Join one hundred million hearts into one!", "We need nothing, only victory!", and, "Damn the American and British devils!" As the war came to an end, however, these words were replaced by "The final battle on mainland Japan!" and "We, one hundred million people of Japan, are ready to die for the Emperor!"

When I was a third-grader in junior high, the school auditorium was requisitioned as a factory for manufacturing earphones. Students were no longer taught in class. Instead they spent their time winding threads on earphone parts. As we could not know when American bombers might attack, the school was evacuated to a Buddhist temple in the suburbs.

As primary and secondary school pupils were in danger of being killed in the air-raids, the government ordered us to be moved to country villages to escape the attack. Young boys and girls were separated from their families. Even little first-graders had to leave their homes. They cried when they were separated from their family members.

On 10 March 1945 downtown Tokyo was attacked by American bombers. Countless firebombs were dropped, and around one-hundred- thousand people were burnt to death in one night. Incendiary bombs were dropped around residential blocks, preventing people from escaping to safety.

Thousands of civilians were trapped as bombs rained down. Crying for their family members, people ran this way and that while being showered with fireballs. Most of them were burned to death. It was hell on earth.

Other parts of Tokyo suffered air-raids, too. Since most of the houses were made of wood they burned easily. The fires spread quickly to nearby areas. Some people narrowly escaped death but lost everything. They dug holes, raised pillars, made roofs with burnt logs, and lived in these poor shanties. I remember I could see as far as I wished for there was nothing around me but the charcoaled remains of houses.

Those children who had been evacuated to country villages had escaped with their young lives. However, many of them lost their parents and became orphans. After the war they roamed the streets of cities and towns like paupers. These 'war orphans' were one of the most serious post-war problems in Japan.

We were informed of the end of the war while staying in the Buddhist temple where our school had been evacuated. A navy officer who had been staying there with us told us that Hiroshima had been attacked with an atomic bomb, and he predicted that the war would end before long. 15 August 1945 was a very hot day. On the radio, we heard the Emperor declare the surrender of the Imperial State of Japan to the Allied Nations. The words the Emperor used to announce the defeat were beyond our comprehension, but we knew it had to be something gravely serious if the living god was speaking directly to the common people. It had to be nothing less than the end of the war.

Thus it was on a glittering summer's day in 1945 that I returned home with my heart made light by the Emperor's announcement of war's end. At home both my parents were waiting for me.

All of a sudden "Damn the American and British devils!" and "We one hundred million people of Japan are ready to die for the Emperor!" slogans disappeared overnight. I wondered if there were other countries where such a drastic change as this had occurred. Almost everyone welcomed the American army of occupation. This is proved by the fact that all postwar reforms were carried out smoothly with little resistance. Democracy, liberty and human rights became idealistic mottos for the Japanese people. Nobody remembered that they had been living submissively and willingly under a fascist regime until just a few weeks earlier. They had forgotten everything that had passed.

My fifteen years of life up to 1945 were spent in wartime, including Japan's attack on China. Therefore that period is sometimes called the 'Fifteen Years' War'. At the beginning of this war, I was a little boy and when the war ended I was almost a young man. Thus my physical and mental foundations were built in wartime Japan. Sometimes I asked myself, "What did that period mean to me?" But each time I found myself at a loss for an answer. This was because I am convinced that the wartime of 1930-45 and the postwar reforms of 1945-60 should not be evaluated independently. Rather, it seems to me, both should be taken as a continuum and should be evaluated as a whole. Endless transformation is the reality of human society.

It is a far cry from the days of the Second World War from the point of view of aerial bombing. Its apotheosis was reached in 1944 and 1945. Both by night, if they could have been seen, and by day the sky was black with aircraft as far as the eye could see. The concept of the large aircraft and ever larger bomb loads was the compensatory necessity for the relative absence of precision of the bombing. Many bombs had to be dropped so that on a statistical basis a percentage of them was bound to find its mark. If the intention was simply to carpet bomb a whole city then the imprecision of the bombing became an asset. Perhaps that very fact encouraged the eventual indiscriminate attacks on cities to develop in the first place. Justification could always be found in the state of total war which the Second Wold War became.

The concept of the heavy bomber has persisted since then. American heavy bombers have been used to shower armaments on ground targets many times since 1945. But as far as the Royal Air Force has been concerned bombing capability has taken a different course. The descendants of the Lancaster, Halifax and Stirling were the Victor, Valiant and Vulcan, which were designed to carry the ultimate in aerial armaments of the nuclear variety. The rapid development of anti-aircraft weapons, such as rocket propelled missiles and heat seeking armaments, however, made large aircraft finally vulnerable.

The Panavia Tornado became the direct descendant of the Lancaster as the strike aircraft of the Royal Air Force. It was able to demonstrate its capabilities for the first time in the First Gulf War and has been used subsequently in the Middle East. It was designed to carry a nuclear weapon in the European theatre of war in the event of a conflict with the Communist powers during the Cold War. It can deliver eight 1,000 pound bombs at low level and with considerable precision, making it an economical replacement for the mass of aircraft that were needed to guarantee effective bombing in the Second World War.

There has been much controversy over the efficacy of Bomber Command's systematic attacks on German or German held targets across the entire Continent of Europe. The gargantuan scale and sight of all that was involved represented a colossal effort of human organisation and sacrifice. The question over its worthwhileness and effectiveness, however, will always remain and be subject to challenge. Those who suffered by it can hardly be expected to agree with its justification.

The grand total of sorties dispatched by Bomber Command for the entire period of the war,1939 to 1945, was 297,663 by night and 66,851 by day. A total of 7,449 aircraft sent by night and a total of 876 of the aircraft sent by day failed to return. The average number of missions per aircrew overall for Bomber Command was 9.1. Only one-third of all bomber aircrews completed a first tour.

Of the operational aircrews involved throughout the war in Bomber Command, 5,582 were killed, 41,548 were missing, presumed dead, and 138 died of the total of 9,784 who were shot down and became prisoners of war. In addition, 4,200 were wounded. Of the aircrews lost on non-operational flights involved throughout the war in Bomber Command, 8,090 were killed, 4,203 were wounded and 215 died of other causes. These figures underlined the risks of training flights in themselves and the attendant exposure to enemy action against aircraft and personnel on the airfields and aircraft on training flights all over Britain, together with the constant danger implicit in handling explosives.

Altogether these figures give a total of 55,573 aircrew personnel who were killed or died in the service of Bomber Command. Of this total, 47,268 were killed or died as a direct or indirect result of operational flying. These figures put bomber aircrews at the forefront among all the different elements of the services in terms of the scale of losses, both as regards absolute numbers and as a percentage of those who were involved.

Among these losses it may be noted that from its small population of three and a half million people during the war years, New Zealand contributed over 11,000 men to the service of The

Royal Air Force, half of whom served in Bomber Command. One-third of those who served in Bomber Command did not return from operations or training sorties, making a total of 1836 New Zealanders killed.

The nadir for New Zealanders serving with Bomber Command was the night of 28/29 July 1942. It was the night for an attack on Hamburg. More New Zealanders died that night than on any other single night or day of the entire Second World War in any theatre of war throughout the world. 75 (NZ) Squadron alone suffered twenty-one dead. In the second half of that year a total of over 360 New Zealand aircrew members were killed. This was the highest loss rate of the war for New Zealand aircrew – it was greater than the total deaths suffered by RNZAF aircrew in the Pacific theatre for the entire war. It was a 4% loss rate, or one in every twenty-five sent out on a mission. When the half way date of the war was reached at 3 September 1942 only one third of the ultimate total deaths of New Zealand aircrew had been incurred, indicating the ascending nature of the loss rate as the war progressed, Bomber Command being able to increase mission numbers at a rate which was unthinkable in the early stages of the war.

Many of those who went as aircrew joined one of the two all-New Zealand squadrons, either 75 (NZ) Squadron or 487 (NZ) Squadron, which respectively produced in Sergeant James Allen Ward and Squadron Leader Leonard Henry Trent acts of supreme courage and sacrifice for which the Victoria Cross was awarded. But most of them served with mixed British, Commonwealth and Allied crews throughout the other 128 Squadrons that made up Bomber Command. In the case of 75 Squadron, between its first operational flight of 27 March 1940 and the end of hostilities in May 1945, the squadron became distinguished for flying 8,017 sorties, more than the number of sorties flown by any other squadron in 3 Group, and for carrying out the fourth highest number of raids of all the squadrons of the entire Bomber Command, in so doing losing 193 aircraft, the second highest loss rate of any Bomber Command squadron.

The quantity of sorties flown by Bomber Command each year varied widely but an overwhelmingly disproportionate number of those sorties both by night and by day took place in the year 1944. This was the year in which the German authorities commissioned a nationwide assessment of the damage which had been caused to its cities and towns and in which, by a massive process of decentralization, dispersal and underground development of the industrial production of war materials, Germany managed to achieve higher production rates of vital war materials than in any other single year of the Second World War.

In that year Bomber Command flew 113,352 sorties by night and 35,096 by day. 2349 aircraft from the night sorties and 224 from the daylight sorties failed to return. My own operational tour lasted from 20/21 April to 10/11 August. During this exact period in 1944 the two squadrons based at East Kirkby, 630 Squadron and 57 Squadron, suffered heavy losses. The latter lost thirty-three aircraft during the period - all except one, which was on an air test, as a direct or indirect result of enemy action. My own squadron lost twenty-three aircraft over the same period, all as a result of enemy action, except for one lost on a training flight. The total losses for the station were therefore fifty-six for the period covering my operational tour.

These losses can be put into perspective. A squadron's normal aircraft strength was twelve. Typically up to four of them would be undergoing servicing at any one time, leaving at least eight available for operational use – making sixteen for the two squadrons based at the station. My operational tour dates lasted for 112 days. The station, therefore, lost an aircraft exactly every two days out of the sixteen available for operations. However, replacement aircraft did not always arrive quickly enough to keep pace with losses, so that the number of aircraft actually available for operations often fell below the standard sixteen, making the en passant loss rate proportionately greater. The loss rate presented a daunting prospect for every incoming new crew to a bomber station. It has been truly said that "To be a member of a bomber crew required persistent fortitude at a time and in circumstances when the stoutest mind and heart would have every excuse to show a natural and normal weakness. The average operation was in darkness and in the early hours of the morning. Every one who took part in it knew that the odds were against the survival of any particular airman".

I was lucky to survive an activity in war which claimed the lives of a high percentage of those who engaged in it. On the national memorial in the Atrium of the Air Force Museum at Wigram, Christchurch, New Zealand are listed the names of the large number of New Zealanders who lost their lives during the Second World War as aircrew. From my own personal group of friends I had known as a young man in New Zealand seven left never to return. Pilot officer H H Bruhns was shot down in Kiel Bay on the night of the 24/25 February 1944 on his fifth sortie with 75 Squadron. Pilot Officer A S Frampton was shot down at Frankfurt on the night of 17/18 March 1944 on his sixth sortie with 115 Squadron. Flight Sergeant J R Garbutt on his very first sortie, flying as a 'second dickie' with 622 Squadron was shot down over Berlin on 13 February 1944. Sergeant J C Gray went to 9 Squadron and was shot down at Wismar in Germany on his tenth sortie on the night of 23 September 1942. Pilot Officer W J Green was on his seventh sortie with 625 Squadron when he was shot down at Culne in France on 11/12 April 1944. Sergeant R A Hamilton was shot down over Germany in 1942 on his fifth operation with 51 Squadron, and Flight Sergeant L L Harrison of 97 Squadron was lost in the North Sea in 1941 on his seventh sortie when his Avro Manchester aircraft developed engine failure.

The loss of these men who were in various degrees well known to me was hard to bear. They had been friends before the war or were made so during our training and the extended travelling time we spent together. In retrospect I can see how inured perhaps aircrews were to having to deal with the loss of their fellow combatants compared with other branches of the armed forces. One's own crew members were close friends and highly esteemed. The loss of one of them to enemy action by ack-ack or the attack of a fighter, as quite often happened during a mission became an immediate psychological blow and tangible emotional experience for the rest of the crew. On station, however, aircrew members drawn from all of the United Kingdom and many other parts of the world were essentially strangers and mostly remained so, the loss rate maintaining the flow of such strangers and preventing relationships of any worth developing with any of them.

The worthwhileness of such a substantial loss of men and of using the massive economic resources needed to produce the Bomber Command offensive has long been debated. The benefits of it really fall into two categories. The indirect benefit category consists of assessing the cost to Germany of devoting resources to its defensive measures against Bomber Command, along with the American Air Force after 1942, that otherwise could have been available for use against the Russian armies in the east and the Allies in the west on the ground. This factor is the more imponderable of the two. The second benefit category is the manifest direct destruction and damage meted out to Germany's war production and resources of all kinds.

In January 1945, when the Russian armies were poised to overrun the eastern parts of Germany itself, Stalin ordered Marshal Konev to preserve the mines, steelworks and factories of Upper Silesia. He described them as gold. Konev obliged by executing a wide encircling movement to prevent the sabotage of the installations and plants by the retreating Germans and to avoid the necessity of fighting through them in the Stalingrad manner. The capture of all that economic industrial capacity in one fell swoop has been compared with the somewhat doubtful impairment of Rhur industry by Bomber Command. However, it must be remembered that Upper Silesia fell when all was already lost for Germany, even though its directorate and diehards either could not or would not recognise the fact. In contrast, Bomber Command's campaign, though remarkably ineffective at first, built up into a means of counterattack and military initiative against a triumphant enemy nation which had carried all before it and which was otherwise unassailable at a time when the future course of the war was not a foregone conclusion. It created an opportunity cost for Germany by which extensive assets and mental preoccupation and creative thinking had to be devoted to variegated means of defence against aerial attack that otherwise could have gone into waging the war elsewhere.

The response made by Germany to the steady and relentless bombing campaign mounted by the RAF Bomber Command indicated that a substantial portion of its material resources and the war effort of its labour force had to be devoted to the purpose of defence against air attack. When the need to produce the aircraft required for defence is considered, alongside the huge demand for anti-aircraft guns and ammunition, searchlights, radar and other equipment, it may be further appreciated that Bomber Command's onslaught tied down a significant amount of military capacity on German soil, and that of the occupied countries.

After the war, Albert Speer said the battle against the bombers was the greatest lost battle of the war. He said that the lost production of military equipment desperately needed on the Russian Front amounted to 10,000 heavy guns, 6,000 heavy and medium tanks, and 4,000 aircraft. He considered that the real importance of the air war was that it opened up a second front long before the invasion of Europe. That front was the skies over

Germany. Fleets of bombers could appear at any time over any large city or important factory, the range and unpredictability of the attacks making the front gigantic. Defence against those attacks required the production of thousands of anti-aircraft guns and searchlights, the stock piling of huge amounts of ammunition throughout the country and the holding in readiness of nearly a million trained personnel as well as the production and organising of hundreds of night fighters with their radio and radar equipment. Such a defence required the increasing diversion of Me 109s, Me 110s, Junkers 88s and other aircraft capable of interception away from the offensive commitment to which they had been devoted during the years 1940 to 1943.

Field Marshall Montgomery said that Bomber Command had done more than any other branch of the armed forces to win the war. His old opponent, Field Marshal Rommel, said during the war, "Stop the bombing or we can't win".

As far as direct destruction and damage are concerned, catalogued records and photographic evidence - added to the unbelievable scenes that were there for those alive at the time to witness - leave no doubt as to the unremitting drain that the bombing inflicted on the population, its material assets and productive capacity. That the trauma it caused in the psyche of Germany was deep and persistent is evidenced by the fact that as recently as 2002, *Der Spiegel* could devote twelve pages of its issue Nr 2/6.1.03 pp 39-50 to the subject, citing the following data resulting from the latest research in Germany itself. On the magazine's front page the article is foreshadowed as Als Feuer vom Himmel fiel, When fire dropped from the sky. On the first page of the article itself was the introduction So muss die Hölle ausehen, This is what hell must look like. The magazine reported the following data.

The total enemy aircraft penetrations into Europe 1940-45 were 1.4 million, mainly made up of 1.35 million to Germany alone, 0.58 million to occupied France and 0.37 million to Italy as Germany's ally. A total of 2.67 million tons of bombs was delivered, given as 10,000 tons in 1940, 30,000 tons in 1941, 40,000 tons in 1942, 120,000 tons in 1943, 650,000 tons in 1944, and 500,000 tons in 1945.

The bombing killed 49,000 people in Berlin, 42,000 in Hamburg, and 35,000 to 40,000 in Dresden but with the possibility that up to 200,000 refugees without identification were buried, incinerated or blown to pieces in Dresden. Other cities also suffered a severe loss of population. For example, 20,000 were killed in Cologne, 20,000 in Pforzheim, 15,000 in Magdeburg, 13,000 in Kassel, 12,300 in Darmstadt, 7,500 in Heilbronn, and 6,300 in Munich. It should be noted that figures like these need to be taken in relation to the size of the city concerned. For example, the heavy attacks on a small town like Wesel must have had disproportionate effects compared with those on a large city like Hamburg.

It appears from other sources that the city which suffered the heaviest physical damage as opposed to loss of population was Krefeld which lost 54% of its total physical stock, which included 37% of industrial property and 62% non-industrial property. This destruction and damage rate was slightly heavier than that of Hamburg and Remscheid, both of which suffered a loss of just over 50%.

I had taken part in this massive manifestation of warfare by the British and American Air Forces. I found myself at first terrified at the prospect of my own imminent violent death. Then I wondered what was happening to the seven human beings inside each of our aircraft I saw shot down. Since it never befell me to try to escape from a burning or exploding bomber, the fate of those who did suffer it was left to my imagination. Thoughts about it haunted me from time to time. I simply had to develop a means to become inured to it. The emotions had to be stifled. It was always the way in war. The first reaction on seeing another aircraft hit and plunge downwards as a fiery furnace was that it wasn't me. Then that thought assailed the mind and gave way to feelings of guilt if one found oneself being in any way uncharitable or bereft of feeling.

There was always the thought that it might have been us but I had to accept that it wasn't us. Therefore there was no cause to worry. That was the reality of it. We ourselves were returning from dropping a load of bombs that undoubtedly must have killed and maimed people - including women and children. The facts of it were unknown to us. It was a case of not worrying about it, not worrying about what you didn't know. It was a grossly hideous world that we had to learn to live in. Although human beings were human beings no matter which country they lived in at that time, other human lives no longer had any value. It was our own lives that were at stake. As long as we were still alive, nothing else mattered. That was war.

The bombing of Germany, begun and continued by Bomber Command throughout the war and powerfully supplemented by the American Air Force from 1942 onwards, inflicted horrendous damage to all kinds of property, a frightful loss of life and injury to the population and the tragic destruction of so many towns and cities of cultural interest and value.

This action however did not have the nature of original initiative that subsequent generations might assume it had. It was in reality a reaction. When Germany had boldly and brilliantly overrun the entire Continent of Europe with the exception of Sweden, Switzerland, Spain and Portugal and crushed the armies of France and Britain that had been sent to halt their advance, whilst their U-boats were sinking British ships on the oceans of the world at a potentially lethal rate, the only means of self-defence left was the ability to attack the Reich from the air at night.

That ability was for so long a puny effort and lacked significant effect in terms of injuring Germany's ability to wage the war, although it had a substantial positive effect on British and Allied morale as well as propaganda value. Nevertheless, it was steadily built up to be a major means for prosecuting the war and reversing the fortunes of the Allied forces, leading ultimately to the cessation of the war. Along that terrible road, Germany suffered unprecedented destruction from the air. It was a road, however, that Germany itself had marked out and used when teaching Europe how to wage war effectively in modern times. The markers were Guernica, Rotterdam and Coventry. When one has sown the wind, one may expect to reap the whirlwind.

Chapter 17

Full Circle

Feelings of relief in having survived a tour of operations were tempered by the sadness we felt on separating from our comrades in arms and going our separate ways Our parting was being brought about because we were still alive and were about to return to normal lives which considerably brightened the outlook. Having examined the records to check on the survival rates, I calculated that during the time we were on the squadron, the average life of a new crew was only a fortnight. Out of the last forty crews who had passed through the squadron eight had survived.

Before we left, we were able to take our ground crew for a celebration at the little village of Old Bolingbroke in recognition of the wonderful work they had done for us, often in appalling conditions. I think that we all felt disappointed that we had had so little time to spend together but like us they were always busy, making it difficult to arrange social occasions.

The next day we said our farewells to East Kirkby. Joe Lennon, Bruce, Griff and I were transported to Boston where we caught a train for Lincoln. From there we travelled by train to Grantham, where we joined a train for London. We had time to spend a while at the New Zealand Forces Club in London where we met a few people we knew, before taking a train again for Aylesbury, finally arriving at RAF Westcott, an operational training station, with a satellite airfield, Oakley, near by. Bruce, Joe's navigator was to be trained as a Navigational Instructor, while Joe and I were to be trained as Pilot Instructors. Since the next pilot instructor's course was not due to start for ten days, we had some time on our hands and were able to take bicycle rides around the district, as well as a week's leave. Joe spent his leave in London and I spent mine with friends in Nottingham.

We moved to Oakley for our training course, where we met Nick Nicklin who was the pilot of the aircraft 'A' Able which had ditched in the North Sea on the way back from our squadron's trip to Wesseling. Nick told us that he was now flying Hurricanes on the fighter affiliation flight at Oakley and that they needed two more pilots. Joe and I had the good fortune to get those two jobs.

Thus began the term which I regard as the jewel in the crown of my Air Force career. My job entailed making dummy attacks on the aircraft flown by bomber crews in training, requiring the bomber pilot to take the appropriate evasive action, while the gunners aimed their guns and pressed the triggers as though it were the real thing. When the gunners pressed their triggers, instead of shooting bullets a cine camera recorded the level of their prowess. When projected on a screen the film revealed the right and wrong deflections that had been allowed.

Flying a Hawker Hurricane was sheer joy for me after flying a heavily laden bomber. Its instantaneous responses to fingertip control made me feel that the aircraft was almost part of me. Every flight was fun. I was being paid to have fun, but best of all my future looked secure. Oakley was only a few miles from Oxford, where many of the London stage shows were first premiered. It took us only about twenty minutes on our bicycles to be there. Consequently we saw many shows that we otherwise would not have seen. We often went to dog races too - a novelty for us since we didn't have dog racing in New Zealand at that time.

Boating on the River Thames was also a pleasant novelty which we often enjoyed. Having rowed up river a while we came to a weir with a ramp alongside it to enable those who wished to go further up the river to pull their boats up to the next level. The weir caused the next stretch of water to be flat where it was easier rowing on pleasing lake-like surroundings. It was also a stretch of the river which was enjoyed by the members of a male nudist society, a fact that didn't seem to be commonly known. Often we would see a boat rowed by a young fellow who had taken his girlfriend for a trip on the river, suddenly head back in the direction from which he had just come, while his red-faced girlfriend studiously looked the other way. In to-day's world I don't think there would be such a reaction.

After a while Jack Warwick was posted to Oakley too, much to our mutual satisfaction, so we were able to share together the pleasures instead of the dangers we had shared in the past. Joe applied to join Transport Command and left Oakley. As Joe and I had spent many hours taking cycle rides together, it was nice for me when Jack who was also a keen cyclist took his place. I was there until the war's end. When that great day came, crowds of jubilant people flocked to the city or village centres for the hoped-for long-lasting peace, security and normal life to replace the fear, anxiety and sadness that had lasted so long. Of course for many the sadness would remain for the rest of their lives but at least peace and security for the survivors would prevail.

Fig. 64. Author (centre), Jack Warwick on the left and alf Dawson (Digger) on the right in 1997.

I was shocked, however, to find myself bereft of emotional response, even though I had so much to be happy about. It just seemed that my emotions were worn out and ceased to respond.

My last job was ferrying aircraft all around England, for them to be parked in fields for future disposal. I thought that when my work was done I would be sent on leave before going home. I was looking forward to being able to say good-bye to my numerous friends around England and Scotland. It was not to be. I was flying one week and the next week I was on board ship, heading for home from England for the second time. I had been in the country in

1939 to hear the first air raid sirens sounding in Kent. I had been in the Oxford and Aylesbury area in 1945 to hear the last of them.

I did consider the possibility of deliberately missing the ship but reflected that if I did that I would not be home for Christmas, so I complied with instructions. Before I went, I flew up to Norfolk, where I had spent some of my leaves. From the air I could not tell them that I was leaving England but I thought that if I flew low over their house they would guess my identity even though I was flying a Hurricane rather than a Lancaster. It was harvest time and they were busy in the fields. I flew round and round to give them time to recognise me and give me a wave. I waved back, then returned to base for the last time.

With my belongings packed in my kitbag I caught a train for London and then for Southampton, where I boarded the MV *Andes*, along with hundreds of other troops from all three Services. Most of them were from Australia but there were many from New Zealand, some of whom I knew. Crowds of people lined the dock area waving farewell as we cast off and moved slowly down the harbour, while four engined Sunderland flying boats flew low across our bows as a good-bye salute. We maintained a fairly slow speed as we sailed down the English Channel while I watched the changing landscape of the country - which had given rise to our adventures, fears and sorrows - slip slowly by.

It was a potentially emotional experience but I seemed capable only of regarding it coldly as a fact. Yet as dusk was fast approaching and we moved out into the Atlantic Ocean, I stood on the stern - as I had done when leaving New Zealand - and watched the coast of England slowly slip below the horizon. It was like the curtain drop on a long and dramatic play but sadly, not one from which all the actors, having removed the equivalent of grease paint and disguises, would return to ordinary life. When we had watched New Zealand sink below the horizon three years previously I had turned and looked at a group of my friends and wondered how many of us would see the coast of New Zealand again. I now had the answer. I seemed to be abandoning them to remain forever in a foreign country, while I was going home to my lovely wife. I found that my heart was full of a mixture of joy and sadness from which I was incapable of creating rational thoughts or feelings. I was very conscious of the meaning of those words "They shall not grow old, as we who are left, grow old". I had been granted the great privilege of being allowed to grow old.

Travelling from England to New Zealand by ship via the Suez Canal took about six weeks. By the time I arrived home I found that there were many people who preferred not to know airmen who had dropped bombs on Germany. Perhaps there was some odd justice in the fact that many of the over 55,500 aircrew of Bomber Command who had sacrificed their lives in protecting their loved ones from an evil and barbarous regime had no graves in which to turn. Harold Bruhns would not be turning because he had no grave. He had been the best man at my wedding. How could we have known that he was to enjoy such a short life while I would survive to celebrate our sixtieth wedding anniversary in 2002 and rejoice over our three children and later the grandchildren for whom we have such love. The years in the end have been kind to my emotions, for which I am grateful.

I was born on 17 November 1916. That was the year in which a handful of khaki-clad young volunteers was trained as pilots to serve in the British Army Air Corps in France in the inferno of the Western Front of the First World War. They gathered at the instigation of Henry Wigram - who was later knighted for his services to New Zealand aviation - after whom the airfield created from the land that he donated was named. The row of tiny wooden huts which served as the humble private accommodation of those first recruits has been preserved and stands today outside the No 1 Hangar at Wigram Airfield in Christchurch, New Zealand, where I completed an important part of my own pilot training, and which reached its apotheosis in training hundreds of aircrew members during and after the Second World War but today no longer serves as an Air Force base. Its life even as an airfield is now virtually over.

For the past few years, after a very long and eventful life, I have returned to Wigram to be a voluntary guide. Its modern atrium, the former hangars and other buildings are all passively employed as an Air Force museum of outstanding quality and for the restoration of vintage and classical aircraft from their wrecked condition. I have stood in the line of succession started by those young men. The time line between them and me seems to be immensely long, yet in spirit and purpose and now physical location it seems that for me a circle has been properly closed.

Fig. 65. Margie watching the MV Andes arriving in the distance at Lyttelton in 1945.

Fig. 66. The MV Andes entering Lyttelton harbour in 1945.

Fig. 67. Reunited

Fig. 68. The author receiving the DFC from the Governor-General of New Zealand. Lt. General Sir Bernard Freyberg in December 1945.

To the left, holding the cushion, is David Roberts, who, as Robbie, piloted the Lancaster in which the author flew as second dickie on his first opertional flight.

Fig. 69. Author arriving home in Christchurch. December 1945

Fig. 70. Author at the Air Force Museum, Wigram, New Zealand.

Postscript

by Jack Warwick, Navigator, 630 Squadron

I always remember how difficult it was to retain my charts and instruments when flying with Doug. As they were not secured even at the best of times they were prone to wander. When we were trying to avoid night fighters or flak or even maintaining the regular weaving pattern that Doug adopted en route to targets, they slid all over the place and sometimes became temporarily irretrievable. For my part, I was kept constantly busy in my cubby hole. I just got on with my work and paid no attention to what was going on outside.

When over the target on one occasion only, I looked outside to see what was happening but didn't like the look of it so I never did so again. When we flew illegally over Switzerland, Doug called me up to see the Alps on a beautiful night. It was a memorable sight, enjoyable in peace away from the war.

Doug was knowledgeable about the machinery and could talk intelligibly with the ground staff about our aircraft. He was meticulous in attitude, a quality which must have contributed to our survival. He was a caring person. He even volunteered to cut my hair once but only made a passable job of it. I told him to stick to being a pilot.

Doug so well exemplified the claim made on behalf of aircrew members generally by W J Lawrence, Historian of 5 Group, Bomber Command that "It never was and never could be a mode of warfare to be conducted in hot blood. The bomber crew was engaged throughout a flight in a series of intricate tasks. Calculations and minute adjustments of machinery had to be made all the time with a clear head and a steady hand".

Bibliography

Aberbach, David (1996)
> Charisma in Politics, Religion and the Media. Macmillan, London.

Beevor, Antony (2002)
> Berlin The Downfall 1945. Viking, London.

Bowyer, Michael J F (1986)
> Air Raid! The enemy offensive against East Anglia 1939-45 Patrick Stephens, Wellingborough.

British Rail Engineering Limited (BREL) (1975)
> Swindon Works. BREL, Swindon.

Caldwell, Donald L (1991)
> JG 26 Top Guns of the Luftwaffe. Ivy Books, New York.

Chorley W R (1992)
> Royal Air Force Bomber Command Losses of the Second World War – Aircraft and Crew Losses Volume 1: 1939-40. Midland Counties Publications, Leicester.

Chorley W R (1997)
> Royal Air Force Bomber Command Losses of the Second World War – Aircraft and Crew Losses Volume 5: 1944. Midland Counties Publications, Leicester.

Churchill, Winston S (1959)
> The Second World War. Cassell, London.

Cooper, Alan (1993)
> Born Leader The Story of Guy Gibson VC. Independent Books, London.

Davies, James Arthur (1994)
> A Leap in the Dark. Leo Cooper, London.

Der Spiegel
> So muss die Holle aussehen, Nr 2/6. 1. 03 pp 39-50.

Dymond FE undated
> A Very Special Lancaster.Pitkin Pictorials, London.

Frankland, Noble DFC (1965)
> The Bombing Offensive Against Germany. Faber and Faber, London.

Franklin, Neville (1961)
> Lancaster Photo Album. Patrick Stephens, Cambridge.

Friedrich, Joerg (2002)
    The Fire: Germany Under Bombardment 1940-45.
Garbett M and B Goulding (1992)
    Lancaster. The Promotional Reprint Company, Leicester.
Garbett, Mike and Brian Goulding (1988)
    Lancaster at War. Ian Allen, London.
Garbett, Mike and Brian Goulding (1988)
    Lancaster at War 2. Ian Allen, London.
Garbett, Mike and Brian Goulding (1988)
    Lancaster at War 3. Ian Allen, London.
Goulding, Brian, Mike Garbett and John Partridge (1974)
    Story of a 'Lanc'. The Lincolnshire Aviation Heritage
    Centre, England.
Harris, Sir Arthur, Marshall of the RAF (1947)
    Bomber Offensive. Macmillan, New York.
Holmes, Harry
    Avro Lancaster : the definitive record.
Jacobs, Peter (1991)
    The Lancaster Story. Cassell, London.
Jefford C G (1988)
    RAF Squadrons. Airlife Publishing, Shrewsbury, England
Lacey-Johnson, Lionel (1991)
    Point Blank and Beyond. Airlife Publishing, Shrewsbury.
Lawrence W J (1951)
    Number 5 Bomber Group RAF (1939-1945). Faber,
    London.
Martyn, Errol W (1999)
    For Your Tomorrow Volume Two: Fates 1943-1998.
    Volplane Press, Christchurch, New Zealand.
Mason, Francis K (1989)
    The Avro Lancaster. Aston Publications, Bourne End,
    Great Britain.
McKee, Alexander (1982)
    Dresden The Devil's Tinderbox. Barnes and Noble, New
    York 1945.
Meehan, Patricia (2001)
    A Strange Enemy people, Germans under the British
    1945-50. Peter Owen Publishers, London.
Moyes, Philip JR (1964)
    Bomber Squadrons of the RAF and Their Aircraft.
    Macdonald, London.

Neillands, Robin (2001)
> The Bomber War Arthur Harris and the Allied Bomber Offensive 1939 – 1945. John Murray, London.

Ogilvie, Gordon (1973)
> The Riddle of Richard Pearse. AH and AW Reed, Auckland

Overy, Richard (1997)
> Bomber Command 1939-45. Harper Collins, London.

Patterson, Dan
> Lancaster: RAF Heavy Bomber.

Perrett, Bryan (1990)
> Knights of the Black Cross. Grafton Books, London.

Radell, Rick and Mike Vines (1993)
> Lancaster: a bombing legend. Osprey, London.

Richards, Denis (1994)
> The Hardest Victory. Hodder & Stoughton, London.

Robertson, Bruce (1964)
> Lancaster - the story of a famous bomber. Harleyford Publications, Letchworth.

Rohwer J and G Hummelchen (1992)
> Chronology of the War at Sea 1939 – 1945. Naval Institute Press, Annapolis.

Scholes, David (1997)
> Air War Diary: An Australian in Bomber Command. Kangaroo Press, Sydney.

Smith, David J (1989)
> Britain's Military Airfields 1939-1945. Patrick Stephens Limited, Wellingborough.

Sterling M D (1992)
> Lancaster NX665. Society of the Museum of Transport and Technology, Auckland.

Terraine, John (1985)
> The Right of the Line. Hodder and Stoughton, London.

The Avro Lancaster 1 undated
> Profile Publications, Leatherhead, England.

Thompson H L (1956)
> New Zealanders with the Royal Air Force Volume II European Theatre January 1943 – May 1945 Official History of New Zealand in the Second World War 1939-45. Oxford University Press, London.

Thompson, Walter (1997)
> Lancaster to Berlin. Crecy Publishing, Wilmslow.

Thorne, Alex (1990)
  Lancaster at War, 4 Pathfinder Squadron. Ian Allen, London.
Tripp, Miles (1993)
  The Eighth Passenger. Leo Cooper, London.
Webster, Sir Charles K, and Noble Frankland (1961)
  The Strategic Air Offensive Against Germany. 1939-45. HMSO, London.
Yates, Harry (1999)
  Luck and a Lancaster. Airlife Publishing, Shrewsbury, England.

57 Squadron and 630 Squadron Association Newsletter October 2003.

The private undated papers of May Calvert, wife of Squadron Leader Roy Calvert, sometime Commander of 630 Squadron in 1944, deceased.

The private diary and Pilot's Flying Log Book (Form 414) of Flight Lieutenant Douglas Hawker DFC.